CHOOSING THE PRESIDENT

 The American Assembly, *Columbia University*

CHOOSING
THE PRESIDENT

Prentice-Hall, Inc., *Englewood Cliffs, N.J.*
A SPECTRUM BOOK

Library of Congress Cataloging in Publication Data
MAIN ENTRY UNDER TITLE:

Choosing the President.

(A Spectrum Book)
At head of title: The American Assembly, Columbia
University.
Background papers for the 44th American Assembly,
Arden House, New York.
  1. Presidents—United States—Nomination—Congresses.
2. Presidents—United States—Election—Congresses.
I. Barber, James David, ed.   II. American Assembly.
JK521.C45   329'.022'0973   74–3067
ISBN 0–13–133561–8
ISBN 0–13–133553–7 (pbk.)

Choosing the President is also the title of a publication of the League
of Women Voters of the United States, the contents of which is
different from and complementary to this publication. We recom-
mend it to those who wish to know more about the step-by-step
process of nominating and electing the President. (© 1972 League of
Women Voters of the United States, 1730 M Street, NW, Washington, D.C. 20036   95 pp. Publication #301, $1.00)

10 9 8 7 6 5 4 3

PRENTICE-HALL INTERNATIONAL, INC. (*London*)
PRENTICE-HALL OF AUSTRALIA PTY., LTD. (*Sydney*)
PRENTICE-HALL OF CANADA, LTD. (*Toronto*)
PRENTICE-HALL OF INDIA PRIVATE LIMITED (*New Delhi*)
PRENTICE-HALL OF JAPAN, INC. (*Tokyo*)

Table of Contents

Preface

The participants in the Forty-fourth American Assembly, at Arden House, December 1973, themselves probably wrote the most suitable preface to this book when they agreed in their final report (which may be had from The American Assembly) that the "Presidency of the United States may be the most powerful office in the world. But it is far from all-powerful; in our multi-centered system it depends—in fact as well as in Constitutional theory —on active cooperation from other institutions. And when the Presidency strays beyond the bounds of law or broad consensus, those other institutions can, if they will, call it to account.

"The fundamental way we enforce accountability is the national election to decide who shall leave and who shall enter the White House. Through a long and not untroubled history the Presidential election process has worked its way every time, determining the peaceful transfer of authority. Such a record in meeting one of government's most difficult problems cautions against radical change in the basics of the system, particularly because history provides so many examples of new rules producing surprising and sometimes unwelcome results." The Assembly report then explored what changes in structure and substance may be needed in the choosing of Presidents.

And so does this book, which was put together under the editorial supervision of James David Barber, chairman of political science at Duke University, to take a hard, long-range look at our Presidential election system. One will not find in it any suggestion for temporary patchwork to meet a current crisis with fashionable solutions. But both scholar and general reader will find some new light on an old subject, which Dr. Barber calls a "political order in disarray." The shedding of new light—that is one of the jobs of The American Assembly. We think this book will help.

The opinions herein belong to the authors on their own and not to The American Assembly, which is a neutral public affairs forum on the national scene. Furthermore nobody should try to see any relationship between the material in this volume and any official stand of the Overbrook and Woodruff foundations, which provided some generous support, gratefully acknowledged herewith, for this American Assembly project

Clifford C. Nelson
President
The American Assembly

CHOOSING THE PRESIDENT

James David Barber

Introduction

The choice of a President is the most important single act in American politics. It is also the most thoroughly studied process in political science. And it is also a subject full of the most striking paradoxes and anomalies to the citizen trying to understand how it happens.

In 1972, Richard Nixon won the Presidency by an overwhelming popular vote. In 1973, thanks in large part to overwhelming popular protest, it seemed not improbable that he would be forced out of office.

Part of the reason Americans voted for Nixon in 1972 was his stand in favor of law and order. Yet by 1973, his Vice President had resigned and been convicted of a felony, his former chief aides were indicted, and long lists of probable crimes by the President himself were circulating. As for order, the attentive public reeled in response to surprise after surprise, and the capitol city was groggy from too much novel experience.

Another reason people voted for Nixon in 1972 was his apparent success in achieving a detente with the Soviet Union. In 1973, the President as commander-in-chief ordered a worldwide alert of United States armed forces to counteract Soviet moves in the Mideast war.

But the puzzles and surprises do not begin and end with the choice

JAMES DAVID BARBER *is professor of political science at Duke University, where he came in 1972 as chairman of the department after teaching more than ten years at Yale. He is the author of* The Presidential Character: Predicting Performance in the White House, *which was nominated for a National Book Award. Dr. Barber has also written several other books and many papers and articles on various facets of American politics, including* The Lawmakers, Citizen Politics *and* Political Leadership in American Government *(editor).*

of Mr. Nixon, as the chapters in this book make clear. Much of the conventional wisdom derived from previous studies and the well-developed common sense of politics now must be called into question. Not only sudden news events, but data emerging over the past few years make necessary a thorough reexamination of the way we choose our chief executive.

That reexamination must reach beyond the immediacies of the general election itself. That is, we see now that the choice of a President begins long before the voting and its implications extend on into the President's action in office. Similarly the choice is strongly conditioned by nonformalities. From 1787 to today, Americans have sought to solve problems by reforming structures. But it is increasingly clear that structures are only part of the equation; they are operated (or not) by human beings whose perceptions, beliefs, and attitudes determine the uses structures are put to. They exist in a cultural context, a context of images and purposes, a context of persuasion. Therefore there is a good deal more to the process than its machinery—there are the mechanics. And there is a good deal more to reform than reorganization—there is, there could be, reformation.

Thus the book begins in the White House, not the ballot box. Erwin Hargrove raises the overriding question—what kind of President do we need, a question not only logically prior to choice but of considerable practical import considering how hard a time the public has had in getting what it wants. Hargrove lays out the criteria for this age of political anxiety. If as it now appears, the public voted for activism in 1960, for peace in 1964, for tranquility in 1968, and for competence in 1972, then somehow our calculus has been defective. The Presidency, Hargrove points out, is run by the President and we had better start paying attention to what kind of person he is. "No one can force the President to use a mechanism he does not want to use," he writes, to which must be added that reliance on mechanisms to restrain Presidents has also proved extraordinarily difficult. Congress can play a checking role (and we should be paying a good deal more heed to what kinds of persons we send to *that* body). But in the end it is a matter of character—of the President's own patterns of self-restraint and self-actualization. Those are not matters so arcane or uncertain that the public cannot grasp them, given real facts by the media and real concern by the king-making politicians.

How do the politicians choose the characters we the people get to choose among? Badly, in recent history, thinks Donald Matthews, and also far earlier than even they may be aware of. The choice must be narrowed—two persons winnowed from the platoons of the ambitious and draftable. To succeed, a candidacy must move, as Robert Colodzin has put it, from conceivable to achievable to inevitable. That process starts long before the convention city is selected. The first trick is to get yourself widely "mentioned" as a presidential possible—no easy task, and one in which the media play a determining part. From there through gathering enough money to seem "serious" on to "front-runner" status as the primaries approach, the choice narrows precipitously. Indeed, the preprimary leader *usually* becomes his party's nominee; that is, the real nomination choice is made before the formal nomination process gets started. To my mind (and Matthews has much more to say about it), this means that political science should be focusing far more strongly than it does on the politics of prominence—on how potential candidates get into the on-deck circle. And it implies that party politicians who hope to have a hand in choosing the President are going to have to get into the act from the start, for instance by "bringing along" promising candidates as the old-time city bosses used to do.

Yet both legal and political *responsibility* for nominations rests with the parties as institutions. They cannot pass the buck, whatever the polls say. At the very least, they legitimize the choice; at most they decide themselves. Of necessity, theirs is a rule-bound process and in the United States the rules are of Babylonian complexity. Austin Ranney (who took time out from political sciencing to help write some of them) analyzes their impact against the background of key questions of democratic theory. Who is a party member and thus eligible to take part at successive stages? Should the popular will be expressed directly or through representatives, and, if the latter, who should the representatives be? And above all, what is the purpose of the national party convention—to mirror its constituency or to win the election? The answers are hard to come by. In 1972, George McGovern was nominated by a convention probably more representative of his party's rank-and-file than any in history—but that November the *national* rank-and-file made him the winner only in Massachusetts and the District of Columbia. The rules will always be there to change, as there can be no legitimacy in anarchy, and candidates will bend them as they can to their own advantage. But it is fair to pose the question: looking back on it all, how much (and what *kinds* of) difference do they make?

A lot of the coyness has gone out of politics. In the old Victorian days, candidates cultivated an appearance of reluctance, as when McKinley wrote a supporter that "I cannot get the consent of my mind to do anything that places me in the position of seeming to seek an office and anything I might say or do would at once be interpreted as an effort in that direction." McKinley waited calmly in his Ohio living room for news from the Republican convention of 1896. Nowadays the candidates typically arrive at convention city thoroughly worn out from long months of campaigning—hoping to win so they can swim on forward into months more of it. The military word "campaign" used to be a recognized exaggeration; now it is almost a euphemism. The whole experience tends to reward martial spirits, to select for presidential advancement those characters attuned to arduous struggle in their own cause.

To win in November the nominee fights through the fall, guided by his campaign strategy. He must hold his own and add millions of others. John Kessel shows how candidates walk the tightrope, balancing the needs and hopes of the activists and the apathetics, the partisans and independents, the insiders and the outsiders. However strong the candidate's want to abjure calculation and simply tell the truth to shame the Devil, sooner or later he must decide (or all do, anyway) to shape his appeals to those appealed to. The standard coalitions inherited from New Deal days are in massive disarray, at least in presidential politics. The Solid South, for example, seems to have shifted to solid Republican without going through a liquid stage. The integuments which used to connect the presidential team to state and congressional party candidates have been broken or severely strained. The arts of political ambiguity—the vigorous assertion of substantive obscurities—are cultivated by candidates desperately trying to whip up their old friends without scaring off new acquaintances. No longer can they count on California neglecting what they say in Connecticut. Therefore they ponder, in the nonrandom ways Kessel outlines, what words to broadcast to lure the marginal, isolate the irreconcilable, and keep the faith at home.

The public the politicians are trying to lure sometimes seem a fickle lot. Public opinion about candidates may fluctuate, but underneath the flux are some deep emotional tides that complicate President-choosing even more. Fred Greenstein, who has been assessing public reactions to Presidents for a score of years, saw that long ago. Americans feel for their President as for no other public officer; he provides —or at least they wish he would provide—sustenance for their needs to understand, to take part, to get together and keep together. So when we search out a new President we are looking for far more than mere professional competence. We want an emotional connection. We want faith beyond works. We want a trustable hero. It would probably be better if we learned, from school days on, that the President is, as Harry Truman said, only a man like the rest of us, one who puts his pants on one leg at a time. But there you are: we don't, and odds are we won't.

Even the disillusionment with President Nixon is unlikely to still the tides of popular emotion that flow toward the White House. Indeed it may increase them. For Nixon's performances highlight the contrast between deed and ideal, throw into sharp relief the high standards Americans demand of their White House hero. There is no sign that a disillusioned public will expect less of Nixon's successor. Absent some revolution in deep public attitudes, Presidents will continue to be chosen in part to satisfy our hunger for a Superman, a hunger made all the more intense by a decade of deprivation.

The public turns for guidance, emotional sustenance, and information, as it tries to get its head straight for the election, to the mass media. The media do much more than simply convey the candidates' message. Indeed the media are increasingly seen not as mere middlemen of the system, but as a powerful and independent force affecting choice from its earliest phases on. The accusations fly: that media trickery and fake propaganda helped get Nixon elected, for example, as Joe McGinniss argued in *The Selling of the President 1968,* and then that media misinterpretation unfairly undercut Nixon's support, as ex-Vice President Agnew propounded. Supposed media-power is recognized in the immense sums of money collected for and spent on television campaigning, probably the main reason presidential campaign financing has become such a significant focus for corruption and reform. Yet very little is known for certain about the impact of media messages on the public; what is known raises suspicions that a great deal of money and talent is being expended to little effect, at least in the short-run (which is the run candidates care most about, at any particular point in time).

Murray Edelman steps back from the immediate and writes about the politics of persuasion, that symptom which distinguishes democracy from its counterparts. Adlai Stevenson joshingly defined a politician as a statesman who approaches every question with an open mouth. But when talk in politics loses its seriousness, we are on our way to 1984—the equating of opposites, the pseudification of the link between event and report—and the death of government by consent. Edelman sees such a threat in the contemporary loosening of social bonds. The shallower the voter's roots in work, family, home place, the more vulnerable he is to phony political advertising. Rootlessness, anomie, persuasibility go hand in hand. But this persuasion is skin-deep. Such "public opinion," measured by polls which show preferences but not intensities, has all the staying-power of last year's skirt length. But its evanescence can be and is manipulated to win elections, especially when voters with stronger social commitments are closely divided. There is no more urgent problem in choosing the President than restoring continuity and rationality to debate on the question.

The urgency escalates as new millions of voters find politics and politicians not worth their time or attention.

All of this comes to a climax in the choice on election day. Presidential voting behavior has been studied from every conceivable angle; some of that calls to mind E. E. Schattschneider's definition of political science as a mountain of data surrounding a vacuum. But the pioneering work of the 1950s set off by Angus Campbell, Warren Miller, Philip Converse, and Donald Stokes had virtues rare in our discipline: the questions did not determine the answers; they would be asked again and again in an institutionalized program of research; the analysis generated definite hypotheses; and, most important, the findings could be tested against the facts of the future.

That test for this era is the work Richard Boyd undertakes in the book's ultimate chapter. The old order of propositions confronts new evidence, building up since 1960 and culminating in 1972, that the interplay of variables is a good deal different now than it was in the Eisenhower years. Boyd's careful assessment produced an apparently schizoid picture of an electorate (a) increasingly disaffected, pessimistic, apathetic, and unfettered by strong party ties, *and* (b) increasingly knowledgeable, issue-oriented, and active in campaigns. How Boyd resolves the seeming clash, I leave to the curious reader. Clearly the most important implication for the process of President-choosing is the ungluing of the parties, not just as political organizations (they always did come unstuck between elections) but in the insides of voters' heads. A new generation of American voters—for which Eisenhower and even Kennedy are historical figures like Roosevelt and James K. Polk—are entering the eligible electorate at a time when "Democrat" and "Republican" have lost their force as symbols of political ethnicity. Unless voters are to choose Presidents unguided by meaningful political identifications, these loci of loyalty will have to be revived or replaced.

The general picture emerging from these essays is, to my mind, a portrait of a political order in disarray, but groping forward toward new modes of choice. Change is inevitable. Progress is not. The President we want next time is out there, somewhere, and it is up to us to find him. Our present system of discovery is infested with kitsch and fakery. But it is only a system, only a pattern of behavior, alterable when there is a will and a way. The organization of will is the province of politicians. What scholars can try to do is to throw some light on the way.

Erwin C. Hargrove

1

What Manner of Man?

The Crisis of the Contemporary Presidency

Problems of the Presidency

If this chapter were being written in 1960 by a political scientist of liberal persuasion it would surely eulogize presidential power. But today the words do not come. The Bay of Pigs, the Vietnam War, and Watergate have taken the shine off of such an exercise. Our optimistic assumptions about the happy fusion of power and purpose have been exploded. It is not only that power has been abused but also that we trusted too much in it.

Political scientists who wrote on the Presidency were under the spell of the progressive interpretation of American history. The lesson of the defeat of Woodrow Wilson in the Senate and the struggle of Franklin Roosevelt against the isolationists was that only the President could lead the nation responsibly in foreign affairs. The fact that President Truman began an American war in Korea without the approval of Congress was not criticized by scholars, and John Kennedy's inaugural address was a call to activism abroad in the tradition of Wilson, Roosevelt, and Truman.

ERWIN C. HARGROVE *is chairman of the Department of Political Science and also of the Public Policymaking Interdisciplinary Concentration at Brown University. Among his many publications are* Presidential Leadership, Personality and Political Style *and the forthcoming* The Power of the Modern Presidency.

The author wishes to thank the following persons who gave helpful advice about improving the essay, not all of which was taken: William Gorham, John Macy, Thomas Cronin, James Patterson, Elmer Cornwell, Dennis Kavanaugh, Fred Greenstein, Peter Billings, and James David Barber.

Parallel with this litany to power and purpose was the belief that only the President could initiate domestic social reform. Victory over Congress was the key to success and we celebrated those traits of toughness, manipulative skill, and sensitivity to the dimension of personal power which would permit a President to carry a resistant Congress and bureaucracy with him.

Franklin D. Roosevelt was the implicit model for much of the literature and Dwight D. Eisenhower was the scapegoat. Of course a conservative President was supposed only to tread water between activist administrations but in 1960 we felt that Eisenhower had gone on too long. It was time for an activist "new generation of Americans" to come to power. And they did.

Now, after thirteen years of the active exercise of presidential power in both foreign and domestic affairs many scholars and citizens are in a revisionist mood. Eisenhower's self-restraint in regard to military intervention abroad, his refusal to get excited about the missile race with the Soviets, and his respect for the prerogatives of Congress are now being praised. There is little to distinguish between Presidents Johnson and Nixon in regard to the unaccountable exercise of military power abroad. And the events of Watergate suggest that the presidential institution itself is in some way beyond external control.

In short, this is a time of fundamental reappraisal of our beliefs about the Presidency and its role in American democracy, and the position that we formulate now may guide us for a generation. Political scientists need to learn what historians have always known, that our perceptions and evaluations of institutions change as our experience changes us and that we are always subject to selective perception. Those aspects of the Presidency which we once praised now frighten us. However the new revisionist models will surely reflect selective biases, or reactions against recent history of which we will only become fully aware with experience.

What problems about the Presidency have emerged since 1960 which require a new model of presidential leadership? One can cite five concerns:

1. We sense more clearly that *at key moments of crisis the personality of the President is* the *decision system*. When he chooses to act, for example to order military action, there are simply no effective collegial checks on him from within his government nor external restraints in the short run.

After the experience of Lyndon Johnson and Richard Nixon we are not so keen to idealize power-maximizing either as motive or skill. We are concerned that the love of office and power may, in some men, mask and serve deep inner fears about the self which require the exercise of power to be abated. Flaws in personality in these two men have had serious destructive consequences for policy and for the conduct of the office.

So, we must begin to ask the question, what kind of presidential personality do we want?

2. The rich firsthand accounts of presidential policy-making processes that have been published in recent years show clearly that *the presidential personal style of authority is the crucial variable in what the top leaders of the executive branch know, consider, and debate and in how discussions at the top are carried on.*

A great deal has been made of models of "bureaucratic politics" and "organizational routine" which are said by some to restrict the information available to the President, limit the options presented to him, and handicap his intentions for implementation. Much of this is accurate but it is even more true that the President himself creates the channels of communication at the top and that he sets the tone and permissiveness within which discussion takes place. His associates learn from him whether they dare think the unthinkable and speak honestly in meetings. We are back to personality because a style of authority flows from personality. But the special problem of the Presidency is that every President must break through the excessive deference which is shown him by associates and subordinates and make clear that he wants plain speaking. Of course, sometimes what appears as deference is in fact bureaucratic cover-up from below but this too is the President's problem.

3. *The White House, including the Executive Office of the President, as an institution presents new problems of accountability*—a number of phenomena cluster together and reinforce each other but they can be separated analytically. Presidential advisers who are not subject to direct congressional scrutiny exercise great personal authority. The White House has become the center for policy development in the executive which has led to a demoralization of the bureaucracy and an effort to do too much at the center. The atmosphere within the White House is too often one of "we-they," and a dedication to the President's interests often actually undercuts his political needs through arrogance toward the other parts of government. And finally, the excessive deference to the President within the White House can produce a myopia which dictates reality for all within, including the President.

4. *Abuses of bureaucratic power congruent with presidential interests occur all too frequently and go unchecked.* We may have constructed a "Garrison State" in Harold Lasswell's prophetic phrase, in which a national security bureaucracy specializing in violence is not accountable to democratic principles. The revelation in July 1973 that

the United States secretly bombed Cambodia in 1969 and 1970, contrary to the public word of the President and at his direction, and the subsequent discovery that Air Force reports of the bombing were falsified to conceal the truth from the Congress, the public, and most of the government make us wonder if we have lost control. This is not a matter of the President being unable to control bureaucracy; that happens but it can be solved by presidential action. Rather, it is a problem of lack of external control by Congress and public of presidentially-directed bureaucratic power. A President who feels that he is primarily accountable to his own conscience and to history for his use of power is not accountable to the democratic principle.

5. *The chronic problem of deadlock between the President and Congress in matters of domestic policy and the great difficulty the White House seems to have in securing responsiveness from the domestic bureaucracy are still with us.* These problems do not seem of a piece with the others. It is as if Aaron Wildavsky's "two Presidencies" of foreign and domestic policy have grown further apart, the one magnifying in power and the other withering.[1]

The experience of the "Great Society" has made us wonder whether we know how to design legislation intelligently and find effective means of bureaucratic implementation even when presidential power over policy is at its height. Many of the Great Society programs were put together in terms of feasibility of legislative passage and wide political appeal without sufficient analysis of the social and bureaucratic problems of implementation that might occur.

There is a great temptation for Presidents to emphasize foreign affairs over domestic problems in their appeals to public opinion—in large part because their symbolic resources are greater in the former and their control over solutions to problems may in fact be greater. Difficult domestic problems are not well understood, and presidential proposals often create new conflict and offer little political capital for a President. Much domestic policy-making has therefore become a combination of imagery and palliative. There is little political credit to be gotten in taking on hard questions like income maintenance for the poor, reform of the tax laws, the busing of schoolchildren; problems of management of the economy, which must be faced, are so difficult that they are often mishandled.

6. The recurring constitutional crises of 1973 having to do with Watergate have revealed that *there is little short of impeachment that the rest of the polity can do to restrain a President who may abuse his constitutional powers, in areas in which he is autonomous.* The Con-

[1] Aaron Wildavsky, "The Two Presidencies" in Aaron Wildavsky, ed., *The Presidency* (Boston: Little, Brown, 1965).

stitution provides no mechanism for the resignation, whether forced or voluntary, of a President who has lost the confidence of the great majority of the people. And impeachment is such a drastic measure that members of Congress shrink from it. The political system relies upon observance of self-restraint and political accommodation by all parties, publics, and interest groups, as well as leaders. When a President lacks this commitment the other principal actors in the system stand baffled. It was evidently only the threat of impeachment in October, 1973, that led President Nixon to accede to a court order that he make the tapes of White House conversations about Watergate available to the court. And this congressional threat was in response to the unanticipated outpouring of public opinion against the President after he directed the discharge of Archibald Cox, the special prosecutor on Watergate matters. This case is cited not to indict President Nixon or to suggest knowledge of his motives but to illustrate the difficulty of restraining a President short of impeachment on certain kinds of constitutional questions. The firing of a special prosecutor by the President suggests that it may be impossible for the Department of Justice to be used as a vehicle to investigate the Presidency. In short, impeachment may be the only method by which presidential wrongdoing can be ventilated. This is a very unsatisfactory situation because of the general reluctance to resort to it. We identify the stability of the nation with strength and continuity in the Presidency. And we lack the simple device of replacement of the Prime Minister by another party leader within the continuity of government available in a parliamentary system.

Remedies

These problems require diverse solutions.

INSTITUTIONAL

Most abuses of bureaucratic power can be corrected by the vigilance of Congress and its committees. The structures for surveillance exist but the political will to use them has often been lacking. There were reports in the press of the bombing of Cambodia in 1970 and some members of the Armed Services Committees may have known of the action. But, the will to resist the President on Indochina in Congress was not strong enough at that time. Public disclosure of the bombing might have made no difference. The truth is that congressional politicians and publics, until 1973, were too ready to defer to the President in crucial matters of foreign affairs, especially in regard to military policy. Surveys of public attitudes toward the President in the Korean and Vietnamese wars show that he had great latitude to conduct a war as he wished. Even in the winding down of an unpopular war, publics rely on the President to choose the best means. American patriotism and the presidential ability to invoke a "rally round the flag" take precedence in the minds of most people over what seem to be abstract ethical considerations about the morality of bombing Asians.[2]

We are faced here with the negative aspect of some of the cultural resources that reside in the symbolic power of the Presidency cited by Professor Greenstein in his chapter. The existence of congressional structures of surveillance is necessary but not enough as an antidote to the misuse of such resources. Even new legislation to require the President to seek congressional approval for the long-term commitment of troops to combat will depend more upon the political atmosphere than on the requirements of the law. We have to hope that the shock of Vietnam, the advent of a generation of congressional leaders less enamoured of the military and distant in time from Cold War ideology, and a genuine public loathing of war will make a difference here.

We should not be optimistic that congressional legislation or action can do much to shape policy-making processes or patterns of authority within the White House and presidential orbit. It might be good to require the congressional confirmation and continuing accessibility and accountability of key White House staff, but such officials can always evade inquiry by invoking presidential privilege as department heads can do. Congress is too remote from what goes on day to day in the White House to have any means of shaping authority relations there. The post-World War II Congress set up the Council of Economic Advisers and the National Security Council with the intention of checking the President. The CEA was also to be accountable to the Congress, through confirmation and the requirement of an annual report to the Joint Economic Committee. However, President Truman simply failed to use the first Council chairman when he attempted to function in such a manner. The lesson was driven home that no one can force the President to use a mechanism he does not want to use. This was also very clear in Truman's initial aloofness from the National Security Council. The Armed Services Committees and the services themselves hoped to exert more control over the President through the structure of a council where each service was guaranteed a seat. But successive Presidents refused to be so bureaucratized and have used the NSC for their own purposes. The fluidity of the institutionalized Presidency, in fact its imperfect institutionalization, gives the President the freedom to impose whatever patterns he wishes upon it.

2 John E. Mueller, *War, Presidents and Public Opinion* (New York: Wiley, 1973).

The problem of the weaknesses of the domestic Presidency is really too great to deal with here. The literature is vast and inconclusive. One current argument is that "party government" which could link President and Congress in accountability would curb the excesses of presidential power and permit effective action in concert. This is a modification of the older view that party government would make Congress responsive to the President. It is not at all clear that any of the claims are true. Party government may be incompatible in theory and practice with vigorous congressional checks upon the executive branch, just as it is in a parliamentary system. Party government seen in terms of positive action would not clearly increase the effectiveness of government. Presidents would be dependent upon a majority party coalition which might inhibit action even more than the present system of appeals to a cross-bench majority. In any event, the likelihood of party government is remote. Both national parties are in an advanced state of disintegration. The historic partisan coalitions are weakening. Traditional party identifications are eroding. A dramatic realignment may eventually take place but its outlines are not at all clear. Presidential candidates and incumbent Presidents in the immediate future will lack the partisan political resources for strong party government because the electoral coalitions behind them will be so wavering.

POLITICAL

A future President may help to bring about a new partisan alignment and create an electoral coalition as a basis for governing. But this will be an act of political creativity on the part of a President and cannot be achieved by the structural engineering of national party committees enamoured of the idea of responsible party government.

The restraining of a President who is thought to have overstepped his constitutional powers has to be worked out through politics because it is only by means of politics that such issues are brought to the courts. Current history suggests that the final sanctions against a President are political rather than judicial in the sense that he can probably successfully resist all legal sanctions against him until such time as Congress decides to impeach him. This is of course speculative because such instances are so uncommon in American history even though we were living through one in 1973. But everything that has been said before about the difficulties of finding institutional means to restrain Presidents applies here. We ultimately have to ask the question of whether the Constitution gives us a virtually autonomous republican monarch in respect to his fundamental constitutional powers.

An analysis of the available institutional and political remedies for possible abuses of presidential power is not heartening. The stunted character of political parties, particularly, as potential agencies of constraint upon and guidance of a President provides little hope in that direction. Congress, as an institution, is the victim of its own virtues. The fragmentation, decentralization, and division of labor which provide institutional strength to the parts prevent a comparable strength for the whole, especially in conflict with a unified Presidency and executive. The problem of the continuing weak institutional and ideological resources for presidential domestic leadership is based on the same poverty of institutional development.

Therefore a more radical question must be posed and answered. Should Americans perhaps think of changing to a parliamentary system in order to eliminate the problems of republican kingship?

A Parliamentary System?

We cannot say how parliamentary government would actually work in the United States because politics and culture would shape it in ways unique to America. But, we can look at Britain and Canada to ask if the operation of the system at its best solves our problems.

BRITISH AND AMERICAN EXPERIENCE

The British do not idealize their Prime Minister. He is a party politician who leads a government of politicians and his virtues and frailties are not seen as crucial to the success or failure of the government. They do not suffer from "President fixation" in this sense. He is responsible to his political colleagues in Cabinet and Parliament and lacks autonomous bureaucratic power of his own. The evidence is mixed but it seems clear that the parliamentary party does exercise constraints and influence over its government, usually behind the scenes. The central link in the entire system is that of party.

All of this is very appealing to us today and we often hear that the British would have handled a Watergate scandal by deposing the discredited leader. Perhaps so but there would probably also have been the continuation of a "cover-up." One Prime Minister would have given way to another and the governing party would have carried on as before with little increase in public knowledge of the facts. Governments no longer fall because of votes in Parliament. This is what happened after Suez in 1956. There would be no Senate Watergate Committee to investigate, for parliamentary committees do not act so impolitely. An officially appointed inquiry could do the job but might also be very circumscribed in its charge.

Each system has the defects of its virtues. British government has been vigorously criticized for some years by reformers because it lacks the virtues of American government. It has been pictured as too secretive and lacking in open, adversary processes for the discussion of policy in the stage of formulation. Parliamentary debate has a certain mock combat quality without genuine discussion of issues and Parliament as an institution is very weak vis-à-vis the Government. There has also been considerable criticism of the dependence of ministers upon civil servants for advice and the absence of the stimulus of new ideas and variety of expertise that American "in and outers" bring to administration.[3]

The reforms of the sixties—specialized parliamentary committees, increase in temporary expert advisers to ministers, and reform of the civil service in the direction of greater substantive and managerial expertise—have had difficulty taking root because they are contrary to the internal logic of the British parliamentary system.

In Canada one sees the same virtues: collegiality, political sensitivity at the top, party accountability for government. But one also sees the same fault of a weak Parliament which cannot compare with Congress in its influence upon government. Party government is also marred by the splintering of parliamentary parties. This may be a consequence of the requirements of parliamentary party discipline in a society of great diversity. More unity is required than can be achieved and the result has been a fragmentation of parties into smaller, more coherent groups. This might occur in an American parliamentary system but does not prevail now because party demands on members of Congress are minimal.[4] In addition the Prime Minister lacks the symbolic resources of office available to an American President for popular leadership and has tended to be a broker figure.

AMERICAN CIRCUMSTANCES

An American prime minister and government would be the children of what is now the Congress. It is uncertain what kinds of leaders would emerge, but it seems likely that seniority, provincialism, and extreme flexibility of style would be strong characteristics of such a government. They would have to appeal to a variegated parliament, perhaps splintered into several parties in the Canadian fashion. The

[3] Erwin C. Hargrove, *Professional Roles in Society and Government: The English Case* (Beverly Hills, Cal.: Sage Publishing Co., 1972).
[4] Leon P. Epstein, "A Comparative Study of Canadian Parties," *American Political Science Review*, Vol. LVII, no. 1 (March 1964) , pp. 46–59.

accountability of the executive to a national electorate might be diminished. Most of the existing congressional institutional checks on the executive would disappear. This assumes that our version of the parliamentary system would emphasize the support of a majority party or party coalition for a cabinet government. Such a system has proved to be incompatible with an institutionally strong parliament. No parliamentary body in the English-speaking world has the division of labor and specialized legislative subparts of Congress. Of course an American-style parliamentary system might be more like that of an older version of a French republic, surely something not intended.

The benefits of a parliamentary system in America are not clear enough to persuade people to support it. Such a system also runs against the grain of our political culture. We venerate the Constitution as our chief national symbol. The Presidency is fused with our national mythology. It is not conceivable that we would abolish the office or turn it into a figurehead.

The lesson need not be labored. The explosive volatility of the American system of government with the coexistence of separation of powers and checks and balances permits a great deal of constructive open conflict and collaboration and forcing out of information and issues in ways uncongenial to a parliamentary system. But it also provides great autonomy and capacity to act irresponsibly for each branch of government, which is again foreign to British parliamentary government.

One can hope very much that in the long run the parties will become stronger in regard to both representation and government, and that ways will be found to blend such change with the reform of Congress to permit its leadership to deal with Presidents on an equal footing without frustrating the effectiveness of government. But these are questions of gradual and difficult institutional change and do not speak to our present concerns. The immediate need is for a President who will restore our confidence that official power will not be misused and who will have a style of authority that will respect the strengths of Congress and draw on it, keep the White House an open institution, and find ways to lead the permanent government of the bureaucracy so that its talents are utilized. It is the task of every President to combine politics with purpose, and the talents required to establish confidence in government are also those needed for policy leadership. In a government of laws, not men, we are ultimately dependent upon a single man.

What are the lessons of the past about the kind of man we need in the White House?

Character

PERSONAL INSECURITY AND POLITICAL SKILL

In the heyday of Lyndon Johnson this writer developed the thesis that personal insecurity and political skill were linked. The creative politician was depicted as the man who required attention and needed to dominate and therefore had developed skills of self-dramatization and persuasion that would serve those needs. The thesis was applied to American Presidents. The two Roosevelts and Wilson were pictured as men especially in need of attention and power, and skill and creativity were said to be related to a perpetual striving to serve these goals. Whereas Presidents lacking such needs were also seen as without abilities—with Taft, Hoover, and Eisenhower as instances. They were pictured as almost too healthy to be good leaders.[5]

The view of the presidential office and the skills required was that presented by Richard Neustadt.[6] The Presidency was seen as institutionally weak in power and each President had to start from scratch in developing political resources. A sensitivity to power and power relationships was therefore essential. Coalitions of support within and outside of government had to be built up out of the perspectives of others who had power in their own right, independent of the President. The argument went further than Neustadt's in asking what kinds of personalities had such power skills.

This thesis assumed that Presidents were guided by moral purpose and it was frankly biased in the direction of the liberal, power-maximizing Presidents. It was assumed that purpose would purify power. To be fair to oneself the argument was made that such power-striving, if rooted in personal needs, could lead to self-defeating eruptions of personality such as Theodore Roosevelt's in 1912, Wilson's rigidity in the League fight, and FDR's plan to pack the Supreme Court. However, it was assumed that institutional checks and balances were sufficient to control such behavior. The price was worth paying because strong political leadership was required. Lyndon Johnson seemed the ideal President in this scheme of things. His voracious needs and insecurities provided the fuel for his great abilities in the service of genuinely liberal values in which he deeply believed. How much of this position needs to be taken back now that we have had a longer and

[5] Erwin C. Hargrove, *Presidential Leadership, Personality and Political Style* (New York: MacMillan Co., 1966).

[6] Richard E. Neustadt, *Presidential Power, The Politics of Leadership* (New York: John Wiley & Son, Inc., 1960).

fuller look at LBJ? And does the experience of Richard Nixon as President add to the difficulty?

"POLITICAL MAN"

The formulation reflected the liberal optimism of the time that power would be used for the right purposes. Therefore, there was insufficient inquiry into possible variations in the personal needs for attention and dominance of creative leaders. The hypothesis about the relation between needs and skills was taken from Harold Lasswell but optimistic conclusions were drawn from the inference—something Lasswell did not do. Lasswell drew a distinction between "political man" and "democratic character." The former sought a political life in order to bolster low estimates of the self. Early feelings of deprivation would be overcome by political successes. A prominent type of "political man" was the "agitator" who taught himself to play on the emotions of audiences, whether large or small, and direct their attention and affection toward himself. The "democratic character" on the other hand had successfully passed through the developmental crises of life and had no such insecurities and needs. He had "outgrown" politics, and in a society conducive to the development of "democratic character" there would be no "political men." [7]

Lasswell did not solve the problem of what to do about selecting leaders until that ideal time. So this writer adapted the model of "political man" to the requirements of democratic leadership, aware that a price might have to be paid. The experience of Johnson and Nixon has increased that concern greatly. The tragedy of each Presidency has been that the basic insecurities of the man, which were one basis for the talent that had been developed, were also the principal reason for failure. The negative effects upon the Presidency have been great.

We do not need to question Johnson's strong desire to do good when we point out that it was always joined to a compulsion to rule others. Those who worked closely with him felt that this compulsion was rooted in an uncertainty and insecurity about the self which seems to have had two dimensions. There was the cultural insecurity of being from Texas, of not having gone to Harvard and feeling ill at ease with intellectuals and Eastern "establishment" figures. But there was also a much deeper uneasiness that showed in his sensitiveness to criticism and the demand for absolute loyalty from subordinates and associates.

His insecurities were less apparent in Congress because the setting was more provincial and his power was limited. He worked well in bargaining situations where he knew he could not dominate by fiat, and the Senate of the nineteen-fifties was his element. He continued

[7] Harold P. Lasswell, *Power and Personality* (New York: W. W. Norton, 1948).

the same style of broker for a consensus in his first year as President—especially in his leadership of Congress, in which he employed the forcefulness of his personality upon its members and yet respected congressional prerogatives.

However, within his own official family a different Lyndon emerged, the one who had always been a bully to his staff. He demanded total loyalty within and lashed back at criticism from without. His excessive reaction to criticism of the Dominican Republic intervention forecast what was to come on Vietnam. As the war grew more frustrating he created an artificial world within the government about the reality outside which led to a public credibility gap. He refused to believe he might be wrong until the very last. Even if we believe his Vietnam policy to have been correct, Johnson's psychology was one of defensiveness and rigidity. He responded with fury to all threats to his self-esteem. The consequences affected not only policy but the entire atmosphere of his administration. The Presidency as an authoritarian force emerged into full view.

President Nixon's troubles stem from deep strains in his character as well. One need not believe that he was an active participant in the Watergate affair to give him responsibility for the atmosphere in the White House which produced Watergate.

Nixon's entire career has been a painful series of efforts to overcome a deep uncertainty about himself. The obsession with facing a "crisis" well reflects a fear that he might fail to meet the test. The persistent theme of a Uriah Heep—such as self-pity and the identification of all his problems with "enemies"—reveals a man who cannot relax in a happy love of self. The awareness that he tires easily and needs time and seclusion to make up his mind shows us a man doubtful of his inner resources.

Behind the Watergate tragedy we see an isolated President who created a White House staff defensive and protective of the President and full of contempt for his "enemies." We had the incredible paradox of people in positions of national power who felt weak and defensive in regard to national "establishments" like Congress, the bureaucracy, the media, and the major universities. The morality tale of Watergate is a pathetic unraveling of the presidential personality.

The great danger is that a President who feels threatened by events or harassed by "enemies" will precipitate a crisis in order to shore up his own inner doubts and confound his opposition.

"DEMOCRATIC CHARACTER"

Yet Theodore and Franklin Roosevelt enjoyed attention and power and needed office and a full political life to realize themselves. How do they differ from Johnson and Nixon? The answer seems to be that despite their insecurities and strong needs these two men sought a life in politics as a self-actualizing quest. They were not so much insecure as needing fulfillment. They were at their happiest when in the saddle, and in fact Teddy Roosevelt's aberrations came when he was out of office and desperate to get back in. John Kennedy was similar to these two in the self-affirming character of his leadership but his needs and drives were not so intense nor were his skills as fully developed.

James David Barber, writing after the experience of Johnson and Nixon, and therefore free of any temptation to idealize the power-seeker, has given us the clue to the differences between these kinds of Presidents. Franklin Roosevelt, Truman, and Kennedy were happy, integrated, self-respecting, and expansive people who were capable of growth and learning. Their energies were directed outward toward achievement, not bound up in defensive postures. Roosevelt in particular shared the characterization of Lasswell's "political man" in their political needs and skills. But they also possessed "democratic character." [8]

Woodrow Wilson, Hoover, Johnson, and Nixon brought a negative cast to their careers according to Barber. Ceaseless striving for place, power, and deference could never be satisfied because the lack of self-esteem that needed strengthening was insatiable. Political style took on a compulsive quality. And sharp threats to self-esteem and position were often met in rigid and ego-defensive ways.

Not all persons who have confidence in themselves and politics are skillful political leaders. Dwight Eisenhower had a basic self-respect and stability which was a source of strength to him as President, but he lacked the personality needs which might have made him a complete politician.[9] John Kennedy fell somewhere between the two Roosevelts and Eisenhower on such a need skill scale.

However, we cannot expect to get brilliant "political men" who are also "democratic characters" very often. A great many extraordinarily able political leaders are not "democratic characters" but "active-negatives," to use Barber's term, who desperately need office and power and can do great harm with power if unchecked. We must particularly be on guard against such people and this is not easy since "active-positives" and "active-negatives" often appear the same to observers on the surface. This is particularly the case in an entrepreneurial political

---

[8] James D. Barber, *The Presidential Character, Predicting Performance in the White House* (New York: Prentice-Hall, 1972).

[9] Barber classifies Eisenhower as a "passive-negative" but I do not agree with that interpretation.

culture in which the politician who would succeed must develop self-dramatizing and power-maximizing skills to a great degree.

Of course individuals do not embody the characteristics of "ideal types." Johnson had an "active-positive" expansive and joyful side to his personality and leadership. Who can deny that Woodrow Wilson was a great President with an enormous gift for moral leadership despite a tragic flaw in his character? We cannot expect to be able to predict what kind of President an individual will be by placing him within a typology. But these crude beginnings in linking character to style should at least make us sensitive to what we wish to avoid. In the immediate future we are likely to emphasize character over great political skill. Truman, Eisenhower, and Kennedy will be our models. They were not great political craftsmen but were rather "democratic characters" who were teaching themselves to be "political men."

Perhaps we have made too much of a sensitivity to power relations as the key to success as President. By putting such a high priority on the ability to manipulate others we make ourselves prey to the "active-negatives" who are good at this. The experiences of Johnson and Nixon show that a heightened sensitivity by the President to his personal power position may actually blind him to the kind of learning and listening required by his official power position.[10] And the positive achievements of all Presidents, and especially the master of tactics like FDR, were not really based upon tactical skill at manipulating others. Rather the basis of influence and achievement was the ability to appeal to others in terms of shared values.[11] There are many bases of power and most important among them is the affirmation of future possibilities in terms of common values. The "active-positive" leader is more likely to lead in this way and these are the qualities of leadership that we must look for.

Democratic Style of Authority

The fruits of "democratic character" are in a style of authority which encourages others to express themselves freely and which promotes discussion processes in which there is a maximum possible variety of viewpoints on both normative and factual questions. Clearly there are limits in time, energy, and world view as well as political

[10] Alexander L. George, "The Case for Multiple Advocacy in Making Foreign Policy," *American Political Science Review*, Vol. LXVI, no. 3 (Sept. 1972), pp. 751–785.

[11] Peter W. Sperlich, "Bargaining and Overload: an Essay on Presidential Power," in Aaron Wildavsky, ed., *The Presidency* (Boston: Little, Brown & Co., 1969).

constraints on such a style and process but it is the basic posture that we demand. We need leadership which will be a catalyst for initiatives and ideas and which will learn from this process. At the end of the day a President must decide for himself and then find ways to persuade others to support his view. But there is a greater likelihood of his decisions being "good" in terms of his own objectives if he has an open style of authority.

Of course there is not a perfect relationship between democratic character and a democratic style of authority. Skill at organizing discussion processes is not necessarily related to character, and even the most skillful President can make a mess of things. Nor will a democratic style guarantee an accurate presidential view of the world or of American society. No President can completely transcend the stock of commonly shared cultural biases nor perhaps should he. Also, under some conditions a secretive authoritative style in a President is necessary. But, on the whole, openness makes for better decisions, and institutions in which all actors feel free to speak out are better than ones bound up in hierarchy, deference, and fear.

CASES

The numerous foreign policy crises of the nineteen-sixties stimulated a search by political scientists for the conditions which produce policy mishaps in which the decision-makers fail to see basic factors in a situation which will ensure failure, judged in terms of their own objectives. In this sense a "good" decision is one which manifests an understanding of the real situation. This is a limited perspective because a group of men could see a situation accurately and yet act in ways we would condemn because our moral standards would differ. But, the model is useful for analyzing the decision process.

The crucial variable in achieving a "good" decision in the sense defined above is presidential style of authority. Theoretical conclusions from experiments with laboratory small groups are confirmed by current history. An authoritarian leadership style saps the initiative of the group and screens out information. A democratic leadership style, which is not so permissive that authority is lost, liberates the energies of a group and permits creativity of response to new situations.

Glenn Paige was the first to develop a theoretical framework for looking at decisions in this way.[12] He developed a model of the properties of a crisis decision out of his study of the United States intervention in Korea. When faced with an unexpected crisis the small group which the President brings together for decision is likely to make

[12] Glenn D. Paige, *The Korean Decision, June 24–30, 1950* (New York: Free Press, 1968).

a "high consensus decision" in which support for the President and group solidarity will be strong. The President will set the limits of possible option by the cues he gives the group. In this case, President Truman made it clear from the beginning that American action against aggression was essential and this inevitably led to a military commitment. In such a group the picture of the world which its members bring is likely to continue to prevail against new information in the short run. And in the moment of crisis little heed is paid to external critics.

Paige does not regard the Korean decision as a bad one but he does point out the dangers in such a decision process. Conformity and group solidarity can rule at the expense of new ideas. Excessive deference to the President can prevail and potential dissent be stifled. Information contrary to the group consensus can be unconsciously screened out. He urges that special pains be taken to build in adversary processes through the use of staff and that an effort be made to solicit external criticism.

The dynamics of such a decision group are obviously capable of great variety depending upon presidential style. The Bay of Pigs invasion and the Cuban missile crisis illustrate Paige's basic insights. In the first case John Kennedy did not encourage the members of the decision group to criticize the assumptions or information supplied by the Central Intelligence Agency nor did he support the efforts of Senator Fulbright and Arthur Schlesinger to challenge the consensus. The President encouraged his associates to close ranks behind a decision that was poorly presented and inadequately scrutinized. The execution of the decision proved this to be so, for much of the intelligence provided was simply wrong. Of course the even greater failure on the part of the President was not to raise the question of the morality of the action.

In the second case Kennedy acted deliberately out of the experience of the first. He had already changed decision styles within his government to promote adversary debate by using McGeorge Bundy as a staff catalyst in this regard and pushing his brother Robert and Theodore Sorensen to be devil's advocates. He was fortunate in having a brother who was completely secure with the President and not afraid to speak out and who could therefore legitimize courage for others. Thoroughly open discussion characterized the executive committee during the missile crisis. The result was a high consensus decision but one of a higher level of synthesis than the Korean decision because it had emerged from a more intense and searching consideration of alternatives.

Of course, Kennedy ruled out a nonmilitary response at the beginning. Had the decision been for an air strike resulting in a nuclear exchange, we would not be praising it. Adlai Stevenson's plea for a strictly political response was ridiculed by some members of the group. The efforts of Secretary McNamara in the same direction stopped when he saw they would not carry the President. But the point is clear, that Presidential style is the critical variable in setting the tone and limits much of the content of group discussion.

COUNTERING CONFORMITY

Irving Janis postulates that there is a strong tendency toward working conformity in small groups. The mechanisms for uncovering and challenging unexamined premises are often lacking.[13] Dissenters are likely to be ignored or ejected. What seems like vigorous debate is usually about instrumental questions rather than basic assumptions. In short, everything about presidential decision-making is likely to serve the President ill unless he self-consciously takes deliberate steps to ensure variety, dissent, conflict and make clear to his advisers that he values honesty above all else. Even then, he may have a hard time getting others to approach him on equal terms. The personal ambition of advisers and plain speaking to the leader are often not compatible unless he rewards frankness.

Alexander George has suggested that the President set a staff "custodian" to watch over the quality of advice and debate, but one must stress the point that only the President can communicate his intentions to others and must do this by his personal relationships with them. No "custodian" can do that for him.[14]

Chester Cooper describes how Lyndon Johnson would poll his principal foreign policy advisers one at a time on questions to do with the conduct of the war. He would go around the table and elicit an "I agree, Mr. President" from each one. Cooper imagined a fantasy in which he would stand up and announce with a flourish, "Mr. President, gentlemen, I most definitely do not agree." But when his turn came he always heard himself saying, "Yes, Mr. President, I agree." [15]

One forms a strong impression from the accounts of Vietnam decision-making that Johnson initially gave his advisers cues that precluded any serious consideration of withdrawal or a political settlement in 1965 and that he promoted a subsequent hardening of commitment to the policy of intervention until 1968 when a series of shocks penetrated his reality world and caused him to pull back. It was largely

[13] Irving L. Janis, *Victims of Group Think* (Boston: Houghton Mifflin Co., 1972).
[14] George, pp. 751–785.
[15] Chester L. Cooper, *The Last Crusade, America in Vietnam* (New York: Dodd, Mead & Co., 1970).

due to the courage of new and old advisers, especially Clark Clifford, that this change occurred. But even that might not have happened had it not been for the Tet offensive and the candidacies of McCarthy and Kennedy.[16]

All of this suggests that a presidential style of authority which sets undue limits on discussion is likely to reinforce all the other factors in government that make for policy mishaps: the timidity and conformity of advisers, lack of sensitivity to external critics, failure to examine the assumptions behind prevailing policies, and adherence to bureaucratic routine. A democratic style of authority therefore is not a weak or permissive posture. It is the insistence by a President that he be well served. He must be tough, ask hard questions, break up comfortable alliances and, above all, encourage those who work with him to strive for fresh views and to have the courage to speak out. Clearly we are in the realm of subjective judgment when we start to say that a given President should have cast his net more widely in a given case or cases. We may simply disagree with his decision and wish that he had given greater weight to our values. It is also true that all Presidents set limits to the ideas they will entertain and that no President likes an adviser who is consistently critical or difficult.

But, we can make a general evaluation of a man's style of inquiry and discourse and here Presidents differ greatly. Theodore and Franklin Roosevelt were superb at reaching out for information from a variety of sources and at encouraging them to provide it. Dwight Eisenhower and John Kennedy had open, inquiring styles but each was limited by the uniformity of his key associates and advisers, in contrast to FDR, for example. However, Kennedy's capacity for growth as evidenced by his initiatives for civil rights and an end to the Cold War in 1963, neither of which were characteristic of the strident cold warrior and cautious politician of 1961, stands in clear contrast to the imperious style of Johnson and the crabbed isolation of Nixon.

There are always intellectual and normative limits to the scope of presidential discourse but we must ask—is a President trying to learn and encouraging others to do so? And the negative cases convince us of the importance of the question.

Institutional Consequences of Democratic Character and Style

We have considered the consequences of personality and style for policy-making, but what of the effect on the institutions themselves?

16 Townsend Hoopes, *The Limits of Intervention* (New York: David McKay Co., Inc., 1969); David Halberstam, *The Best and the Brightest* (New York: Random House, 1972); Cooper, op. cit.

Since the Second World War an institutionalized Presidency consisting of the White House staff and an Executive Office of the President has developed out of the practical necessities of the President doing his job. A great honeycomb of separate sets of staff advisers sit in concentric circles around the President and they are his primary agents in dealing with the bureaucracy and Congress. This institution however is only imperfectly institutionalized if by that we mean displaying regular, set, recurring patterns of activity. Rather it is malleable and few of its members have independent political or governmental status of their own. They rely upon the President for that status, and his attitudes toward them shape the way they relate to him, to each other, and to the rest of government. There is no prescribed pattern by which a President will or should relate to these advisory groups. He will eventually feel his way to a comfortable relationship. However, there are consequences for government of any such pattern.

IDEAL VS. REAL

Ideally the institutionalized Presidency should be specialized to communication and learning. It has all the attributes which the literature on innovation in organization ascribes to a bureaucracy which is well geared to learning from and adapting to its environment. It is composed primarily of professionals, economists, lawyers, scientists, who are in close touch with constituencies outside of government specializing in the development of knowledge and innovation and who bring a restless desire to improve things to government and are not mired in the routines or loyalties of bureaucracy. It provides for a mixture of professional roles in problem-solving in ways that encourage friction, within set limits, and therefore are conducive to the generating of new ideas. There is a flatness of hierarchy and relative equality among foreign policy, economic, scientific, budgetary, and political advisers and the collegiality that goes with professional styles reinforces this equality. The innovative institution is said to have a high degree of professionals, a rich mixture of roles, low stratification and formalization, and an atmosphere of collegiality. This is the potential structure and character of the White House.[17]

However, a number of forces that are perhaps found in all presidential institutions, whether public or private, run counter to these tendencies. The chief factor is the semiroyal character of the Presidency itself. The President is always addressed by title rather than by his first name. He is accorded the deference given to a monarch in the

17 Jerald Hage and Michael Aiken, *Social Change in Complex Organization* (New York: Random House, 1970).

steps that are taken for his comfort and security. He travels around the country in a sort of insulated royal procession by helicopter and presidential plane. A picture in *Life* magazine which showed President Nixon being greeted by the standing applause of his Cabinet and chief aides after a television speech on the bombing of North Vietnam in the spring of 1972 summed up this exaggerated deference. As George Reedy has put it, there is no one around to tell the President to "go soak his head" when he is wrong.[18] These magical properties of the office are congruent with the natural effects which great authority and power will have on those who serve it. Alfred Speer records the slavish deference that the unwilling Hitler was able to extract from his principal lieutenants even in the last days of the war because they still felt a mingled awe and fear of a man who had power over them.[19] This is commonplace court politics and it operates in the White House, in competition for the President's attention, in telling him what one thinks he wants to hear, in being afraid to tell him unpleasant news for fear of the effect on one's own ambitions. The drive for status and power strongly undercuts the learning qualities of the institution.

The men who serve Presidents are usually drawn from the ranks of the "successful" in a success-oriented society and they are likely to be arrogant about it. David Halberstam perhaps overdoes the importance of the "machismo" complex of the American male in his characterization of Vietnam decision-making, but certainly the White House has been "blessed" since 1961 with a succession of bright, arrogant young men who felt they had the key to history, whether it was the "new generation" of the Kennedy team or the true believers in the "zero-defect system" of H. R. Haldeman. Toughness and demand for results, qualities valued among American elites, have been the hallmark of such "in and outers." [20]

Of course there are functional, programmatic reasons why these attitudes develop. The necessity for the President to keep a close, personal supervision over foreign policy and the fact that national security matters cut across a number of departments have increasingly required the development of a White House national security apparatus. The same has been true for domestic program innovation in the sixties and seventies. The departments have not been geared to the development of ideas and plans for new programs which have cut across a number of fields and jurisdictions and the initiatives have inevitably gravitated to the White House.

18 George E. Reedy, *The Twilight of the Presidency* (New York: World Publishing Co., 1970).
19 Albert Speer, *Inside the Third Reich: Memoirs* (New York: MacMillan, 1970).
20 Halberstam, op. cit.

However, a series of vicious circles have been the result as authority and power for program initiation and implementation have been drawn to the White House. The departments have withered even more into those routinized, unimaginative patterns which led to the original presidential mistrust. The State Department is the classic case. Imaginative program innovation in the White House has sometimes resulted but a serious overload at the center has also occurred, and the basic tasks of reforming the departments to make them more innovative and better able to serve the President have been avoided.[21]

NEED FOR DEMOCRATIC STYLE

We cannot deny that the President needs help but his helpers can be his worst enemies if he does not control them. It is increasingly clear that the White House staff is standing between the President and the rest of government and has got to be cut down to size. Staff should be lean, inquisitive, and catalytic. They should serve as inquirers for the President and coordinators of his business. But, they cannot displace the departments. The reversal of the trend of power toward the White House and back to the departments would be only the first step in a number of reforms necessary to revitalize the departments which cannot be discussed here. But such action can only come from a President who is determined to draw upon the widest possible variety of sources of advice. Presidential style will set the dominant patterns of attitudes and relationships within the White House and between the White House and the rest of government.

We have seen all the worst features of the trends of the sixties at work in the Nixon White House. The privacy of the President, loyalty in the White House hierarchy from the top down, enforced by command and central mechanisms, were the order of the day. The effort to run a "zero defect system," in Haldeman's words, reveals an incredible naiveté about the inherent and desirable sloppiness of government in which one learns from the mistakes that one made. The efforts to create a hierarchy of White House counselors-department heads who would direct the rest of the Cabinet again ran up against the pluralist reality of government.

In the wake of Watergate there was talk in the White House of opening up the Presidency so that the President would see and deal

---

[21] Thomas E. Cronin, "Everybody Believes in Democracy Until He Gets in the White House—An Analysis of White House Departmental Relations" in Norman C. Thomas and Hans W. Baade, eds., *The Institutionalized Presidency* (Dobbs Ferry, New York: Oceana Publications, 1972); Robert C. Wood, "When Government Works," *The Public Interest*, No. 18 (Winter, 1970).

directly with many more people such as department heads and congressional leaders. This was an implicit admission that something had gone wrong before and a recognition of the fact that a President draws support from personal and political relationships throughout government rather than from a managerial system.

Only a breath of presidential fresh air in the form of a genuinely democratic style of authority can reverse these trends. And it is not only a question of the President getting the information he needs. That is only the first step toward his taking hold of the levers needed to govern. The chief lever is the capacity to move and excite others in terms of shared values. This is the only way a President can ultimately get the bureaucracy on his side. There is a great deal of slack and untapped energy in the permanent government which a President can draw on. In Philip Selznick's phrase, the executive becomes a statesman as he moves from administrative management to institutional leadership, and this means providing a sense of institutional purpose.[22]

The same lessons apply to policy leadership in Congress and the country. A President must listen to and learn from Congress in his own interest and when he decides not to do so, as President Nixon so decided in the heady flush of victory in early 1973, he sows the seeds of his own defeat. But, even more important, a President carries the Congress with him only by appealing to shared perspectives and values. He must have that ability to reach out and catch others up in his design.

This is the chief moral of the essay. The kind of President whom we need to establish a new constitutional morality and reverse the trends of closed hierarchy is also the kind of President who can build the political conditions for the resolution of our policy dilemmas. We are now living with a fragmented and divided policy system. Neither major party can amass the political resources to confront our difficult domestic problems. New electoral and policy coalitions will have to be put together. This is the most crucial task of the Presidency and everything that we have said about democratic character and style is prerequisite to it. Coalitions for lesser and meaner purposes will be put together but solution of our problems in terms of the ideals of the nation will require more than that. This kind of creativity requires empathy for the values and beliefs of others and the ability to invoke the deepest values of American life in support of programs of action. Such ability matches democratic character and style.

[22] Philip Selznick, *Leadership in Administration, a Sociological Interpretation* (New York: Harper & Row, 1957).

CRITERIA OF DEMOCRATIC STYLE

How can we know such men when we see them? The literature on innovation in organizations sets forth a model which bears a close resemblance to the kind of President we need.[23] The similarity is due to the functional imperatives that are common to all organizations, public and private, that would adapt to the modern world. Warren G. Bennis calls this the "agricultural" style of leadership. The central requirement is that the leader have the capacity to stimulate the efforts of others to give their utmost to the work of the organization. He does this by sowing the seeds of ideas, challenging others to develop initiatives, and so structuring the patterns of authority that equality and collegiality predominate. He must be able to bring it all together in policies most will accept because they have had a hand in their formulation. This is not a permissive style of leadership but one strong enough to keep its authority in the face of dissent, disagreement, and challenge. But authority resides in style rather than position.

This manner of leading is seen as functional for modern organizations because it enhances the creativity of response to problems. It is the contrast to a hierarchical style which stands on formal position and relies on levers of managerial command and administrative sanctions to get results. Such leadership is likely to lack the legitimacy that comes from direct involvement with others. And such organizations are not likely to be flexible enough or sufficiently capable of learning about reality to adapt to their problems.

A model of leadership which stresses psychological health, an open and democratic style of authority, and the ability to draw the best in the way of ideas and aspirations from others is very much a reaction against a Machiavellian ideal and practice of a manipulative leader who resorts to deception to gain his way. We came too close to embracing Machiavelli in our implicit expectations about Presidents. Skills in the maximization of power have been shown to be sterile and destructive unless joined to commonly accepted moral purposes. The personal need for power and respect in a political leader has a double-edged quality to which we were not sufficiently sensitive. Therefore the model of "democratic character" is a revisionist idea. But, as such, it is incomplete. It is too much of a nonpolitical ideal of a good man but a great deal of the necessary equipment for political leadership is left out. The idea of the "agricultural leader" itself was developed from the study of leadership in business corporations and other non-

23 Hage and Aiken, op. cit.; Warren G. Bennis and Philip E. Slater, *The Temporary Society* (New York: Harper & Row, 1968); Bertram Gross, ed., *A Great Society?* (New York: Baris Books, 1968).

political institutions in which the authority of the leader is more assured than is that of political executives. A corporation president can afford to be more permissive about fermentation below because in most circumstances he knows that he can get his way in the end. A President can never be sure of that in a government of countervailing powers. Therefore Neustadt is quite correct to call for the political arts of persuasion and maneuver in his President. The model of "agricultural" leadership is a valid and necessary insight but it does not call for the leader himself to have ideas about what ought to be done and a craft at moving others to accept those ideas. A President who attempted to be nothing more than an "agricultural" leader and did not exercise skills in moving men in desired directions would lose control of the governmental process. He would fail to be aware of the inevitable conflicts of interest and goals among men and would lack his own sense of direction and purpose.

Therefore we need both a democratic character and a political man. We do need an "agricultural" leader but he must also be a person who can hold something of himself in reserve, who can see through the designs of others, and who can play on both the low and high motives of men in persuading them to act. However, the evidence of history is abundantly clear that the most reliable and strong base of political influence and power for a President is the ability to persuade others to do something or support a measure because it is felt to be the morally right thing to do. Often this must be joined to appeals to self-interest but such appeals by themselves are often insufficient. It is difficult to define such moral leadership but we know it when we see it. Lyndon Johnson exercised it in 1965 when he stood before the Congress to call for voting rights legislation and joined the language of the civil rights movement—"we shall overcome"—to the basic right of every American to vote. Of course there can never be a guarantee that what a President and others feel to be the right action is in fact what is morally correct. We can only call for aspiration, not certainty.

What manner of man are we seeking? A full model of a democratic character and political man will inevitably contain a tension between the two guiding principles, and different facets will be given priority at different times depending upon the felt necessities of the period. Therefore a model is an ideal type which will never be fully realized in any individual leader. However, there are minimal requirements for each dimension of the model which must be met by acceptable candidates for the Presidency. These are the touchstones by which we must judge those who aspire:

1. They must give every sign of so loving themselves in the biblical sense that they are free to have concern for others. Any signs of self-pity, the

personalization of conflict and issues, fundamental self-doubt, and rigidity and defensiveness under attack are danger signs.

2. Concern about the health of personality as phrased above is not enough. We must also ask about old-fashioned moral character and integrity. Is a man good to his word? Does he tell the truth? Recent history has shown that these are not idle questions.

3. There must be evidence of a democratic style of authority drawn from actual leadership positions and experience. We are taking a risk when we select men who have not had the opportunities to develop such a style.

4. The ability to persuade others that a moral question is at stake in given matters is elusive and difficult to define or discern, but it is vital. There will always be disagreement about the content but a man who can move others with moral appeals can usually affect even his opponents in a positive way.

5. The leader must be able to think and act politically and to devise strategies and tactics of persuasion that draw upon diverse sources of support.

No individual will embody all of these fully but we must insist that any man who would be President must possess the first two attributes in full. Individuals will vary in the degree to which they embody the latter three but these are criteria by which candidates may be compared and evaluated. In 1973 we were emphasizing character and democratic style and downplaying skill and even moral leadership because we did not see a time of dynamic positive leadership ahead. Rather, we were anxious to restore respect and legitimacy to the Presidency. A time will come in the future when there will be a strong call for positive moral leadership and political skills and at that time it will be most important to also ask about character and style of authority. We must not be beguiled again by men of power. The most important lesson may be the negative one that we must guard against "political" men without democratic characters, who are hollow and destructive.

The criteria of this ideal type are separate attributes of personality and none follows automatically from the possession of another. A healthy, self-confident character is necessary but not sufficient for a democratic style of authority. Skills of leadership are important as well. A democratic style of authority facilitates moral and intellectual leadership but it cannot provide correct understanding of the world or moral and ideological purpose. These derive from a man's beliefs and values. So we need all three—character, skill, and beliefs.

It is not the intention of this chapter to claim that character and style are more important than moral and policy purpose in a President. These things are equally important. The continuing crises of confidence in the contemporary Presidency have been both crises of character and of ideology and these have often been fused. For example, the experience of Vietnam has caused us to reconsider our Cold War ideology at the same time that we begin to question presidential war powers and see the critical importance of presidential personality in crisis decisions. The questions are ultimately inseparable. The emphasis of this essay is upon character and style but that does not deny the importance of purpose.

SELECTING LEADERS WITH "DEMOCRATIC CHARACTER"

The normal processes of presidential selection operate on the political level and have to do with a candidate's coalition and his policy ideas. Little explicit attention is given to his character although his style of authority is sometimes considered if he makes obvious blunders as did George McGovern. The American people are not interested in a weak or indecisive leader. However, there does not seem to be any way to institutionalize a concern with the qualities of character and style of authority which have been stressed here. The selection process is far too open and unpredictable for there to be elite gatekeepers who would bar the way to men who did not meet these kinds of criteria. Nor can one be sanguine that we can ever have sufficient knowledge of a given individual to describe him in these terms or that such knowledge can be widely disseminated and understood if it existed. There is no real training ground for the Presidency and most men have not developed the full range of talents required for the office in their previous work. We will therefore not always know of deficiencies which have not yet emerged.

The best that we can hope to do is to emphasize democratic styles of leadership in all the organizations of our society as a functional imperative so that the selection of leaders, including Presidents, will be implicitly guided by a search for "democratic character." If these ideals are strong and operative in everyday institutional life, destructive personalities are likely to fall by the wayside in the presidential contest. This is an idealistic hope. It is not comfortable to have to rely on the character of a man for the health of our democracy. We have something of the dilemma of medieval monarchy in our need for a "good king." One would wish that our institutions of government could make it otherwise.

Donald R. Matthews

2

Presidential Nominations:

Process and Outcomes

The recent history of American presidential nominations is dismal. Both parties, the Republicans in 1964 and the Democrats in 1972, have nominated candidates who were virtually certain losers. The Democratic national convention of 1968 was accompanied by bloody skirmishes between antiwar protestors and the Chicago police; what went on within the convention hall was not much more reassuring about the party's ability to govern itself or the nation. One leading contender for the presidential nomination has been killed and a second badly crippled by assassins. A vice-presidential candidate was dumped from the Democratic ticket in 1972 after a record of emotional instability and psychiatric treatment came to light a few days after his nomination; his successful Republican opponent resigned the Vice-Presidency after pleading no contest to income tax evasion (rather than face charges of extortion and bribery). And now the Watergate hearings have revealed widespread criminal activities directed by presidential associates and White House assistants calculated to insure Richard Nixon's reelection. The American people have cause for concern over the adequacy of both the processes and the outcomes of recent presidential nominating politics.

Professor of political science and faculty associate, Institute for Social Research, University of Michigan, DONALD R. MATTHEWS *was senior fellow in governmental studies at The Brookings Institution from 1968 to 1973. He is the author of* U.S. Senators and Their World *and numerous other publications. He recently edited* Perspectives on Presidential Selection *and is working on a volume on presidential nominating politics (with William Keech) for The Brookings Institution.*

As Austin Ranney points out in chapter 3, both major parties have begun to respond to these concerns. The Democrats embarked upon one of the most sweeping programs of party reform in their long history after 1968; the Republicans are moving cautiously in the same direction. Undoubtedly, the Watergate scandals will intensify this reevaluation of established ways and lead to more reform.

But what is wrong with American presidential nominating politics and what to do about it are not clear. There is an unfortunate tendency for party reformers to focus on "what went wrong last time" and for practical politicians to be exclusively concerned with winning "next time." As a result, the more persistent and basic problems of presidential nominating politics are ignored. Now is thus an especially propitious time to examine existing nominating arrangements in some historical depth and to seek to determine how various processes affect the type of person who ordinarily becomes a presidential candidate.

Some Properties of Nominating Decisions

Nominating decisions differ from other collective choices, especially elections, in significant ways. Unless we fully appreciate these differences we are not likely to grasp how they are made, or might be made better.

NOMINATIONS ARE MORE CRITICAL THAN ELECTIONS

Nominations are the most critical stage of the entire process of presidential choice. Once the major parties have made their nominations only two out of the millions of persons meeting the constitutional requirements of the office have a realistic chance of entering the White House: more eligible persons are eliminated from the presidential contest at this early stage of the process than at any other. Viewed qualitatively, nominations are equally important. If the two major parties select well-qualified candidates, the voters cannot make a really bad choice; if the two parties both nominate fools, the electorate cannot win.

The nominating decision is one of the major determinates of who wins in November. Of the trinity of variables affecting voter choice—party identification, issues, and candidates—the last is most subject to change. Victory or defeat is often shaped by forces over which politicians have little control, at least in the short run. But the major parties must nominate presidential candidates every four years. Once they have done this job, the results of the November elections have been fairly well predetermined about half the time since 1936 (i.e., 1936, 1952, 1956, 1964, 1972).

NOMINATIONS ARE MORE COMPLEX THAN ELECTIONS

In the November election, the nation is presented with a forced choice between two presidential candidates, one a Republican and the other a Democrat.[1] The selection of a presidential nominee is an inherently more difficult matter.

The Two Roles of the Nominee—In the first place, a nomination is a provisional choice. When a party selects its presidential nominee, it has chosen him to perform not one but two roles—President of the United States and *candidate* for President of the United States. While the qualities necessary to perform successfully in these two roles are similar, they are not identical. Since a campaign must be won in order to become President, electoral considerations usually loom larger in nominating decision-making than estimates of probable performance in the White House. But the relative weight assigned to these two factors can and does vary according to the situation and from individual to individual. Certainly the major parties do not invariably choose the man with the best general election prospects at convention time. Politicians may want to win, but "winning" is not always defined as attracting more votes nationwide than the other party the following November. Factional or ideological triumphs within the party, victory for the state and local ticket, and so on, can be more important to some than winning the Presidency.

"Arrow Problems" and All That—While presidential elections present a forced choice between two alternatives, the number of persons who might be nominated runs in the millions. Of course, only a relative handful of persons have a chance of being nominated or actively seek it. But our parties ordinarily must choose between more than two alternatives when they make a presidential nomination. Arriving at a collective choice between four or five possible nominees is vastly more difficult than deciding between two. Indeed Kenneth Arrow and others[2] have demonstrated that there is no invariably satisfactory way for a

---

1 This, of course, ignores the existence of minor party candidates. So few votes are cast for them in the typical presidential election that it is safe to assume that most voters usually perceive the voting situation as a forced choice between the two major party candidates.

2 Kenneth Arrow, *Social Choice and Individual Values* (New York: Wiley, 1963) and Duncan Black, *The Theory of Committees and Elections* (Cambridge University, 1959) for mathematical demonstrations of this point. V. O. Key, Jr.'s criticism of one-party politics in the South was based, in large part, on his view that a multiplicity of unlabeled candidates resulted in voter confusion and irrationality. See his *Southern Politics* (New York: Knopf, 1949), Ch. 14.

group to arrive at a choice between more than two alternatives in a reasonably democratic way.

If, as is true in both parties, the choice of presidential nominee is made on the basis of absolute majority rule, the selection of a nominee often requires the combination of first, second, and even third choices before a winner can emerge. When this is the case, assessments of the competitors' likelihood of winning the nomination must be combined with their relative attractiveness as candidates and potential Presidents in order to make a reasonable choice between them. It makes no sense to most people to back a first choice candidate if he has little chance of nomination compared to their second choice; to do so may contribute to the selection of a quite unacceptable man. *Anticipated* outcomes thus play a large role in nominating decisions; they are irrelevant in decision-making in the normal American two-man plurality election.

The Absence of Party ID and Other Decision Aids—These inherent difficulties must be faced without some handy aids to reasonable decision which exist in the general election context. Party identification is a short-cut way of deciding who "the good guys" are, but all the contestants belong to the same party in the nominating contests. The amount of information available about alternative nominees varies widely—some have been in the public eye for decades, others are not well known when the nominating contest begins.

Given these inescapable problems, it is not surprising that presidential nominating politics is extraordinarily subtle, ambiguous, and complex.

A MISLEADING METAPHOR

We try to understand complex phenomena by comparing them to simple and familiar things. The vocabulary of American politics contains one dominant metaphor used to describe presidential nominating processes. Presidential nominations, our language suggests, are like horse races with "front-runners," "stretch-drives," "dark horses," "packs," "sweepstakes," "finish lines," and the rest. The image is pleasing—one can almost taste the icy mint julep and hear the roar of the crowd. And yet, as we shall see, presidential nominations are a crazy kind of horse race. The contenders do not start at the same time or at the same place on the track, there is often doubt about how many horses are entered or who will join the chase somewhere along the way. The winner must do far more than beat his competitors to the finish line: he must run a greater distance than all the other horses combined.

I shall, from time to time, use the lingo of the track in attempting to describe the presidential nominating process for the metaphor is so deeply imbedded in political language that it is awkward to communicate without doing so. But the reader is forewarned that the implied similarity between presidential nominating politics and horse-racing is about as close as that between an elephant and a whale.

If the dominant metaphor used to depict American presidential nominating contests is profoundly misleading, what are presidential nominations like? The next three sections of this chapter are devoted to answering this question. I shall draw heavily upon my research on presidential nominations since 1936 conducted at The Brookings Institution in collaboration with William Keech.[3] The nominating process will be divided into three stages: the emergence of "presidential possibilities," the definition of the competitive situation, and the formal/legal nominating process itself. My basic thesis will be that developments occurring during the first two stages of this process ordinarily determine the final outcome. Officially, presidential nominees are selected by delegates to the national party conventions but the convention decision is usually a symbolic culmination of a process that began much earlier and whose decisive stages occurred long before.

The Emergence of "Presidential Possibilities"

The formal nominating process in the United States is unusually open to candidacy. Nonetheless, few men and women have been considered as possible presidential nominees in recent years. How one becomes a member of this ill-defined group is a mysterious process. And yet the gross contours of the process are dimly discernible as are the personal qualities of those who regularly are perceived as "presidential possibilities."

THE NUMBER OF "PRESIDENTIAL POSSIBILITIES"

Agreement on the alternatives from which a choice is to be made often does not exist in the nominating situation. This not only complicates the collective choice process but also confounds the analyst. The best (although by no means the only) way of operationally defining the group of presidential possibilities is by means of the public opinion polls. *All* the presidential nominees since 1936 have shown some support for the Presidency in Gallup polls before their nomination. And yet only 62 Democrats and 47 Republicans have attracted

3 While my intellectual debts to Professor Keech are far greater than this acknowledgment can convey, he should not be held responsible for the content of this chapter. Nor should the officers and staff of The Brookings Institution and The Ford Foundation be held accountable, although I am indebted to them for providing the setting and the resources for this research.

the support of 1 percent or more of their fellow partisans in Gallup polls on presidential candidate preferences during the last 36 years.[4] Of course not all these were "real" presidential possibilities, but we can be reasonably confident that virtually all the serious possibilities are included in a group so defined.

The number of persons with a reasonable chance of being nominated for the Presidency by the Democratic and Republican parties is thus very small. Moreover, almost all of these persons showed up in the polls *before the formal nominating process began:* all but eight of the Democrats and four of the Republicans first surfaced in the polls during the three years stretching from the last presidential election to the beginning of the next election year.

Not only were there few potential presidential candidates at the beginning of the formal nominating process, but many of them had been around quite some time. Almost 60 percent of the Republican group were considered presidential possibilities in one or more previous election years. Harold Stassen's name crops up in seven different election years; Thomas Dewey, Richard Nixon, and Henry Cabot Lodge, Jr., each had measurable support in five different contests; Arthur Vandenburg, Robert A. Taft, and John Bricker in four; Herbert Hoover, General Douglas MacArthur, Earl Warren, Leverett Saltonstall, Dwight Eisenhower, Nelson Rockefeller, and Barry Goldwater in three. The Democrats displayed a notably higher rate of circulation, yet about a third of those showing up in the polls in an average year had been a presidential possibility in one or more previous presidential nominating contests.

The size of this group varies from year to year within each party. The series of electoral disasters experienced by the Republicans during the early New Deal years so decimated the ranks of prominent and experienced GOP officeholders that Governor Alfred E. Landon of Kansas had little opposition for the nomination in 1936. In 1940, Wendell Willkie's last minute nomination was greatly facilitated by the fact that his most serious opposition came from a 37-year-old district attorney

[4] The Gallup question is not an open-ended one. The initial list of potential nominees is prepared by the Gallup organization on the basis of their own judgment and pretest results. At irregular intervals, poll respondents are encouraged to add names to the list. Potential candidates who show significant support in this way are added to the list while those who do not are dropped. Additional names are sometimes added by Gallup in response to the flow of the news. These procedures result in some chance that persons with measurable popular support for a major party nomination are missed. Such errors are quite unlikely except at the very lowest levels of popular support. Nonetheless, the list of 109 persons receiving more than 1 percent support from fellow partisans should be viewed as only approximately correct.

who had yet to win a statewide election (Thomas E. Dewey) and a freshman senator (Robert A. Taft). Nor does a long string of party victories automatically result in a plethora of presidential prospects. Franklin Roosevelt dominated the national Democratic party for so long that the party contained few persons perceived as being of presidential stature upon his death in 1945. The most serious potential threat to Harry Truman's renomination in 1948 came from efforts to draft Dwight Eisenhower as the Democratic nominee! The anti-Truman Democrats had nowhere else to turn when Ike refused and the President was renominated in the face of apparently inevitable defeat.

While the pool of presidentially prominent persons can thus become dangerously shallow, it does not necessarily follow that the more presidential possibilities the better. Our present nominating procedures were severely strained, for example, by the unusually large number of rather evenly matched candidates the Democrats had in 1972. It is hard to imagine the chaos that might have ensued if there had been two or three times more. The principal alternative to present nominating procedures—a direct national presidential primary—seems no more able to handle the problem of majority choice between numerous candidates satisfactorily.[5] In either system, numerous candidates make it difficult to aggregate the broad-ranging support needed to win the nomination and subsequent general election. Indeed, under either present institutional arrangements or a national primary, too many candidates in the race can disadvantage those seeking a broad coalition of supporters in favor of those appealing to highly motivated and active party minorities. Given the nature of the coalitions needed to win general elections in America this scarcely seems desirable.

Thus, the real problem is not that too many potential candidates are screened out before the formal nominating process begins but that those who survive may be less well qualified and less representative of the divergent views of the nation than some of those who fall by the wayside.

THE "GREAT MENTIONER": THE MASS MEDIA

Without massive, nationwide publicity no person can become a "presidential possibility." Not just any kind of publicity will do. If that were the case, presidential politics could be dominated by enter-

---

[5] The usual "solution" to this problem is the run-off election. Not only does this seem infeasible for a national primary but it also does not guarantee that the most popular candidate (counting second choices) gets into the run-off. This difficulty is soluble in theory by allowing voters to indicate their second, third, and so on, choices on the ballot. Americans are quite unused to this form of voting, which has some special problems of its own. See Arrow, op. cit., Black, op. cit.

tainers, athletes, and other celebrities, many of whom are more widely known and admired than most presidential aspirants. There does seem to be a growing tendency in recent years for such "stars" to seek to capitalize on their notoriety in elective politics. But by no means all celebrities turned politician have been successful and, to date at least, none have sought to move directly into presidential contention without serving in lesser office first. The publicity which makes presidential possibilities must be received in a political, preferably a presidential, context.

For the most part, this kind of publicity is not for sale. An advertising blitz can sometimes make a previously obscure figure into a plausible contender for lesser offices, but so far the sheer volume of nationwide media exposure necessary in order to become a presidential possibility has ruled out this approach to the Presidency. Millions of dollars are spent on advertising by candidates for presidential nominations once the formal campaign begins, but these sums are modest compared to the costs of achieving sufficient public prominence to emerge as a plausible candidate in the first place. The publicity which makes men and women into presidential possibilities is mostly embedded in the regular news and editorial content of the press and broadcasting media.

The press thus plays a very large—and controversial—role in the making of presidential possibilities. First of all, the ability to make or break potential Presidents is largely concentrated in the hands of a few newsmen and news organizations—the prestige newspapers, wire services, news magazines, and radio-TV network news organizations. These organizations cover national political news when no one else, including most of the press corps, is very interested. And yet it is during the interelection period that almost all presidential possibilities emerge. Secondly, a consensus on the relative desirability of candidates and potential candidates tends to develop within the press corps. In 1972, for example, the press found Democratic candidate Muskie indecisive and hot tempered, McGovern a "lightweight," Humphrey a has-been, Jackson a right-winger, Wallace a racist demagogue. In 1968, Republican Romney was sanctimonious and naive, Nixon, secretive and untrustworthy. How accurately these images reflect reality is debatable—in my own view rather well as stereotypes go. But there can be little doubt that these collective evaluations are hung on presidential possibilities by the media and that they have an impact on presidential nominations.

The evaluations of the press corps may be less important than whom they pay attention to. Publicity linking a person to the Presidency tends to come most easily to those whom the press views as "serious." While newsmen are uncharacteristically inarticulate about what they mean by the concept, it seems to include their estimation of a person's capacity to wage a respectable nomination campaign. Persons who already rank high in the public opinion polls tend to receive more attention than those who do not—and yet without national publicity impressive poll standings are impossible. And those who have (or appear likely to have) easy access to the resources needed to run are viewed as more "serious" than those who do not (or who appear unlikely to attract such resources). Both these criteria make it difficult, although not impossible, for new faces to emerge on the presidential landscape.

THE ROLE OF MONEY

If the press serves as a screening mechanism in defining the small group of persons perceived as presidential possibilities, so do those who control political money. Presidential nomination campaigns are enormously expensive. A presidential aspirant must be able to raise (or appear to be able to raise) millions of dollars in order to be considered "serious." And yet the financial resources needed to make a plausible start are only a small fraction of those needed to win. If "start-up" costs can be met, a strong early showing in the polls and/or primaries will generate more new resources. But investing in the beginning stages of a presidential nominating campaign is a risky business, since both a nominating contest and a general election campaign must be won before it can bear fruit, symbolic or otherwise. Few Americans simultaneously control such great wealth and are interested enough in electoral politics to take such gambles. Those who are play a major role in presidential nominating politics.

Money tends to flow most plentifully to those who look like winners at the start, thus providing still another advantage to those already prominent and popular at the beginning of the electoral season. Potential candidates whose policy views are held by the politically-minded rich, the business community, and organized labor have a like advantage. Candidates and potential candidates who experience difficulty in raising funds from these traditional sources must develop new financial constituencies. Both Senators Goldwater and McGovern succeeded at this difficult task, but the batting average of potential candidates without much appeal amongst the traditional sources of political money is low.

THE STRUCTURE OF PRESIDENTIAL OPPORTUNITIES [6]

The route to presidential prominence is overwhelmingly political —90 percent of the persons surfacing in the polls between 1936 and

[6] The approach adopted in this section was stimulated by Joseph Schlesinger's *Ambition in Politics: Political Careers in the United States* (Chicago: Rand-McNally, 1966).

1972 were public officeholders. Even those who had held no public office at the time they were first "mentioned" as possible Presidents were still linked in one fashion or another to public affairs. Most of them were distinguished generals (Douglas MacArthur and Dwight Eisenhower), close relatives of Presidents (Milton Eisenhower, Theodore Roosevelt, Jr., James Roosevelt),[7] newspaper publishers (Frank Knox, Frank Gannett), or other media spokesmen (Eric Johnston, one-time "czar" of the motion picture industry). Only Wendell Willkie and Charles A. Lindbergh could claim none of these advantages; both were active and prominent spokesmen for their political viewpoints while private citizens.

The complex federal system of government in the United States results in an unusually large number of responsible public offices from which potential Presidents might be expected to come. In fact, recent presidential nominating politics has been dominated by the incumbents of only three: the Vice-Presidency, the United States Senate, and state governorships (table 1). All the Vice-Presidents, 10 percent of all senators, and 6 percent of all state governors who have served since 1936 have surfaced in the presidential polls. All those actually nominated since then (save Willkie and Eisenhower) came from one of these three public offices.

Vice-President—The Vice-Presidency is an especially advantageous position from which to receive publicity within a presidential context. While in most ways the office may not be worth a pitcher of warm spit (as the genteel John Nance Garner once observed), the incumbent automatically becomes a serious possibility for the next presidential nomination even if he has weaknesses which otherwise might bar him from serious consideration. John Garner was a southerner, Henry Wallace had little independent following and many powerful enemies. Alben Barkley was too old, Spiro Agnew was previously unknown nationally —yet all stood near the top of the polls during their tenures as Vice-President.

Under ordinary circumstances, the Vice-President's chances of gaining the nomination are heavily affected by the actions and inactions of the retiring incumbent. Seeking a presidential nomination as Vice-President is thus an awkward business—at times the effective target is the one man who still resides in the White House, at others it must be the convention delegates and the rank and file partisans they represent.

[7] The extraordinary political advantages of having had a President in the family are not confined to those who have not held public office. Among the politically experienced presidential possibilities showing up in the polls are Eleanor Roosevelt and Franklin D. Roosevelt, Jr.; John, Robert, and Edward Kennedy as well as their father, Joseph; Robert A. Taft and Robert A. Taft, Jr.

TABLE 1. LAST PUBLIC OFFICE BEFORE POLLING ONE PERCENT OR MORE SUPPORT OR BEING NOMINATED FOR PRESIDENT, 1936–72

Public Office	Percent of All Persons Polling 1 Percent or More Who Held Office[a]		Percent of All Persons Who Held Office Polling 1 Percent or More		Percent of All Nominees Who Held Office[b]	
Vice President	2	(2)	100	(8)	31	(4)
U.S. Senator	35	(38)	10	(368)	23	(3)
Governor	23	(25)	6	(434)	31	(4)
Cabinet Officer	17	(19)	17	(113)	0	
U.S. Representative	6	(7)	c		0	
Mayor	4	(4)	c		0	
Supreme Court Justice	2	(2)	6	(35)	0	
All Others	1	(11)	c		0	
None	10	(11)	c		15	(2)
Total	100	(109)	—		100	(13)

a Last or current office at time *first* polled 1 percent or more support for presidential nomination among fellow partisans.

b Last or current office at time *first* nominated.

c Not computed. A small fraction of 1 percent in each case.

But the batting average of those who have lived through the ordeal is high. Usually, the Vice-President is the best known party leader short of the retiring President, a proven vote-getter, and the "natural" candidate for the Presidency.

United States Senators—A seat in the Senate is a less automatic boost towards the Presidency, but it provides unique opportunities for those who wish to try. Senators are located at the heart of the nation's political communications network, their activities are covered by a large and prestigious press corps which finds the Senate a rich source of news. The chamber's lack of control over debate and weak party discipline make it easy for a senator to become an independent national political figure.

Not all senators can or do take advantage of these opportunities, of course. Many of them—including the lion's share of the chamber's most powerful members—are too old to be seriously considered. (Those who are first elected to the Senate after serving as state governors frequently begin their service in the Senate at too advanced a stage in life to think of it as anything but a glorious end to their careers.) The senators who become prominent presidential politicians are rather young by Senate standards. Some—for example Johnson, Hubert Humphrey, Barkley among the Democrats and Taft and William Knowland among the Republicans—have been important party leaders in the Senate but few have been among the chamber's seniority leaders. The point is that one need not be very powerful in the Senate in order to make quite a splash in the papers or on TV.

But senators have other advantages in the contest for a presidential nomination. They have a better chance of becoming Vice-President than anyone else—ten senators have been nominated for the office since 1936, compared to only three state governors, three federal executive officials, and two United States representatives.[8] More members of the Senate have followed this route to the presidential nomination than have made the jump directly (see figure 1).

Fig. 1. *Pattern of Public Office-Holding by Presidential Nominees, 1936–1972*

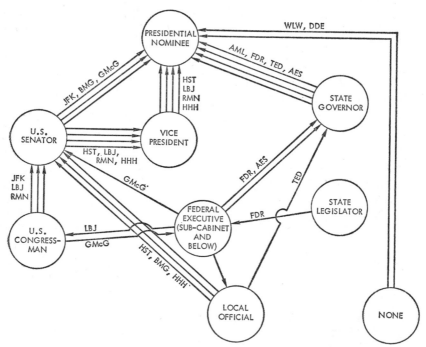

Senators are proven vote-getters in statewide elections, the nearest equivalent to a national campaign. Their normally long, continuous

[8] These figures include both Thomas Eagleton and Sargeant Shriver in 1972. Frank Knox, the Republican's vice-presidential nominee in 1936, had no prior office-holding experience.

service permits them plenty of time to emerge as a presidential possibility—by contrast governors must achieve national acclaim quickly, get elected to the Senate, or forget about the Presidency. The six-year term provides Senate members with still another advantage, "free shots" at the Presidency without giving up their seat in the Senate since they come up for reelection in presidential years only half the time. The only senator since 1900 to lose his seat because he sought the Presidency was Barry Goldwater in 1964.

Senators belong to a collegial body which conducts most of its public business Tuesdays through Thursdays. Short campaign trips are easily combined with their routine, and long periods of absence from Washington are scarcely noticed in a group of one hundred men. A senator with presidential ambition, can, in effect, launch a four-year campaign for the nomination; few other officials can.

Since World War II, American Presidents have been preoccupied by the nation's relationships with the rest of the world. Foreign and military policy issues have loomed large in the news. Some association with these matters has become a valuable asset to a presidential contender, and all senators can claim at least a superficial familiarity with foreign policy and national defense. Those who serve on the Senate Foreign Relations or Armed Services Committees can rightly claim some measure of expertise, a fact which has not escaped the attention of the presidential aspirants in the Senate who seek assignment to these committees eagerly.

Thus senators not only have tremendous advantages in attracting nationwide publicity but are in a very favorable position, relative to others, to translate their political prominence into convention victories.

State Governors—Relatively few governors are so well advantaged. While a governor may be the focal point of his state's politics, few state capitals are at the core of a national communications network as Washington is. It is a great deal easier for, say, Senator Birch Bayh of Indiana to become a national figure than it is for Governor What's-his-name in Indianapolis. Most governors who have become prominent as presidential possibilities since 1936 have been from large, metropolitan states. While Albany, Sacramento, and Springfield are not exactly communications crossroads, New York, Los Angeles, and Chicago are. And the big states are politically important—in the Electoral College and thus in presidential elections, at the national party conventions and thus in presidential nominating politics. A small state governor labors at a disadvantage that a small state senator does not have. Landon in 1936 was the last small state governor to be nominated; few governors of small to medium size states have been seriously mentioned as presidential possibilities since.

Even the big state governors seem to be at a disadvantage compared to their Washington-based competitors: the last big state governor to be nominated was Stevenson in 1952. This is not the result of a lack of public prominence: an impressive 22 percent of all big state governors have polled 1 percent or more support for a presidential nomination compared to only 10 percent of the senators. But state governors have experienced greater difficulty in capitalizing on this prominence than have senators. For one thing, a state governorship is not an office a politician can count on holding for very long. Even in the absence of constitutional constraints most governors serve only one or two terms. A governor who aspires to the Presidency has fewer chances to make his move than does a senator. And, for the governors chosen at the mid-term elections, the first chance comes embarrassingly early (after only two years' service, he is still learning the job) or distressingly late (after six years as governor, how many men still appear to be miracle workers?). Governors chosen in presidential years are disadvantaged in another way: they must choose between seeking another term as governor (if this is permitted by their state's constitution) or running for President.

As chief executives of their respective states, governors are far less dispensable and geographically mobile than senators. Prolonged absence from the state is out of the question while their state legislature is in session—an increasingly large portion of their term in the larger states. It is clearly awkward the rest of the time.

Moreover, when governors do campaign, the issues and themes which they can more authoritatively address and with which they are identified are state and local ones. The problems of New Jersey may light few fires in the hearts and minds of the residents of Iowa or Maine. And these issues are not the same as the national and international areas confronting the President.

Other Public Officials—Cabinet officers, especially secretaries of state, defense, treasury and the attorney general, are among the more widely publicized officials in the land; they benefit from a relatively close association with the President and his programs. Supreme Court justices enjoy a prestige which rivals that of the President. The Court deals with some of the nation's most pressing problems and is a major source of national news. The tradition of signed court opinions (and dissents) makes it possible for justices to establish individual reputations and followings. Both the Cabinet and the Court, in fact, show up as sources of publically perceived presidential possibilities. Indeed a larger proportion of all Cabinet members since 1936 have surfaced in the polls (17 percent) than has been true for either senators (10 percent) or governors (6 percent). Despite the traditional separation of the Supreme Court from partisan politics, both William O. Douglas and Fred Vinson have figured in recent presidential speculation (the two men make up 6 percent of the justices since 1936). Despite their visibility and prestige, no Cabinet member has been nominated for the Presidency by a major party since Herbert Hoover in 1932. The Supreme Court has not furnished a presidential candidate since Charles Evans Hughes in 1916. Obviously more than political prominence explains the preeminence of Vice-Presidents, senators, and governors over the Cabinet and the Court as a source of presidential candidates.

For one thing, Cabinet officers and Supreme Court justices are appointed officers, and relatively few of either have been elective politicians in the past. Given the importance and scarcity of presidential nominations, prudence suggests that the parties go with proven winners in contests as nearly like presidential elections as possible.

Often factors disadvantage would-be-Presidents on the Court. Its insulation from partisan politics means that no justice can actively seek the presidential nomination and hold his seat on the Court, too. Trading life-tenure on the Supreme Court, with its great power and prestige, for the high risks and heavy costs of a presidential nomination campaign followed by an election of uncertain outcome is not much of a bargain. Only a relative sure-thing would be attractive to even the most politically-minded judge.

Rather different barriers confront Cabinet officials. Their average tenure is short, and entirely dependent upon the President's pleasure. Presidents tend to be suspicious of Cabinet members with independent political followings, and with good reason. If he resigns to run without the President's approval, a Cabinet officer alienates his party's most powerful figure. (If he forces the President to fire him, the result is the same, only more so.) The Cabinet officer's presidential future is controlled by the President.

Most observers agree that the power and prestige of the Cabinet have eroded in recent decades. The development of an institutionalized Presidency and the transfer of much power and policy initiative to the White House staff has diminished the significance of the Cabinet secretary. This trend has been accompanied by a sharp reduction in the proportion of Cabinet officers publically perceived as potential Presidents. Before 1949, 35 percent of all "inner Cabinet" members polled 1 percent or more support for a presidential nomination before, during, or after their services in the President's official family. Since 1949, only 17 percent have achieved that degree of prominence and popularity. Incumbents of lesser Cabinet posts have suffered an equally sharp drop in their opportunities to achieve mass popularity in a presidential context: before 1949, 17 percent of them surfaced in the polls at the 1 percent level or better, since then only 4 percent of them have. The Cabinet increasingly has become isolated from presidential politics.

Very few members of the House of Representatives end up as presidential possibilities for a still different set of reasons. The average member of the House of Representatives is an anonymous fellow compared to his counterpart in "the other body," for he has been elected from a smaller constituency. The important work of the House is done in committee, and the tight control over debate and greater party discipline in the House provide few chances to make publicity on the floor. Only a few members of the House—the Speaker, majority and minority party leaders, and chairmen of a handful of the more important committees—are perceived as national political figures and routinely receive national press attention. A few of these men surface in the presidential polls. But important House positions go to senior members, often too old to be considered for the Presidency and usually committed to a lifetime career in the House. Ambitious younger members of the House can either seek continuous reelection until they achieve enough seniority to gain power in the House or run for the Senate or a governorship. The structure of the office predisposes the members toward staying put: their two-year term means they must abandon a career in the House in order to run for higher office. Some members take this chance every election year, of course, and three of them (Kennedy, Johnson, and Nixon) have recently become President. But, increasingly, congressmen are locked into a career in the House by the relative security of House seats, the allocation of power in the House on the basis of seniority, and the growing specialization of members in a limited range of public policy. The route to power in the House leads away from, not towards, the Presidency.

Big city mayors preside over governmental units which equal or surpass most states in size and complexity. They have demonstrated an ability to appeal to urban electorates in a predominantly urban nation. Moreover, the mayors of New York, Chicago, or Los Angeles are better situated to obtain massive national publicity than almost any governor. And yet only Fiorello La Guardia, John Lindsay, and Sam Yorty polled more than 1 percent support for President since 1936; none were taken very seriously as presidential contenders.

The reasons for the mayors' poor showing as presidential possibilities and presidential candidates seem fairly clear. The politics of a number of large American cities is sufficiently unsavory, at least by reputation, that a man who succeeds at it is widely viewed as lacking in sufficient rectitude to be considered for the highest office in the land. Certainly a politician who can win elections in our central cities is likely to have much less appeal in suburban and rural areas. This, of course, becomes progressively more true as our central cities become increasingly impoverished and black. The problems of American cities today are immense; few mayors have had the resources or the power to make much of a dent on them. The office of mayor, under these conditions, seems to be a graveyard for higher political ambitions. Few men with presidential aspirations are attracted to the office, even fewer have much hope left once they have served in it. Only one former mayor, Hubert Humphrey of Minneapolis, has achieved the presidential nomination since 1936 and he only after long service as senator and Vice-President.

Prospects for Change—These patterns tend to be self-perpetuating. The fact that Vice-Presidents and senators have much better presidential chances than anyone else creates presidential ambitions among those who hold these offices and encourages already committed presidential aspirants to contest for them. The media, party leaders, and others who regularly provide resources to would-be candidates reinforce this tendency: in their continuing search for new presidential ambition and talent they tend to look where they have found them before.

But it would be a mistake to assume that this structure of presidential opportunities is immutable. The current pattern of opportunities is quite new—Estes Kefauver and John Kennedy seem to have been the first to exploit the advantages, under modern conditions, of a Senate seat for a presidential aspirant. If changes in communications organization and technology and/or the definition of "news" dispersed access to nationwide publicity, if preoccupation with foreign and military policy should diminish, if the power and prestige of state and local governments could somehow be enhanced, if the isolation of the Cabinet from presidential politics could be reduced by greater presidential reliance on its members rather than the Executive Office, if lateral mobility between high public offices rather than the pursuit of specialized and largely separate political career lines became the norm, then our heavy reliance on the Senate and the Vice-Presidency for presidential talent might be reduced. Here is an aspect of presidential nominations which reformers do not talk about very much. They should; the political opportunity structure probably has more impact on nomination outcomes than the legal machinery of the formal nominating process itself.

A way out remains for those who are concerned by this heavy reliance on senators and Vice-Presidents—the recruitment of nonpoliticians as presidential candidates. The technological revolution which has contributed to the narrowing of presidential opportunities to a few federal officials has also made instant fame possible. Wendell Willkie emerged from near obscurity to great popularity in a matter of weeks —*before* the advent of television. The technological capacity to gain massive popular support quickly, without years of prior public service, is in being. Media-based campaigns by previously unknown amateurs and nonpolitical celebrities have succeeded for lesser office with some regularity. Certainly, if the pool of politically experienced potential Presidents becomes too narrowly circumscribed, the tendency to look to ambitious men from outside the political arena is enhanced.

Defining the Competitive Situation

Slowly but surely the beginning of active (if not always acknowledged) candidacies, press attention to and public awareness of presidential nominations is creeping backwards toward the previous election four years before. Indeed the 1972 Republican convention—thanks to its lack of contests, the Twenty-second Amendment, and Nixon's lead in the polls—was rife with speculation and maneuvering over the 1976 nomination. Some politicians blame this development—for it is almost universally deplored—on Theodore White's influential series of books on presidential elections which devote much attention to this phase of presidential choice. A more likely explanation is modern technology combined with the American calendar system of elections.[9]

Today it is possible for a party to arrive at a tentative and unofficial agreement on a candidate without ever meeting face-to-face, or selecting representatives to arrive at a choice on behalf of its members. Instantaneous communications and rapid transportation allow fellow partisans to communicate with one another, and candidates and potential candidates to communicate with them, with ease and intimacy. The development of scientific public opinion polling in the 1930s provided another essential ingredient to this capability for decentralized early choice—reliable estimates of mass sentiments and rank and file preferences. Potential candidates communicate with potential followers

[9] Obviously there is no way of shortening the period of informal and unofficial campaigning for the Presidency except by shortening the President's term or by making the length of his service unpredictable. The latter approach has problems as Elijah Kaminsky points out in his "The Selection of French Presidents" in D. R. Matthews, ed., *Perspectives on Presidential Selection* (Washington: Brookings, 1973), Ch. 4.

through the media, the polls tell all how well they are doing (and sometimes even why).

These interactions between the mass media, party leaders, and rank-and-file frequently produce an early consensus on the relative desirability and opportunities of the presidential possibilities. Movement toward one candidate tends to be self-perpetuating. If the media give more favorable attention to one of the possible candidates than to the others, party leaders begin to talk of him as a "viable" candidate, the party rank-and-file become better acquainted with the potential candidate, his poll standings improve, and this causes the media to pay still more attention for he is "serious." As George Romney and Edmund Muskie can testify, this system can work both ways, either generating additional new support or eroding existing support rapidly. In either case, early collective agreement on candidates is enhanced.

Usually tentative agreement is reached about who will and who ought to be their party's nominee *before the formal process of nomination begins early in the presidential year*. Usually (although after 1972, we scarcely need to be reminded, not invariably), this consensus "man to beat" survives the pitfalls of the formal nominating process and goes on to win at the convention a year or so later.

The record since 1936 is summarized in table 2. Since the situation is significantly different for the party controlling the White House and the party out of power, the records of the in-party and the out-party are listed separately.

THE PARTY IN POWER

The early stages of in-party nominations revolve around the incumbent President. In nine of the last ten election years (the exception was Eisenhower in 1960), the President was constitutionally eligible to run for another term. In every one of these nine cases, the incumbent President was the front-running candidate to succeed himself before the formal nominating process began. Even when there was substantial doubt about the President's intentions (as in 1940, 1952, and 1956), he remained the man to beat. In seven of these nine cases, the President went on to win the nomination. Truman and Johnson's withdrawals in 1952 and 1968 will be discussed below; for now it is enough to know that no President who persisted in seeking renomination was denied the opportunity of running—even when, as in 1948, his prospects of winning seemed very poor.

Moreover, the eligible Presidents usually faced no serious challenge during the critical three years before the New Hampshire primary. Only Roosevelt in 1940, Truman in 1952, Johnson in 1968, and Nixon in 1972 faced open and avowed opposition candidates by the begin-

TABLE 2. CONTINUITY AND CHANGE IN PRESIDENTIAL NOMINATING POLITICS,
1936–72

Year	Leading Candidate at Beginning of Election Year	Nominee
Party In Power		
1936 (D)	Roosevelt	Roosevelt
1940 (D)	Roosevelt	Roosevelt
1944 (D)	Roosevelt	Roosevelt
1948 (D)	Truman	Truman
1952 (D)	Truman	Stevenson
1956 (R)	Eisenhower	Eisenhower
1960 (R)	Nixon	Nixon
1964 (D)	Johnson	Johnson
1968 (D)	Johnson	Humphrey
1972 (R)	Nixon	Nixon
Party Out of Power		
1936 (R)	Landon	Landon
1940 (R)	?	Willkie
1944 (R)	Dewey	Dewey
1948 (R)	Dewey-Taft	Dewey
1952 (R)	Eisenhower-Taft	Eisenhower
1956 (D)	Stevenson	Stevenson
1960 (D)	Kennedy	Kennedy
1964 (R)	?	Goldwater
1968 (R)	Nixon	Nixon
1972 (D)	Muskie	McGovern

ning of the election year. Trial balloons, unofficial travels to sound
out public opinion, announcements of "availability" if the President
should decide to lay down the burden were common. But politicians
willing openly to take on a sitting President for the nomination were
rare, even when the President was in serious trouble.

Under these circumstances the early stages of in-party presidential
nominations often degenerate into guessing matches—will he or won't
he run again? Presidents typically remain silent on this matter until
the formal nominating process begins, thus making it difficult for candidates unwilling to face the possibility of a head-on confrontation to
launch early campaigns. The Twenty-second Amendment, by requiring Presidents to retire after eight years, has ruled out this strategy for
second-term Presidents—the result may be more open competition in

the future. But in the one instance so far since the amendment has taken effect, Vice-President Nixon was provided such important and timely opportunities to further his presidential stature that he had the nomination wrapped up before the New Hampshire primary even without Eisenhower's open endorsement.

Given the psychological and symbolic importance of the Presidency described elsewhere in this volume, the President's dominance over in-party nominations is not surprising. But it is well to remember that half of all presidential nominations are made by the in-party, that few of these nominations are the result of competitive processes, and that the in-party is twice as likely to win the general election as the out-party.

THE OUT-PARTY

The competitive situation within the party out of power is less clearly structured and predictable. No single figure stands so automatically and authoritatively at the center of the stage as the President does for the in-party. Nonetheless, the historical record shows that a single "man to beat" had emerged in six of the last ten out-party nominations *before* New Hampshire. Five of these six early leaders went on to win at the convention. Twice, the contest for the out-party nomination had boiled down to two evenly matched contenders (Dewey and Taft in 1948 and Eisenhower and Taft in 1952) by the beginning of the presidential year; both times, one of these men was nominated while the other came in second. Only in 1940 and 1964 did the out-of-power Republicans begin the presidential year with a confused competitive situation. In 1940, the muddle resulted from a lack of plausible candidates, in 1964 the problem was a large number of quite evenly matched possibilities. Thus the *normal* competitive situation within the out-party is similar to that found in the in-party—one (or two) prospects are perceived as being so far ahead of the others that nominating politics tends to revolve around them. The central question of most out-party nominations is: can the initial front-runner hold his lead until the party convention makes him its official candidate?

That the early leaders usually do should not be surprising—anticipations of victory tend to be self-fulfilling in ways I have described above. Many of the same skills and resources needed to become the initial leader are also required to do well in primaries, state conventions, and at the national convention itself. Indeed, the anticipation of performance in the upcoming series of primaries and conventions has a major impact on how strong early candidates and would-be candidates are thought to be beforehand. Thus while the early stages of the nominating process occur in a highly unstructured environment, the formal organization and rules of the game have an indirect impact on the competitive situation from the very beginning.

BECOMING THE EARLY FRONT-RUNNER

How one becomes the initial leading contender for the out-party nomination is obviously of critical importance. Dramatic breakthroughs in popular recognition and support frequently occur during the nomination and election contests held two or four years before. Before losing the contested vice-presidential nomination at the 1956 Democratic convention, John F. Kennedy was merely an attractive and ambitious junior senator from Massachusetts; from that point on he was a leading contender for the 1960 nomination. Nelson Rockefeller's big victory in the 1958 New York gubernatorial race made him a national political figure almost overnight. But there is also a large element of chance involved. Edmund Muskie's performance as the Democrat's vice-presidential nominee in 1968 contributed heavily to the fact that he was viewed as the party's most likely nominee in early 1972. And yet if Robert Kennedy had not been assassinated, if Edward Kennedy had not been involved in the accident at Chappaquiddick, if Hubert Humphrey had not (apparently) retired from presidential politics, it seems unlikely that Muskie would have been the party's front-runner. Thomas E. Dewey was seen as the sure Republican nominee as 1944 began, but he would have been in a far less favorable situation if Robert A. Taft had not withdrawn from contention in favor of his less impressive colleague from Ohio, John Bricker. And so it goes. The status of front-runner, by definition, is a relative matter—who the alternatives (and potential alternatives) are makes a tremendous difference. This, in turn, is often affected by essentially chance factors.

The Formal/Legal Nominating Process

The United States must have the most elaborate, complex, and prolonged formal system of nominating candidates for chief executive in the world. The selection of delegates to the national party conventions is spread over approximately six months. The states decide when and how this is to be done, with few limitations on their discretion imposed by the national parties or federal law. The result is mind-blowing complexity and variety in delegate selection methods and the extent to which delegates are mandated to support specific presidential candidates at the convention. The winning candidate must somehow attract the votes of 50 percent plus one of these delegates, chosen under 50 different sets of laws and political arrangements.

THE ROLE OF THE PRIMARIES

Most public attention is focused on the presidential primary states. The massive publicity which these contests receive makes it possible for a little-known politician to become a national figure by a strong showing in a single state, thereby helping him capture convention delegates in other states whether they hold primaries or not. Similarly, a primary performance which falls below expectations can erode a candidate's support across the entire nation. Under modern conditions, state presidential primaries are national events.

Despite the lack of any central coordination, the system of primaries which has evolved has two important properties: the primaries take place over three or four months and the early ones tend to be held in states smaller than those of the later primaries.

An important consequence of these two factors is to reduce the significance of inequalities in resources between presidential contenders. The "start up" costs of a primary campaign are relatively modest. One or two early victories in relatively small states like New Hampshire and Wisconsin can generate enough publicity and plausibility as a possible winner to make the accumulation of the vast resources needed to contest later primaries in bigger states much easier. This feature of the primary system favors those who are not near the top of the list at the start.[10] But there is a somewhat countervailing consequence of the serial nature of today's primary system: victories scored in the late primaries can make up for early defeats. This tends to advantage candidates who were in or near the lead at the start of the primary season because outside challengers who suffer early defeats rarely survive as plausible candidates long enough to attempt a comeback. The primaries both encourage challenge to front-runners and give the early leaders a second chance. Let us examine the net effects of these potentially off-setting characteristics.

The In-Party—The overall impact of the presidential primaries on in-party nominations is not very impressive quantitatively, and largely negative in character. In eight of the last ten in-party nominations, the dominant position of the preprimary front-runner (all of them incumbent Presidents except Nixon in 1960) remained essentially unchanged at the end of the series of preliminary elections—indeed no serious primary challenge was launched against any of them. This does

---

10 A one-shot national primary would ordinarily have the opposite effect. Given the infrequency with which initial front-runners are seriously challenged, and the even greater rarity of their defeat under the present system, this could be a very serious drawback.

not mean that everyone was happy in the President's party but rather that a high threshold of discontent must be reached before prominent and ambitious men with manifest presidential qualifications are willing openly to challenge the President in the primaries.

In 1940, 1952, and 1968 serious challenges to the renomination of incumbent Presidents were launched. John Nance Garner's challenge to Franklin Roosevelt in 1940, inspired largely by the third term issue, did not get very far. But Estes Kefauver's challenge to Truman in 1952 and Eugene McCarthy's and Robert Kennedy's challenges to Lyndon Johnson in 1968 did. Both Presidents were quite unpopular, presided over a deeply divided party, and faced bleak electoral prospects in November. Both of them had given serious consideration to withdrawing from presidential politics before the primaries began. Both did withdraw after suffering humiliating defeats in early primaries. A strong challenge in the primaries increases the incentives for an unpopular President to retire. Given the President's extraordinary power—both Truman and Johnson probably could have been renominated if they had persisted in seeking it—this is a significant result of the primaries. They can raise the costs and reduce the value of renomination to a point where a deeply troubled President may decide to withdraw.

The presidential primary system seems more successful at this than as a means of building up a successor to a President who "voluntarily" retires. Kefauver emerged from the 1952 primaries as the most popular presidential prospect among rank-and-file Democrats; the convention picked Adlai Stevenson, who had entered no primaries at all. Much the same thing happened sixteen years later; the President's successful primary challenger, Eugene McCarthy, was passed over in favor of Hubert Humphrey, who had avoided personal involvement in the primaries altogether. The most success a challenger to a sitting President has had since 1936 has been to throw the nomination to someone other than the President or himself.

The Out-Party—The impact of the primaries on out-party nominations since 1936 has not been much, if any, greater. In six of the last ten out-party nomination contests, there was a single front-running candidate for the nomination before the primary season began. In five of these cases, the pre-New Hampshire leader remained in front at the end of the primaries. In most cases, active primary opposition to the initial leader was weak. Borah (in 1936), Kefauver (in 1956), and Humphrey (in 1960) were quite unlikely nominees but they were the most prominent primary challengers in those years. In 1968 Nixon, the early leader, faced no significant primary opposition at all. Willkie was internationally famous when he challenged Dewey in 1944, but he was so weak within the Republican party that a single primary defeat destroyed his campaign. More often than not, the most dangerous alternatives to the preprimary leaders have preferred to play the free rider game, to let less established politicians challenge the leaders, and hope to pick up the pieces if they succeed. The number, variety, and strength of the challengers to Muskie in 1972 were quite unprecedented. So were the covert efforts by the Committee to Reelect the President to subvert the Muskie campaign.[11] And, of course, so was the outcome: Muskie was the only clear front-runner since 1936 to be destroyed by the primaries, McGovern the only long-shot candidate to parlay a string of primary victories into a presidential nomination.

Sometimes, the out-party fails to achieve consensus on a single "man to beat" in advance of the primaries. When this situation prevails, the primaries have done little to clarify matters. In 1948, Dewey and Taft were about even when the primaries began. Taft avoided the primaries leaving Dewey and Harold Stassen actively to contest the primary states. Stassen's strong early showing nearly deprived Dewey of his claim to being the party's most popular candidate, but the New Yorker recouped his losses toward the end. The competitive situation at convention time was about the same as it was before New Hampshire. In 1952, Taft and Eisenhower were well ahead of the others at the beginning of the primaries. They split the primaries down the middle. While Ike crept ahead of Taft in the polls during this period, the primaries did little to clarify who would be, or who ought to be, the party's nominee. In 1940, Willkie overcame both Dewey and Taft without entering a single primary. Finally, in 1964, the Republicans entered the primary season with four to six potential candidates of approximately equal strength. At the end of the primaries there were still four candidates—Goldwater, Nixon, Scranton, and Lodge—all within two percentage points of one another in the polls. Goldwater had the most pledged delegates, and hence had the best chance of winning the nomination, but this was not the result of his performance in the primary states.

The record of the presidential primary system as it has operated in the out-party since 1936 can be summed up as follows: when the out-party has a single leading contender before the primaries, which is most of the time, the primaries rarely change the situation. When they do alter matters, it is more often to strengthen the claim of the initial leader than substantially to weaken it. When the preprimary competi-

---

11 While there is no way of knowing how much CRP's "dirty tricks" contributed to the collapse of the senator's campaign, the set of challengers Muskie faced in 1972 was so imposing that it seems probable that he would have been defeated without any "help" from CRP.

tive situation within the out-party is more confused, the primary system has done little, if anything, to facilitate the emergence of a single leader of the party.

THE CAUCUS/CONVENTION STATES

Until the 1970s a majority of national convention delegates were selected by indirect party processes—precinct caucuses, county, congressional district, and state conventions. Even after the recent proliferation of presidential primaries, a third or more of national convention delegates are still selected in this way. It is a rather different game than primary state politics.

Ordinarily only the party faithful attend these meetings: it takes a far greater commitment to one's party or candidate to attend these dreary affairs than to cast a vote in a primary election.[12] (Those who bother to attend are frequently rewarded by being elected to another caucus or convention!) National convention delegates selected in these states are often chosen on bases which have little if anything to do with the fate of presidential contenders. Nonetheless, presidential candidates with a strong appeal to party regulars are normally advantaged. Of course party regulars can and do support a mixed bag of presidential aspirants—long established party leaders like Robert A. Taft or Hubert Humphrey, favorite sons, presidential candidates who appear likely to unite the party or carry the local ticket to victory, and so on.

But the McGovern, Goldwater, and (to a lesser extent) Eugene McCarthy campaigns have demonstrated that a different kind of candidate can do very well in nonprimary states. Presidential contenders with an ability to inspire great enthusiasm among previously inactive amateurs and to organize their impressive energies into effective grass roots organizations can beat the party regulars at their own game. Richard Stearns, the director of Senator McGovern's highly successful 1972 delegate hunt in the nonprimary states, estimated that a pro-McGovern turnout of 5 or 6 percent of registered Democrats would be enough to dominate precinct caucuses. This both McGovern and Goldwater succeeded in doing in a surprising number of areas. The intensity of their followings more than made up for their initially limited size.[13]

The Goldwater, McCarthy, and McGovern experiences suggest that

[12] Turnout in presidential primaries is far lower than in general elections. See Austin Ranney, "Turnout and Representation in Presidential Primary Elections," *American Political Science Review*, LXVI (1972), pp. 21–37.

[13] Goldwater had a very substantial following among regular party politicians which McGovern did not. The achievements of the South Dakotan's amateur organization was therefore even more impressive than the Arizonan's.

the way to build a deeply committed following is by taking relatively far out, anti-establishment, ideological policy positions. But looking further back in history, this presumed association is less clear. Not all "extremist" challengers have succeeded in creating active grass roots organizations—Estes Kefauver did not in 1948, for example. And some "centrist" establishment candidates—Eisenhower and Stevenson in 1952 are examples—were helped substantially by the enthusiastic activities of grass roots amateurs.

It would be hard to find a better illustration of how the same institutional arrangements can have different consequences for nominating outcomes depending on the nature of the candidates and the competitive situation. The most that can be said in general about the impact of nonprimary delegate selection systems on presidential nominations is that they favor candidates supported by those who care strongly enough to participate in them.

THE NATIONAL CONVENTIONS

Viewed as deliberative bodies, the national party conventions are an abomination—huge and disorderly assemblies of often inexperienced strangers faced with difficult and important decisions to make in a few days. But usually national conventions are not called upon to make decisions; most of the time they meet to legitimize and celebrate a decision that has already been made.

This is particularly the case, of course, when a sitting President seeks renomination. The smallest share of the first ballot vote (*before* switches) received by any incumbent President since 1936 was Truman's 75 percent in 1948—and he was believed to be leading the party toward certain defeat. The other six times incumbent Presidents sought renomination, the conventions endorsed them with near or actual unanimity. The three remaining in-party nominations since 1936 were less cut and dried, but Nixon in 1960 and Humphrey in 1968 effectively wrapped up their nominations well in advance of the convention. Only in 1952, when the Democrats picked the reluctant Stevenson, did the in-party convention operate as a decision-making body. Out-party nominations more often go down to the wire. Republican conventions actually picked Willkie in 1940, Dewey in 1948, and Eisenhower in 1952. The other seven out-party conventions were essentially ratifications of decisions made earlier. Thus only four of the last twenty national party conventions have clearly operated as decision-makers.

But those presidential nominations which remain unresolved at convention time are particularly difficult ones and the conventions are not well designed to make decisions easily or in a democratic way.

Huge, temporary assemblies are prone to be run by a relative handful of leaders, and the American party conventions have been organized in such a way as to strengthen those oligarchical tendencies.[14]

One might reasonably assume from this that the perspectives and candidate preferences of party leaders would prevail in those rare years when conventions decide. That seems to have been the case at the 1952 Democratic convention when the party leaders vetoed their *bete noir*, Estes Kefauver. But if Stevenson had been an active and avowed candidate for the nomination prior to the convention, Kefauver's claim to be the popular choice might well have evaporated. And Stevenson, while acceptable to the party professionals, was scarcely one of them himself. In all three of the other conventions which made a choice, the ultimate nominee was the rank-and-file party members' favorite, not the party politicians'. And two of these winners had never held elective public office before.

There are good and sufficient reasons for making the national party conventions as "open" and "democratic" as possible,[15] but a propensity for unreformed party conventions to select unpopular party hacks is not one of them. And most of the time, the internal organization and procedural rules of the party conventions do not make much difference to nomination outcomes, except insofar as the anticipation of their possible relevance in the (unlikely) event of a competitive convention affects the relative strength of the contenders during the pre-convention period.

Outcomes: The Presidential Nominees

Presidential candidates of the Republican and Democratic parties have won the curious contest described above. They were the first to attract 50 percent plus one of the delegate votes; if they had not succeeded, someone else eventually would have. Since the qualities required to win in presidential nominating politics are not necessarily the same as those needed in the White House and since most of the winners started the race well in the lead, it is hard to know whether "the best man won." A brief look at some of the characteristics of the winning nominees since 1936 will not give us a final answer to that question, but it may clarify some of the issues and provide some of the

[14] Carl and Ellen Baar's comparison of American and Canadian party conventions is illuminating on this point. See their "Party Convention Organization and Leadership Selection in Canada and the United States" in D. R. Matthews, ed., *Perspectives on Presidential Selection*, Ch. 3.

[15] A good introduction to these problems may be found in Judith Parris, *The Convention Problem* (Washington: Brookings, 1972).

facts needed to evaluate the outcomes of the presidential nominating process.

PARTY POPULARITY

A presidential nominee probably ought to be the most popular person in his party. On this score at least, the performance of the presidential nominating system is strikingly good. Only once in the last twenty nominations has the leader in the final poll of party rank-and-file preferences failed to win the nomination—the exception was Kefauver in 1952. In 1964, the final poll of the Republican rank-and-file resulted in a tie: Goldwater was the first choice of 22 percent, 22 percent were for Nixon, 21 percent were for Ambassador Lodge, and 20 percent for Governor William Scranton. McGovern's lead among Democrats in the last 1972 poll was narrow, and probably reflected to a degree the near certainty of his nomination after the California primary. If second and third choices had been taken into account along with first choices, other candidates may well have stood highest on the average in these two cases (and perhaps a few others as well).

Nonetheless, there have been few times since 1936 when the nominee's claim to being the popular choice of the party was in any doubt. And when the party leadership and party rank-and-file diverged in their candidate preferences, the latter prevailed every time except 1952 in the Democratic party.

STRENGTH AS CANDIDATE

Most of the time, the nominee is also the party's strongest potential vote-getter in the November elections. There was little doubt about this each of the seven times the parties renominated incumbent Presidents—although in 1948 this was more a testament to the lack of Democratic presidential timber than to Truman's popularity. Similarily, the polls showed Landon, Dewey (1944), Eisenhower (in 1952), Stevenson (in 1956), Kennedy, and Nixon (in 1960) running well ahead of the other potential nominees in trial-heat match-ups with their presumed opponents in the other party. In 1940 and 1944 the polls were too sketchy to be of much help, but it seems likely that the GOP picked their strongest vote-getter both years.

In the other five contests, however, the parties *probably* did not pick their most likely November winner from among the available alternatives. In 1964, no Republican came within hailing distance of President Johnson in the polls, but Goldwater was the weakest of all the possible candidates. Four years later, the Republican trial-heats were confusing; most of them showed Rockefeller running stronger against likely Democratic opponents than Nixon, although the last Gallup poll narrowly reversed this finding. Given Rockefeller's greater popularity in the big states, it seems probable that he would have proven more difficult to beat than Nixon, but the Republicans were not about to nominate the New York governor in any event. While Humphrey was the more popular among Democrats in 1968, Eugene McCarthy ran stronger against both Rockefeller and Nixon in trial-heat polls. McGovern showed a modest edge over Humphrey and Muskie when paired against Nixon in 1972. In retrospect, it seems clear that he was not the strongest candidate the Democrats had. Apparently, when the most popular person in the party and the party's strongest vote-getter in November are not the same, the parties usually pick the more popular person within their own party.

REPRESENTATIVENESS: DEMOGRAPHIC

Presidential candidates are far from a sample of ordinary Americans. Rather they have been males, WASPs, well-to-do if not rich, and considerably older than the 35 years required by the Constitution. In this sense, the outcomes of presidential nominations are quite unrepresentative of the nation. People differ in how important they consider this to be, and I do not intend to enter this argument fully here.[16] Nonetheless, a few (hopefully) clarifying points seem to be in order.

The Presidency is no place for an average man. One of the most complex, demanding, and powerful offices of all times the modern Presidency demands extraordinary talent from anyone who seeks to fill it. It seems altogether appropriate, therefore, that the Democratic and Republican parties chose presidential candidates from among those who have already demonstrated a capacity to fill high public office and to win the popular elections which lead to them.

But the opportunities to achieve these positions of political prominence are grossly unequal in the United States. Since the positions from which presidential possibilities emerge are overwhelmingly held by well-to-do, middle-aged, white, Anglo-Saxon males, then presidential candidates are well-to-do, middle-aged, white, Anglo-Saxon males, too. The solution to this bias in the recruitment of presidential candidates requires basic change in American values and social structure more than tinkering with nominating procedures.

True, the present mode of funding presidential nominating campaigns advantages candidates who are wealthy or who have wealthy friends and supporters. But those who look like winners in the presidential sweepstakes have lots of friends and supporters no matter what

16 I have dealt with these issues in *The Social Background of Political Decision-Makers* (New York: Doubleday, 1954).

the state of their personal exchequers. Personal wealth is of especial importance, then, to those who challenge front-runners; when the odds are long the money does not come in easily. A Rockefeller, a Harriman, a Kennedy can persist in the pursuit of the presidential nomination when those with fewer personal resources would be forced to withdraw by a lack of contributions.

The disproportionate power of money in presidential politics ought to be ended. But care must be taken not to make effective challenge to initial leaders impossible or to open the floodgates to unmanageably large numbers of candidates in the process. And it must be further realized that, even after this is done, presidential candidates will still remain a very privileged group so long as American society is characterized by its present inequalities in the distribution of opportunities and resources.

Actually, the representativeness of American presidential candidates has increased noticeably in recent years. A Roman Catholic, a divorced man, and a southerner have been nominated. The shift in political opportunities toward senators and Vice-Presidents has opened up access to the White House to politicians from smaller states. The standards of "availability" used to define the circle of possibilities in the past has largely eroded,[17] thanks in good part to the development of scientific polling. The personal attributes of presidential contenders do not matter much any more so long as the polls show that he or she is popular. When American society is the kind of place where a woman or a Jew or a black or a poor man can become more popular than other presidential prospects, the parties will not waste much time before nominating that person.

REPRESENTATIVENESS: POLITICAL

American presidential nominees have tended to be moderates. Their ideological appeal—if the modest issue content of most presidential nominating campaigns can be dignified by the term—has been broad. The policy differences between the nominees of the two parties are not ordinarily large. Tweedledum, Tweedledee.

The landslide defeats of Goldwater and McGovern have not been encouraging to those who would like to see a greater difference between the two parties and their premier spokesmen. Of course both men lost for a variety of reasons. But there can be little doubt that Goldwater's and McGovern's relatively clear cut and relatively extreme policy posi-

17 See Gerald Pomper, *Nominating the President: The Politics of Convention Choice* (New York: Norton, 1966), pp. 122–133. This book was first published in 1963.

tions, so valuable in attracting their initial amateur supporters, came to haunt them after the conventions were over. The conditions which permitted their nominations—the absence of a strong early leader combined with a large number of evenly matched competitors—can happen again. Convention delegates and party activists tend to be more ideological, and more sharply divided about issues along party lines, than ordinary Americans.[18] But until such time as the electorate is more deeply divided on public issues than it usually has been, most politicians will see little point in offering voters policy alternatives which most of them cannot be persuaded to support.

QUALIFICATIONS

The Presidency is a quantum leap in power and responsibility for any man, no matter how experienced he may be in high affairs of state. It demands a level and variety of skill far beyond that required by any other office in the land. Thus there is no entirely adequate training and testing ground for the Presidency. Vice-Presidents gain much experience at handling ceremonial and partisan chores but ordinarily are kept at a safe distance from the important responsibilities of the White House. Governors and mayors have had to cope with the complexities of being a chief executive, but gain no experience in the foreign and defense policy areas which have consumed the bulk of recent Presidents' time and energy. Senators may have an acquaintanceship with national and international problems and policies that governors and mayors do not, but this exposure can be superficial and the job itself provides no executive experience. Cabinet officers, especially the more important ones, may develop savvy about bureaucratic politics in Washington and considerable knowledge of that segment of public policy with which their departments deal, but they are mostly without significant electoral experience.

The lopsided experience which service in these offices provides might be compensated for by lateral mobility between them. But save between the Senate and the Vice-Presidency, there is little lateral mobility between these offices and not too much prospect of encouraging more without basic change in the political opportunity structure. The truth of the matter seems to be that all Presidents, without regard to their prior experience, have to learn a very great deal on the job.

There are difficulties in drawing conclusions about the qualifications of would-be Presidents from their previous office-holding experi-

---

[18] See Herbert McCloskey, et alia, "Issue Conflict and Consensus Among Party Leaders and Followers," *American Political Science Review*, LIV (1960), pp. 406–427.

ence. It is a mistake to assume that all those who hold the same office emerge from it with the same skills. Some governors are poor administrators, some senators would make good ones. And the personal qualities and skills required to be a successful President are not always the same. Without the Great Depression, Herbert Hoover might have been a successful President and Franklin Roosevelt a failure. Given all these complexities and ambiguities, facile generalizations about all governors (or senators) being better qualified for the Presidency than all senators (or governors) at any point in history are absurd. There is a greater diversity of presidential talent within each of these groups than there is between them.

What then *can* be said about the relationship between the opportunity structure and presidential performance? No matter what one means by presidential "success" a national election must be won in order to be one. A President, be he of the *laissez-faire* or activist variety, must be able to represent and lead millions of people and to inspire their confidence and trust. While he enjoys massive power, the President works within extraordinary political and legal constraints found only in government. Previous experience in high elective public office is not absolutely essential in order to do these things well nor it is a guarantee of adequate performance. Most of the time, though, some experience helps.

There is still another reason why previous service in high elective office is desirable for presidential candidates: it increases the opportunity for voters to make an informed judgment about their capacities. A well-publicized career in public office may or may not equip a man for the rigors of the Presidency, but it gives the electorate a better chance of making a wise judgment of him either way. The information level of the American electorate is not high under the best of circumstances. To ask voters to judge men without public records (no matter how dissimilar the offices they have held are to the Presidency) is to reduce this information level still further.

A presidential system of government in which future chief executives need serve no apprenticeship in comparable office is a risky venture.[19] But a system of leadership selection requiring a long period of training and testing in a prescribed set of offices has problems, too—the dangers of stagnation, of inflexibility to changing times and circumstances, and the development of a self-perpetuating elite perspective. The

[19] For a comparison of the American system with the British apprenticeship mode of recruitment see Hugh Helco, "Presidential and Prime Ministerial Selection" in D. R. Matthews, ed., *Perspectives on Presidential Selection*, Ch. 2.

American system for selecting Presidents is something of a compromise between these two extremes. While the Presidency is formally open to anyone who meets a few constitutionally imposed qualifications, only a few experienced public officials have much of a chance ever to be President. Sometimes this pool of potential Presidents contains no one with much appeal, or a bright and attractive new figure emerges who is able to gain a major party nomination without previously demonstrating any political accomplishment at all. Despite the risks (the voters can know less about the man, the chances that he will prove inept are higher), I believe it wise not to rule out the possibility of lateral entry *directly* into presidential contention.

Finally, the nationalization of the presidential opportunity structure has resulted in the Vice-Presidency—once viewed as a political dead end—becoming the most likely source of Presidents. If the office were filled in the normal way—in an open competition for popular favor between self-starting aspirants—the growing presidential opportunities of Vice-Presidents should tend to increase the qualifications of its normal incumbent. But, of course, Vice-Presidents are not chosen that way. Vice-presidential nominations are, in effect, decided by presidential nominees and their intimate advisers within a few hours of their convention victory. Not only is this decision made hurriedly by a few tired men, it is also made without a prior opportunity to view the various possibilities competing against one another in an open campaign. The presidential candidate and his close advisers, understandably enough, select the President's running mate on the basis of his probable contribution to electoral victory in November. A certain plausibility as a successor is needed, of course, before a man is considered for a vice-presidential nomination. But which of the fairly numerous persons meeting this minimum standard is chosen depends heavily upon quite arbitrary electoral considerations. And whether a vice-presidential nominee becomes Vice-President depends almost entirely upon the relative popularity of two other people—the presidential candidates. Under these circumstances, the presidential opportunities associated with the office of Vice-President can increase without an improvement in the capacity of its incumbents to serve as President of the United States. The risks involved in placing a man selected in this fashion so close to the Presidency—whether the President serves out his full term or not—are grave. Unless the office can be made into a real apprenticeship or filled in a more reasonable way, it ought to be eliminated altogether.[20]

---

[20] Provision could be made for a caretaker, Acting President to serve, in the event of a President's death in office, until the next federal election.

Implications for Reform

The basic thrust of this analysis has been that the early stages of the presidential nominating process are the crucial ones. More often than not, the game is just about over before it officially begins.

This fact of American political life should not be interpreted to mean that recent efforts to reform the major parties and their nominating procedures are meaningless. The internal operations of the Democratic and Republican parties ought to be fair, open, and democratic even if they have no consequences for nomination outcomes. But, of course, the formal organization and rules of the major parties *do* have an impact on who wins and loses when, as sometimes happens, the parties fail to arrive at an unofficial choice in advance of the selection of convention delegates. And even when an early consensus on a nominee is achieved, the front-runner owes his status in good part to the *expectation* that he would win if a serious contest developed under the existing rules of the game. Thus the formal-legal rules of the game have an indirect impact on presidential nominating politics well before they come into play.

But relatively little thought seems to have been given to the direct and indirect effects of reform on nomination outcomes. Many of the most popular reform ideas—shorter preconvention campaigns, strict limitations on preconvention campaign expenditures, a national presidential primary, for example—would tend to favor early front-runners over their challengers. The competition for presidential nominations is already so lopsided, and the process of becoming the early leader so profoundly affected by chance, that such "reforms" seem absurd. An ideal set of rules are of limited value if no serious contests are carried on according to their prescriptions. At least some reformers should try to figure out how to achieve a more *competitive* presidential nominating process. Stronger incentives and more resources are needed before men of manifest presidential caliber will be willing and able to challenge early leaders. What I would like to see is not a vast multiplication of active candidacies (I have argued above that too many candidates can have unfortunate results) but strenuously contested battle between two or three well-qualified aspirants for the presidential nomination. Such "horce races" have been exceedingly rare in our recent history; ways need to be found to encourage them.

Moreover, improving both the process and the outcomes of presidential nominations will require far more than changed party organization and formal-legal rules. If this analysis is anywhere near correct, the qualities of the persons who win presidential nominations are also shaped by America's social and economic structure; by the values and beliefs of its citizens and the issues they think are of paramount importance; by modern communications technology; by political reporters and their definitions of "news"; by the shifting distribution of power, prestige, and opportunities for self-advancement within the governmental structure itself. Many of these things are not easily changed simply because they stand in the way of a more rational choice of chief executives. And yet, taken together, factors such as these go a long way toward defining who the "presidential possibilities" are and which ones become early leaders. And the early leaders usually win.

Those who wish to improve the choosing of American presidential candidates cannot stop with *party* reform.

Austin Ranney

3

Changing the Rules
of the Nominating Game

The nominating game is the most important stage of the presidential selection process. For one thing, it makes possible the popular election of the President by setting before the voters a number of alternatives small enough to permit a meaningful choice. At present over 80 million Americans satisfy the constitutional requirements for being President, but the electorate faces no such impossible range of choices. Their ballots offer only the quite manageable options of the Democratic and Republican candidates, supplemented by the nominees of a few minor parties.

For another thing, few would doubt that the Republicans' 1968 nomination of Nixon over Rockefeller and Reagan and the Democrats' nomination of Humphrey over McCarthy and McGovern were more critical in determining who would occupy the White House and with what kind of mandate than was the voters' narrow choice of Nixon over Humphrey in the November general election. This sharply illustrates the point that the parties' nominating processes eliminate far more presidential possibilities than do the voters' electing processes.[1]

AUSTIN RANNEY *is professor of political science at the University of Wisconsin (Madison). He served on the Democratic National Commission on Party Structure and Delegate Selection which completed its work in 1972. Dr. Ranney is the author of* The Governing of Men *and* The Doctrine of Responsible Party Government *as well as other books and frequent articles. He was managing editor of the* American Political Science Review, *1965–71.*

1 For other statements of this view, see E. E. Schattschneider, *Party Government* (New York: Farrar and Rinehart, 1942), pp. 50–53, 64; and chapter 2 by Donald Matthews in this volume.

So it is in all democratic elections. Yet American presidential elections differ from most others in the world. In the other democracies the parties' nominees, and therefore the nation's rulers, are chosen largely or entirely according to short and simple sets of rules established and enforced by the parties themselves with little or no interference by parliaments or courts.[2] But in America the presidential nominating game is played under by far the most elaborate, variegated, and complex set of rules in the world. They include national party rules, state and local party rules, state statutes (especially those governing presidential primaries), and a wide variety of rulings by national and state courts.

Many political scientists and most politicians have no doubt that these rules constitute one of the prime forces, though not the only one, determining the nature of the nominating game. They also act on the corollary belief that changing the rules changes the game—and thus the various contestants' relative chances of winning.

The Rules and the Game

RULES ARE NOT NEUTRAL

Rules governing political conflict are never entirely neutral; unlike rain, they never fall on the just and the unjust alike. Any particular set necessarily makes some contestant-characteristics assets and others liabilities. Therefore it necessarily favors some contestants over others. So it is not surprising that most proposals to change the rules are evaluated not alone according to whether they are deemed right or wrong with reference to some eternal and abstract principle of justice but also—perhaps even mainly—according to what candidates and factions they seem likely to help or hurt. This does not make those who argue for or against rules changes knaves or fools; it only shows that they recognize the facts of political life.

The history of party reform in America offers many illustrations. In the 1824 fight over abolishing presidential nominations by congressional caucus the supporters of William H. Crawford supported the caucus system because they believed it offered his best chance for victory. The supporters of John Quincy Adams, John C. Calhoun, Henry Clay, and Andrew Jackson entirely agreed with the Crawford faction's analysis, and consequently demanded an end to nominations by caucus. In 1824, then, a person's presidential preference was an almost perfect predictor of his stand on the caucus system.

[2] The most comprehensive survey is Leon D. Epstein, *Political Parties in Western Democracies* (New York: Frederick A. Praeger, 1967), Ch. VIII.

Robert M. La Follette launched his movement for nominations by direct primary in 1897 only after Wisconsin Republican state conventions had twice denied him the party's gubernatorial nomination. If you were for La Follette you were for the direct primary, and if you were for the "Stalwarts" you favored retaining the convention system.

More recently, the donnybrook in the 1972 Democratic national convention over whether California's 271 votes should be given *en bloc* to pro-McGovern delegates or distributed among the various candidates in proportion to their shares of the popular vote in the June primary was decided almost entirely along candidate-preference lines. As the New York *Times* reported, both sides couched the debate in terms of high principle, but "almost no one who supported Mr. McGovern voted for the challenge; almost no one who supported anyone else voted against it." [3]

But the history of such affairs is far from finished. Americans in the mid-1970s are right in the midst of the greatest ferment over changing the rules of the presidential nominating game since the congressional caucus was dumped and the national conventions established in the period 1824–1832.[4] The changes made since the late 1960s have already substantially altered the nature of the game, and the end is not in sight. Yet many past rules changes have not produced the kind of game sought by their advocates or feared by their opponents, and we today operate under the same uncertainties.

ENDS, MEANS, AND UNCERTAINTY

I well remember that the first thing we members of the Democratic party's McGovern–Fraser commission (1969–72) agreed on—and about the only matter on which we approached unanimity—was that we did *not* want a national presidential primary or any great increase in the number of state primaries. Indeed, we hoped to prevent any such development by reforming the delegate-selection rules so that the party's nonprimary processes would be open and fair, participation in them would greatly increase, and consequently the demand for more primaries would fade away. And most of us were confident that our guidelines would accomplish all these ends.

But we got a rude shock. After our guidelines were promulgated in 1969 no fewer than eight states newly adopted presidential primaries, and by 1972 well over two-thirds of all the delegates were chosen or

---

3 New York *Times,* June 30, 1972, p. 20.
4 The contests over rules changes from the 1790s to the 1970s are described in some detail in my *Curing the Mischiefs of Faction: Party Reform in America* (Berkeley, Los Angeles, and London: University of California Press, 1974).

bound by them. Moreover, in 1973 Congress was considering a national presidential primary more seriously than ever before. Of course, it cannot be said that the guidelines were the sole cause for the proliferation of primaries. But we do know that in a majority of the eight cases the state Democratic parties, who controlled the governorships and both houses of the legislature, decided that rather than radically revise their accustomed ways of conducting caucuses and conventions for other party matters, it would be better to split off the process for selecting national convention delegates and let it be conducted by a state-administered primary which the national party would have to accept.

So here was a case in which we had a clear objective in mind; we designed our new rules to achieve it; we got them fully accepted and enforced; and we accomplished the opposite of what we intended. In hindsight it is clear that our rules operated, as rules always must, in a maelstrom of other triggering and contagion factors. Some of these supported the intent of our rules, but others diverted, bypassed, or cancelled them. So it is only too clear that political scientists or party reformers or those of us who sometimes try to be both have only a very limited ability to forecast accurately the political and legal consequences of changes in the rules.

MANIPULATING THE MANIPULABLE

If the effects of rules changes are so uncertain, then, why do we bother with them? The answer, I believe, is both clear and sensible. Of all the many forces affecting the character of the nominating game, the rules are the most manipulable. After all, we can change the voters' cognitive maps only very slowly if at all. We have even less control over the mysterious process by which some persons "emerge" as serious contenders and others fall back. But if we muster the necessary political strength we can change or preserve our party's rules and get Congress and the state legislatures to pass or reject laws.

In short, it is all very well for the detached outside analyst to point out the complexities of cause-and-effect relationships and the consequent uncertainties about the effects of proposed rules changes. Political scientists are very good at that, as they should be. But those of us who want to see the process changed to maximize some greater value cannot wait for the slow story of history to unfold or take the chance that it will tell only tales of frustration and defeat. So we try to manipulate the rules because they are the most manipulable elements of the process and because we feel we must do what we can.

Issues Before the Nation[5]

As noted above, more Americans today than in many years are locked in a series of struggles over the rules of their parties' nominating games. All of us, noncombatants as well as combatants, have a stake in their outcome, and so we should understand what the issues are. In my judgment, the principal issues are the following.

WHO SHOULD CHOOSE THE NOMINEE?

No American who wishes to be taken seriously dares to argue right out in public that our presidential nominees should be chosen by a few party bosses making secret deals in air-conditioned (no longer smoke-filled) rooms. To be sure, such nominees as Thomas Jefferson, James Madison, James Monroe, Henry Clay, Abraham Lincoln, Grover Cleveland, and Woodrow Wilson were chosen that way. But then so too were William Henry Harrison, Zachary Taylor, Franklin Pierce, James Buchanan, and Warren Harding; so the bosses-and-deals method is not guaranteed to produce or prevent a nominee of top quality, and in any case it runs sharply counter to the *Zeitgeist* of the 1970s.

That *Zeitgeist* requires us all to affirm that the nomination should be made by, or at least in accordance with, the wishes of a much larger group—the "party members," the "rank and file," or simply "the people." But when one probes this article of faith the least bit he runs right up against one of the most enduring and vexing issues in all of American electoral politics. That is the issue of just what persons are entitled to be treated as party "members" in the sense that they have a right to participate in making its nominations. I have come to believe that one's position on this issue is an excellent predictor of his position on several others, so let me briefly describe, in order of increasing inclusiveness, the main positions taken on it.[6]

Party Regulars—People who have earned the right by regular and faithful past service to the party and a firm commitment to serve it in the future regardless of whether their candidates or policy preferences prevail in any particular year. Nelson Polsby and Aaron Wildavsky, in their shrewd analysis of convention delegates in both parties' 1964 and

[5] Useful discussions of these issues from various points of view are presented in: Alexander M. Bickel, *Reform and Continuity* (New York: Harper Colophon Books, 1971); Judith H. Parris, *The Convention Problem* (Washington, D.C.: The Brookings Institution, 1972); Nelson W. Polsby and Aaron B. Wildavsky, *Presidential Elections*, 3rd ed. (New York: Charles Scribner's Sons, 1971), Ch. 4; and John S. Saloma III and Frederick H. Sontag, *Parties: The Real Opportunity for Effective Citizen Politics* (New York: Random House Vintage Books, 1973).

[6] They are described more fully in *Curing the Mischiefs of Faction*, Ch. 5.

1968 conventions, found this view predominant among the supporters of Lyndon Johnson and Hubert Humphrey. To illustrate it, they quote the views of some Humphrey delegates about their pro-McCarthy opponents:

> The McWhinnies [McCarthy supporters] are like little boys with marbles; you don't play by their rules—they want to break up the game. . . . The party structure is always open to people who are interested in working. . . . It's just that we have a sort of seniority system like Congress; those who make the most contribution get the largest say in what we do. That's only fair. . . . The problem is that while the McCarthy kids want into the party they want in at the top. They aren't interested in the status which the beginner usually gets licking envelopes and things like that, which we did, all of us, when we were coming up.[7]

Candidate and Issue Enthusiasts—People who work in primaries and conventions because they are devoted to a particular candidate or cause in the year of the nomination and without regard to past party service or future party commitment. Polsby and Wildavsky found this view characteristic of the Goldwater and McCarthy delegates. These delegates felt that the question is never whether *they* deserve a share of the party's power, but always whether the *party* deserves their support this year. If it nominates a good candidate on a good platform, it does; but if it nominates a bad candidate on a bad platform, it is downright immoral to support it.

This view clearly underlay the McGovern–Fraser commission's (and the Republican DO committee's—see below) prohibitions against automatic or ex officio delegates, and their insistence that no delegates be chosen prior to the year of the convention.

Self-designated Adherents—People who become eligible to vote in a "closed" party primary by registering as a "member" of the party. Each of the 41 states using the so-called "closed" primary has some kind of legal test of each registrant's bona fides: e.g., affirmation of past allegiance or present affiliation or future support of the party. But in practice the tests are all but meaningless. The election laws jealously guard the secrecy of the ballot, and so there is simply no effective way of checking the validity of the registrant's affirmation. Registration officials and courts have to take the voter's word for his party membership. And even if they did not, the courts have held that any voter has the right to switch his party registration at *some* time between primary elections.[8] So, in effect, advocates of presidential nominations by

[7] Quoted in Polsby and Wildavsky, op. cit., p. 44.

[8] In *Pontikes v. Kusper*, 345 F. Supp. 1104 (1972); and *Rosario v. Rockefeller*, 93 S. Ct. 1245 (1973).

"closed" primaries favor giving control to anyone who wishes it enough to register with the party. And once registered the voter acquires the right to participate in the party's most important decision without assuming any obligation to it whatever.

Any Voter—Michigan and Wisconsin have no party registration at all, and so their laws lodge their states' share of the power, say, the Democrats' presidential nomination in *any* voter—Democrat, Republican, or Independent—who happens to pull the levers on the Democratic side. The 1972 Democratic national convention ordered its Michigan and Wisconsin affiliates to make "all feasible efforts" to change these laws; but it seems most unlikely that they will succeed.

Those, then, are the four main competing views of party membership. Which is the *right* one? I freely confess an incurable preference for linking rights to obligations, and so I prefer the party-regulars position. But a political scientist should recognize facts whether he likes them or not, and the fact is that even in the party conventions the candidate-enthusiasts view now prevails. In the primary states—which, remember, choose or bind over two-thirds of the conventions' delegates —the self-designated adherents or the any-voter view prevails; and if Congress adopts a national primary, one or the other will be the rule everywhere.

DIRECT DEMOCRACY OR REPRESENTATIVE CONVENTIONS?

One of the oldest arguments in the history of democratic ideas concerns whether true democracy demands direct, unmediated decision-making by the people or allows governing by the people's elected representatives. Not surprisingly, this has been and continues to be one of the main issues in disputes about presidential nominating rules. Most advocates of a national presidential primary, from Woodrow Wilson to Mike Mansfield, have argued that no convention or other form of representation can possibly express "the will of the people" (the parties' registered voters? all voters?) as accurately as the direct vote of the people themselves. And this view now commands more support than ever before, not only in Congress but among the mass public. A Gallup poll of May, 1972, found 72 percent of Americans in favor of a national primary, with only 18 percent against it, and the rest undecided.[9]

Other Americans, however, believe that a national primary would do more harm than good. It would put an even greater premium than at present on large-scale mass-media advertising, polling, public relations

[9] Reported in *Congressional Quarterly Weekly Report,* July 8, 1972, p. 1651.

expertise, and all the other costly features of "the new politics." And this, in turn, would put a premium on big money. Moreover, it would restrict most citizens to just one form of participation in the nominating process, and that would not be healthy for them or for the nation. People of this persuasion therefore agree with the McGovern–Fraser commission's conclusion that "purged of its structural and procedural inadequacies, the National Convention is an institution well worth preserving." [10]

How, then, do we purge the conventions of their inadequacies? The best way, many believe, is to make them more truly *representative*. But that proposition opens up other and even more difficult issues.

WHAT KIND OF REPRESENTATION?

The questions of what constitutes true representation and how to achieve it in our nominating conventions and delegate-selection processes have bedeviled recent party reformers more than any other issue. It is not surprising, for questions of the nature and institutionalization of representation have bothered many of our greatest political theorists for centuries. What, they have asked, is the essence of true representation? The fact that the representative's constituents have authorized him to speak and act in their place? Or that he is accountable to them in periodic elections? Or that he shares their ethnicity or religion or economic status? Is he justified in doing what he thinks best even if they have contrary views? Or is he rightly confined to doing only what they have instructed him to do? And so on.[11]

Several of these questions go to the heart of the 1970s reformers' greatest problems. The most criticized of all the McGovern–Fraser commission's guidelines, for example, has been their quota system for minorities, women, and young people. Guidelines A-1 and A-2 ordered that "State Parties overcome the effects of past discrimination by affirmative steps to encourage representation on the national convention delegation of minority groups, women, and young people in reasonable relationship to their presence in the population of the State." [12]

But why only these groups? Why not also old people, poor people, union members, Catholics, Jews, or other kinds of people important to

[10] Commission on Party Structure and Delegate Selection, *Mandate for Reform* (Washington, D.C.: Democratic National Committee, 1970), p. 12.

[11] The best single analysis of the many different views on these questions is Hanna Fenichel Pitkin, *The Concept of Representation* (Berkeley, Los Angeles, and London: University of California Press, 1967).

[12] *Mandate for Reform*, p. 40. A footnote to these guidelines states: "It is the understanding of the Commission that this is not to be accomplished by the mandatory imposition of quotas"; but most state delegations chose to play it safe by making sure they had close to the required percentages of each favored group.

the party and the nation? The factual answer, though not the moral justification, is that the commissioners who favored quotas (the key vote was only ten to nine in favor) felt that only these groups needed this kind of compensatory protection. They also believed that full proportional representation of the favored groups was too important to be left to the uncertainties of free competition in state and local conventions and primaries.[13]

Many democrats continue to feel that guaranteeing delegate positions for women, youth, blacks, and Chicanos is simple justice, and they are fighting what now appears to be a losing battle to preserve the quotas. Others, including some former members of the commission like myself, have come to feel that the views and interests of women, youth, and ethnic minorities are not represented only, or even necessarily represented best, by delegates with the same biological characteristics. Even more important is the argument that any form of prearranged election outcomes is incompatible with either the principle of fair competition or the principle of accurately representing the candidate and issue preferences of the party's rank and file, however the latter may be defined. We conclude that the party, and indeed the whole presidential nominating system, should place its basic faith in truly fair and open competition. And this, we believe, precludes not only any form of discrimination against any person with a right to participate but also any kind of guaranteed result.[14]

Many Americans, of course, would like to have it both ways—fair and open competition which would regularly result in the winners being, like the general population, 51 percent women, 11 percent black, and 27 percent between the ages of 18 and 30. But in fact it rarely works out that way, and for some time to come the winners of open competitions are likely to be disproportionately male, white, and middle-aged. So the nation, like the parties, must decide whether the essence of democracy, equity, and representation lies in purified procedures or in prearranged outcomes. This choice is tough enough, but the parties have an additional problem which makes their choice even tougher.

THE SPECIAL ISSUE BEFORE THE PARTIES:
EXPRESSIVENESS OR EFFECTIVENESS?

I have no doubt that the leaders and workers of both parties, like most Americans, want rules that will make our presidential nominating

---

13 One of the best accounts of the commission's debates and actions is Theodore H. White, *The Making of the President 1972* (New York: Atheneum Publishers, 1973), pp. 21–33.

14 See, for example, the argument in the manifesto *Toward Fairness & Unity for '76* issued in 1973 by the Coalition for a Democratic Majority.

game the fairest and most democratic possible. Consequently they are as plagued as anyone else by the tough problems of how best to achieve these great ends.

But most major-party activists have an additional goal and thus face a special issue. They not only want to choose their nominee by fair and democratic procedures, but they also want to win the election. And it may be that party rules which guarantee the most faithful expression of the activists' demographic characteristics, life styles, and candidate and issue preferences will tend to produce nominees and platforms unappealing or downright offensive to many of the voters whose support they must have to win. What happens then? What *should* happen then?

For Democrats, at least, this is no hypothetical question. Their massive reform movement of recent years originated in the widespread conviction that their nominating processes in 1968 and before were unrepresentative, undemocratic, and unfair. As the McGovern–Fraser commission put it, "meaningful participation of Democratic voters in the choice of their presidential nominee was often difficult or costly, sometimes completely illusory, and, in not a few instances, impossible." [15] To be sure, the nominee produced by these reprehensible processes did very well in the election: Humphrey received 49.6 percent of the two-party popular vote, carried fourteen states with 191 electoral votes, and might well have won had the election been held two weeks later.

To many of the party's reformers, however, this was largely or wholly beside the point. The old rules and practices were *intrinsically* wrong, regardless of the electoral results they brought. They had to be changed, not solely or even mainly to improve the party's chances of winning in 1972, but to make them fairer and more democratic. It is instructive in this regard to note the McGovern–Fraser commission's statement of the basic reason why their reforms were necessary:

> The Guidelines that we have adopted are designed to open the door to all Democrats who seek a voice in their Party's most important decision: the choice of its presidential nominee. . . . If we are not an open party; if we do not represent the demands of change, then the danger is not that people will go to the Republican Party; it is that there will no longer be a way for people committed to orderly change to fulfill their needs and desires within our traditional political system. It is that they will turn to third and fourth party politics or the anti-politics of the street.[16]

These reformers had their way about as fully as reformers ever have. The delegate selection and convention rules were radically revised and

---

[15] *Mandate for Reform*, p. 10.
[16] Ibid., p. 49.

tightly enforced. Many more people participated in the 1972 nominating game than ever before. The convention's delegates included far higher proportions of women, blacks, and young people than any in history. Their nominee well expressed their triumph in his acceptance speech by declaring, "My nomination is all the more precious in that it is the gift of the most open political process in our national history." [17] Yet in the election he won only 38.2 percent of the two-party popular vote, carried only one state and the District of Columbia for seventeen electoral votes, and suffered one of the most horrendous defeats in history—and this at a time when other Democratic candidates were more than holding their own in elections for Congress, governorships, and state legislatures.

How, then, do Democrats evaluate the 1972 reforms? If Polsby and Wildavsky are correct, it probably depends on the extent to which they are "purists" or "professionals." As we noted above, the purists believe that a party should advocate what is right even if it is unpopular and nominate a candidate who will stand firm for his principles without trimming or pandering for votes. They have no objection to winning elections, of course, but it is not their prime objective and they feel it is certainly not worth the sacrifice of their policy commitments. As one Goldwaterite put it in 1964, "I'd rather stick by the real principles this country was built on than win. Popularity isn't important: prestige isn't important: it's the principles that count." And a McCarthy delegate in 1968 said that if Humphrey were nominated there would be "a crushing and complete defeat this fall. And I'm glad of that. Get rid of a lot of deadwood. Then we can really take over." [18]

On the other hand, the professionals, while they may not feel that winning the election should be the party's only goal or even its most important goal, certainly feel that winning is a necessary if not sufficient condition for achieving all other party goals—whether those be enacting party policies or filling government jobs with party faithful. Most professionals are thus unwilling to pay *any* price for victory— such as, say, supporting a candidate they feel would be disastrous to the nation or breaking into the opposition party's headquarters. But the first criterion they typically apply to an aspirant for the nomination or a proposed platform plank is: will it help us win?

"Purists" and "professionals" are, of course, Weberian "ideal types," and few people can be found who are pure professionals caring only for victory, or unalloyed purists caring nothing for it. But Democrats who are mainly "purists" are likely to feel that the 1972 defeat, if rele-

17 *Congressional Quarterly Weekly Report,* July 15, 1972, p. 1781.
18 Quoted in Polsby and Wildavsky, op. cit., pp. 39, 42.

vant at all, is not important in deciding what the party should do now with its rules. And Democrats who are mainly "professionals" are likely to feel that the party should ask first to what extent the new rules produced the defeat and then what changes are needed to prevent a repetition.

Both sides, however, would do well to take a hard look at the question of just what impact the new rules actually had on the outcomes of both the nominating contest and the election. It is widely said that they made inevitable McGovern's nomination, and without them he could not possibly have been nominated. But is either proposition true? Remember that in 1964 the Republicans made a similar nomination of a candidate identified with one of his party's ideological extremes rather than its center. Like McGovern, Goldwater did not do very well in the primaries but won mainly because his candidacy was pressed effectively by a large and hardworking body of amateurs dedicated to his policy stands. Goldwater's nomination, like McGovern's, repelled many of the voters his party needed to win. And Goldwater, like McGovern, suffered a crushing defeat in the general election. But there is one crucial difference between the two nominations: McGovern was nominated under the new, reformed rules, but Goldwater was nominated under his party's old, *un*reformed rules.

This is not to say that the Democrats' new rules had no effect whatever on their 1972 nominating outcome. They may well have made it easier for McGovern, especially since his organization understood and worked with the new rules much better than did any of their rivals. But it is to say that the similar triumph of Goldwater in 1964 strongly suggests that the rules were by no means the *only* factors affecting the game's outcome. Their impact relative to other factors is hard to isolate in retrospect and hard to predict for the future. The point is so often important and so seldom mentioned that it deserves special emphasis at this point in our argument, and should be borne in mind in the following review of recent rules changes and the agenda of unfinished business.

Principal Rules Changes, 1956–1973

IN THE DEMOCRATIC PARTY

Since the establishment of regular two-party competition for the Presidency in the 1830s, most changes in the rules governing nominations have been initiated by the out-party. There is no mystery why. A party which has just lost an election is more likely to be dissatisfied with procedures producing a loser than is a winning party with procedures that just produced a winner. Moreover, the in-party can realistically consider only those changes which its incumbent President allows it to consider, while the out-party is constrained by no such veto power.

Thus it is not surprising that most, though not all, of the recent rules changes have been initiated by the Democrats in the two periods following their losses of the Presidency in 1952 and 1968. They can be classified under two headings.

National Party Control of Delegate Selection—From the first Democratic national convention in 1832 until the 1950s the principle was firmly established that the party's national agencies, the convention and the national committee, would decide how many votes each state and territorial party would have in the next convention, but it was entirely up to the state and territorial parties and legislatures to decide how the delegates casting those votes would be selected. This long-standing principle was first successfully challenged in the early 1950s by nonsouthern Democrats seeking to prevent southern Democrats from repeating the 1948 Dixiecrat strategy of keeping the party's national ticket off state ballots or listing it under some label other than the regular Democratic label. Their efforts induced the 1956 convention to pronounce:

> It is the understanding that a State Democratic Party, in selecting and certifying delegates to the Democratic National Convention, thereby undertakes to assure that voters will have the opportunity to cast their election ballots for the Presidential and Vice-Presidential nominees selected by said Convention, and for electors pledged formally and in good conscience to the election of those Presidential and Vice-Presidential nominees under the Democratic party label and designation.

This potentially radical switch to national control of delegate selection rules was accelerated by the 1964 convention, which added:

> It is the understanding that a State Democratic Party, in selecting and certifying delegates to the Democratic National Convention, thereby undertakes to assure that voters in the State, regardless of race, color, creed or national origin, will have the opportunity to participate fully in Party affairs. . . .[19]

And the switch was completed in 1968 when the convention actually denied seats to the entire "regular" Mississippi delegation because it was found to have violated this national party rule despite its compliance with Mississippi law.

[19] The two quotations are taken from, respectively, the Call for the 1960 Democratic National Convention and the Call for the 1968 Democratic National Convention.

National control of delegate selection received its greatest boost to date in the period 1969–72. In 1969, acting under a mandate from the 1968 convention, national chairman Senator Fred Harris appointed a 28-member Commission on Party Structure and Delegate Selection (generally known since as the "McGovern–Fraser commission" after its two chairmen, Senator George McGovern, 1969–71, and Representative Donald Fraser, 1971–72). This commission produced a set of eighteen guidelines intended to govern the state parties' procedures for selecting their national convention delegates.[20] The national committee then incorporated all eighteen guidelines in its call for the 1972 convention. Despite many predictions to the contrary, all of the state and territorial parties eventually surrendered their traditional power to make their own delegate-selection rules. By the opening of the convention the commission declared that 45 of the affiliated parties were in full compliance with the new rules, 10 were in substantial compliance, and none were in substantial noncompliance.

The 1972 convention went two steps beyond the guidelines. First, it directed that the call for the 1976 convention include provisions to ensure that no delegates would be selected by direct primaries in which persons other than Democrats could vote (as has been the case in Michigan and Wisconsin). Second, it ordered that all 1976 delegates be chosen "in a manner which fairly reflects the division of preferences expressed by those who participate in the Presidential nominating process," which would rule out winner-take-all primaries such as those in California and South Dakota.

We have already reviewed the main issues emerging in the Democrats' continuing disagreements over these rules. But we should note here that by the mid-1970s the national agencies of the Democratic party had established firmly, and probably irreversibly, the principle that they, and not their state and local affiliates, have the final word on the rules governing the selection of national convention delegates. Quite aside from the rules' particulars, the successful assertion of the national party's supremacy was in itself a drastic change in the rules of the nominating game.

Streamlining and Democratizing Convention Procedures—In pursuance of another mandate from the 1968 convention, the Democratic national chairman also appointed in 1969 a 28-member Commission on Rules, chaired until its discharge in 1972 by Representative James G. O'Hara of Michigan. Although it received less publicity than the McGovern–Fraser commission, the O'Hara commission was every bit as

---

[20] The most complete account of this commission's origins, mandate, guidelines, and underlying rationale is its report, *Mandate for Reform,* cited in footnote 10.

innovative.[21] A sample of its innovations includes: (a) apportioning the delegations' votes according to a new formula giving 53 percent weight to each state's electoral votes and 47 percent to the state's proportion of the party's popular vote for President averaged over the preceding three elections; (b) abolishing the old rule of equal representation for each delegation on the convention's standing committees and replacing it with representation proportional to the delegations' votes in the convention; (c) ending "favorite son" nominations by requiring that each person put in nomination have the written support of at least 50 delegates from at least three different delegations, with no more than 20 coming from any one delegation; (d) determining by lot each delegation's location on the floor and order in the roll call; and (e) perhaps most radical of all, requiring that each delegate's vote "be recorded as polled without regard to any state law, Party rule, resolution or instruction binding the delegation or member thereof to vote as a unit with others or to cast his vote for or against any candidate or proposition." This not only ended the old "unit rule," but presumably also relieved any delegate from being bound by a state primary law to vote for a candidate the delegate did not personally favor.

The cumulative effect of the O'Hara commission's rules and the McGovern–Fraser commission's guidelines was a 1972 convention attended by persons and acting according to procedures quite different from those of any previous national convention in history. Some Democrats have come to view this as small consolation for the near-record defeat of their reformed convention's nominee in the 1972 election, but no one can deny that in recent years the party has been, at least in its internal affairs, the "party of change" as few others have ever been.

IN THE REPUBLICAN PARTY

In sharp contrast to their Democratic competitors, the Republican national party in 1968 achieved a harmonious convention, a united party in the campaign, and a winner in the November election, never mind by how tiny a margin. Thus few observers would have been surprised if the Republicans had stood pat on their presidential nominating rules. But they did not.[22] Their 1968 convention directed the appointment of a committee of the national committee to consider ways of improving the convention's procedures and also ways of

---

21 The most complete account of the O'Hara commission's new rules and the reasoning behind them is its report: Commission on Rules, *Call to Order* (Washington, D.C.: Democratic National Committee, 1972).

22 The best accounts of the Republicans' rules changes are in the *Congressional Quarterly Weekly Report*, April 29, 1972, pp. 943–946; and ibid., August 12, 1972, pp. 1998–1999.

implementing the party's rule 32, which provided that "participation in a Republican primary, caucus, or any meeting or convention held for the purpose of selecting delegates to a County, District, State or National Convention shall in no way be abridged for reasons of race, religion, color or national origin." Accordingly, the Committee on Delegates and Organization (generally referred to as the "DO" committee) was appointed in 1969.

The DO committee had no authority to make rules for the 1972 convention, but was instructed to make recommendations which, if accepted in 1972, would apply to the 1976 convention. The committee met in closed sessions, and about the only publicity it received was the remarks by Democrats about how inactive it was compared to the McGovern–Fraser commission—the "DO-nothing committee" some called it.

But this gibe proved to be less than accurate or fair. The committee made ten recommendations to the 1972 convention, many seeking the same goals as the McGovern–Fraser guidelines, and some even using similar language. They included proposals to open up all state and local caucuses and conventions to all qualified citizens, prohibit proxy voting, and abolish automatic or ex officio delegates. Most significant of all were recommendations 8 and 9:

> . . . each State [shall] endeavor to have equal representation of men and women in its delegation to the Republican National Convention. . . . each State [shall] include in its delegation to the Republican National Convention delegates under 25 years of age in numerical equity to their voting strength within the State.[23]

To the surprise of many party-watchers, the 1972 convention adopted seven of the ten recommendations and broadened number 8 and 9 by calling upon the national and state committees to

> take positive action to achieve the broadest possible participation for everyone in party affairs, including such participation by women, young people, minority and national groups and citizens in the delegate selection process.[24]

Thus even though they lacked the Democrats' incentives to change their nominating rules, the Republicans nevertheless made several major changes. Their implementation is likely to play a significant role in the Republican game in 1976.

[23] Quoted in *Congressional Quarterly Weekly Report,* April 29, 1972, p. 943.
[24] Quoted in New York *Times,* August 23, 1972, p. 26.

IN THE STATE GOVERNMENTS

Between 1969 and 1972 a number of states altered their laws relating to the selection of national convention delegates so as to get into compliance with the McGovern–Fraser guidelines. A few refused to do so: the most notable instances were California's rejection of a bill to end the winner-take-all feature of its presidential primary, and New York's refusal to print the presidential preferences of candidates for delegates on its official primary ballots.

The states' main contribution to the torrent of recent rules changes, however, has been the sudden proliferation of presidential primaries. A bit of history highlights this development. Presidential primaries were first widely used in 1912, when seventeen states held them. By 1916 nine more states had added primaries, but the tide soon ebbed. Between 1920 and 1968 five states and territories adopted presidential primaries, but ten abandoned them.[25] Thus in 1968 fifteen states and the District of Columbia held some kind of primary, which resulted in about 41 percent of the delegates to each convention being chosen or bound by primaries. Between 1969 and 1972, however, no fewer than seven states newly added primaries, and the proportion of delegates so chosen or bound rose to 66 percent. In 1973 Georgia became the eighth state to join the crowd, so in 1976 the proportion of primary delegates will approach 70 percent.

This particular rules change has produced an obvious and significant change in the game. Whether before 1972 primaries were "eyewash," as Harry Truman claimed, or one of the more important of several tests a candidate must pass, as some political scientists said, the primaries have now become perhaps the most crucial of all the hurdles to the nomination. Any candidate who sweeps all or most of them will lock up the nomination beyond challenge, and it is unlikely that a candidate who enters no primaries can ever again win, as did Adlai Stevenson in 1952 and Hubert Humphrey in 1968.

The densening of the primaries thicket has also made life much tougher for all serious candidates for contested nominations. It has greatly multiplied the need for workers and organizations, polling and media expertise, and therefore for money. Indeed, the present hodgepodge of locations, states, and rules now makes the primaries so difficult for contenders that various proposals for superseding them with a national presidential primary are being considered more seriously than ever before. We shall consider the issues involved in a moment.

25 James W. Davis, *Springboard to the White House* (New York: Thomas Y. Crowell Company, 1967), pp. 24–37.

IN CONGRESS

Between 1969 and 1973, Congress's main contribution to changing the rules was enacting the Federal Election Campaign Act of 1971, which went into effect on April 7, 1972. As it pertained to presidential *nominating* contests, the act required all presidential candidates, all candidate-supporting committees with contributions totalling over one thousand dollars, and all individuals contributing over one hundred dollars to file periodic reports with the General Accounting Office (GAO) disclosing the sources and spending of campaign funds. It also limited the amount a candidate could spend on all mass media advertising to ten cents times the resident voting-age population, and stipulated that no more than 60 percent of that amount could be spent for advertising on television and radio.[26]

The new law was something less than a total success. Some observers and campaign directors thought the expenditure limits were absurdly low and thus almost demanded to be violated. Others felt the reporting requirements put an impossible burden on campaign finance directors. Still others complained that it added considerably to the already excessive advantages of incumbent Presidents.

Certainly there were many violations. Between June, 1972, and July, 1973, the GAO issued fourteen reports of apparent violations, twelve of which were referred to the Justice Department for further action. Many other violations were reported in testimony before the grand jury and Senate committee investigating the Watergate scandals in 1973. The Committee to Reelect the President (CRP) was, hands down, the most frequently cited violater, though not the only one. Investigators turned up such episodes as the committee's failure to report a $200,000 contribution from indicted financier Robert Vesco; the unreported fund of $210,000 secretly raised by President Nixon's personal attorney, Herbert Kalmbach, for attorneys' fees and family support for the Watergate break-in defendants; and the transfer of $350,000 in cash to White House aide Gordon Strachan just before April 7, 1972, in an obvious effort to evade the law's application. Many people were shocked even more by testimony in the Watergate hearings that the CRP allocated a fund of $199,000 to G. Gordon Liddy, in part for his "department of dirty tricks" including the attempted burglary of the Democratic National Committee's headquarters, and the use of espio-

---

[26] The act's main provisions are summarized in the *Congressional Quarterly Weekly Report,* June 17, 1972, pp. 1459–1460. Most of them also applied to primary and general election campaigns for senator and representative, but these are outside our present concerns.

nage and forgery to discredit the primary campaigns of some Democratic aspirants, especially Edmund Muskie.

Some anti-Nixon forces also violated the law. John Loeb pleaded no contest to a charge of having made illegal indirect contributions to Hubert Humphrey's campaign funds. The National Committee for Impeachment of the President was cited by the GAO for failing to register as a political committee. And the Sanford Carolina Campaign Committee was cited for knowingly filing false reports.[27]

These relevations have had many repercussions and will continue to have them for years to come. One of the main results has been a greatly intensified concern with the whole problem of campaign finance and practices in presidential nominations and elections. Later we shall review the issues raised.

IN THE COURTS

National Party Rules vs. State Laws—Aside from the 1971 campaign finance law and its predecessors as they applied to presidential primaries, Congress has passed no laws regulating how presidential candidates are nominated. Consequently, almost all of the many statutes regulating presidential nominations are state laws, particularly presidential primary laws and laws regulating the organization and conduct of state and local party conventions and caucuses. So there has long existed a tricky question about the legal rights and wrongs if a national party rule contravenes a state law. The question was largely moot until the 1960s, because, with rare exceptions, the national party rules, conventions, and committees accepted state laws as binding.

But all this has changed. In 1968, as we saw earlier, the Democratic national convention denied seats to the entire "regular" Mississippi delegation despite the unchallenged fact that it had been chosen in full compliance with Mississippi law. The credentials committee held that the Mississippi party's procedures violated the national party rule against racial discrimination, and that the convention had the final power to rule on the qualifications of its delegates regardless of state laws. The convention's majority agreed, and no court intervened.

In 1972 the Democratic credentials committee and convention refused to seat Mayor Daley's 59 delegates from Cook County, all admittedly elected in full compliance with Illinois law, because they violated the McGovern–Fraser prohibitions against secret slating and endorsement of slates by party officials. The Daley 59 challenged these

27 The citations and indictments are summarized in the *Congressional Quarterly Weekly Report,* July 14, 1973, p. 1881.

rulings in the federal courts, but the Supreme Court ultimately refused to intervene in the dispute. Thus the supremacy of national party rules over state laws was, in effect, upheld, though the constitutional issues involved have yet to be authoritatively settled by the Court.

The Constitutional Status of National Party Rules—Hardly anyone disputes that Congress has full constitutional power to regulate national party rules and nominating procedures, but so far Congress has used that power very little. Hence the constitutional question posed by the Illinois case (and its California companion case) in 1972 is whether, in the absence of congressional legislation, the national parties' nominating rules are purely private affairs or public matters subject to review and revision by the federal courts.[28] The Supreme Court's 1972 decision merely postponed the issue until a case comes before it allowing adequate time to make an authoritative decision. Such a case seems likely to arrive in 1976 if not before. The Court's ultimate decision will determine the legal status of the national parties and thus whether most future disputes over presidential nominating rules will continue to be settled by the parties themselves or by the federal courts.

It is an important point to settle, for a great many decisions still must be made about the rules of the nominating game. Let us turn now to a brief review of the major items of unfinished business.

Unfinished Business

THE AGENDA

As we have seen, since the mid-1960s America has made far more sweeping changes in its presidential nominating rules than at any time since the period from 1824 to 1832. Even so, many proposals for further changes remain on the nation's agenda, some but not all of which will be acted on by the time of the 1976 national party conventions. The agenda's main items are the following.

Party Rules and Participation—The 1972 Democratic convention directed the appointment of a new commission to review the McGovern–Fraser guidelines, to make "appropriate revisions after due consideration of their operation during 1972," to "give special attention to implementing . . . the requirement that the National and State Democratic Parties take affirmative action to achieve full participation of minorities, youth, and women in the delegate selection process and all Party affairs," and to report by January 1, 1974. Seventy-

[28] The two cases were decided together in *O'Brien vs. Brown,* 409 U.S. 1 (1972).

three commissioners were appointed; Baltimore councilwoman Barbara Mikulski became chairperson, and it was clear that the new commission's report would have as great an impact on the 1976 Democratic convention as the McGovern-Fraser guidelines had had on its predecessor. It was also clear that whatever rules emerged from the Mikulski commission would not necessarily remain unchanged after 1976.

It also remains to be seen what difficulties the Republicans will encounter in implementing their new delegate-selection rules and to what extent, if any, they will make the 1976 Republican convention different from those before it.

State Laws and the Primaries—We noted above that in 1973 Georgia became the eighth state since 1969 and the twenty-fourth overall to adopt a presidential primary. Several other states are also considering moving to primaries, so there is no doubt that the role of primaries in the nominating game will be greater in 1976 than ever before. Moreover, the 1972 Democratic convention's directives require California and South Dakota to abandon the winner-take-all feature of their primary laws, and Michigan and Wisconsin to restrict participation in their primaries to registered party members—although their Democratic parties will not be barred from participating in the 1976 national convention if they have made "all feasible efforts" to get the laws changed. If, as seems likely, not all of these states make the required changes, then the question becomes whether their parties have in fact made "all feasible efforts." If the national party answers no, then presumably the four states' delegations will not be seated at the convention, state laws to the contrary notwithstanding.

Congress: National Primary and Campaign Finance—Sometime before 1976 Congress is likely to decide whether to establish a national presidential primary. If it decides to do so, it will have to choose among several quite different alternatives. The Mansfield–Aiken and Ford–Conte bills propose a national primary without regard to state lines, with the nomination going to the candidate with the largest plurality, and a runoff if no candidate receives at least 40 percent of the votes. The Packwood bill divides the nation into five regions, requires primaries in all the states of each region, orders the regions to vote in successive months in an order determined by Congress, and allocates convention votes to each candidate proportional to his share of the popular votes in each state. The Udall bill compels no state to hold a primary, but requires those which do to hold them on one of the only three permissible dates.[29]

[29] The bills are summarized in detail in the *Congressional Quarterly Weekly Report,* July 8, 1972, pp. 1650–1654.

Congress is not likely to adopt a presidential primary before 1976, but the probabilities are much higher that it will make substantial revisions in the Federal Election Campaign Act of 1971, the contents, operation, and violations of which we noted earlier. The revisions could take one or more of several directions. They could lower, raise, or even abolish the ten-cents-per-voter expenditure limit. They could tighten the disclosure and reporting provisions and increase the penalties for noncompliance. They could limit the size of contributions. They could even go the final step urged by a number of political scientists by providing partial or complete public subsidies of both nomination and general-election campaigns.[30] Whatever course Congress may take, one thing is perfectly clear: the revelations of shady financial dealings and "dirty tricks" campaign tactics emerging from the Watergate investigations have reinforced the conviction of many Americans, including me, that this aspect of the presidential nominating and electing process is the one most in need of reform.

The Courts and the National Parties' Legal Status—In the brief period between 1971 and 1973, quarreling factions in both national parties took their disputes out of party-arbitrating and -decisional machinery and into the courts more often than ever before in history. The resulting litigation involved a number of matters basic to the nominating rules: the proper legal definition of a party member; permissible ways of preventing members of one party from "raiding" the primaries of the opposition party;[31] and convention apportionment rules that satisfy the equal-protection clause of the Fourteenth Amendment.[32] The most publicized and potentially the most important litigation centered on the issue of the relation of national party rules to state laws and the larger issue of whether the national parties should be treated as private associations or public agencies. As we have seen, the Supreme Court refused to rule on the merits of these issues because of lack of time for full consideration.[33] But the issues remain unsolved, and sooner or later the Court will have to decide them. Their decision will go far toward determining whether the many issues remaining about the proper rules for the nominating game will be made mainly by the parties themselves, the state legislatures, Congress, or the federal courts.

[30] The various proposals and issues are summarized in the *Congressional Quarterly Weekly Report,* July 14, 1973, pp. 1877–1886.
[31] *Pontikes vs. Kusper* and *Rosario vs. Rockefeller,* cited in footnote 8.
[32] *Georgia vs. National Democratic Party,* 447 F. 2d 1271 (1971); *Bode vs. National Democratic Party,* 452 F. 2d 1302 (1971); and *Republican State Central Committee of Arizona vs. Ripon Society,* 409 U.S. 1222 (1972).
[33] In *O'Brien vs. Brown,* cited in footnote 28.

Conclusion

Opaque as the future may seem in most respects, one forecast, at least, seems safe: for some time to come Americans of many different persuasions will continue to seek changes in the rules of the nominating game. Pandora's box was cracked wide open in the mid-1960s, and nothing in view seems likely to close it in the near future. Perhaps the best advice this particular participant-observer in party reform can give to anyone who enters the lists is: whatever changes in the rules you advocate, keep your fingers crossed. If they are adopted and enforced, they may produce a game more to your liking. Or they may produce something very different, perhaps something worse than what you have now.

But none of us should feel too disheartened by our inability to predict accurately the effects of all changes. After all, in the 1970s an optimist is one who believes the future is uncertain.

John H. Kessel

4

Strategy for November

Anyone who cares to join us in all sincerity, we welcome. Those who do not care for our cause, we don't expect to enter our cause in any case. And let our Republicanism, so focused and so dedicated, not be made fuzzy by unthinking and stupid labels. I would remind you that extremism in the defense of liberty is no vice. And let me remind you that moderation in the pursuit of justice is no virtue. . . .
—Barry Goldwater, July 16, 1964

I see another child tonight. He hears a train go by. At night he dreams of faraway places where he'd like to go. It seems like an impossible dream. But he is helped on his journey through life. . . . And in his chosen profession of politics, first there were scores, then hundreds, then thousands, and finally millions who worked for his success. And tonight he stands before you, nominated for President of the United States of America.
—Richard Nixon, August 8, 1968

From the prejudice of race and sex, come home, America. . . . Come home to the affirmation that we have a dream. Come home to the conviction that we can move our country forward. Come home to the belief that we can seek a newer world. And let us be joyful in that homecoming. . . . May God grant us the wisdom to cherish this good land and to meet the great challenge that beckons us home.
—George McGovern, July 14, 1972

JOHN H. KESSEL *is professor of political science at The Ohio State University. He has been active in the Republican party and was director of the Arts and Sciences Division of the Republican National Committee prior to the 1964 election. He is editor of the* American Journal of Political Science *and is the author of* The Goldwater Coalition: Republican Strategies in 1964, The Domestic Presidency, *and coeditor of* Micropolitics: Individual and Group Level Concepts.

These summertime words summon back memories. Not the sharp, fixed recollection of where one was when he first heard of the death of Franklin Roosevelt or the assassination of John Kennedy. Perhaps memories of straining to hear the words amid the babble of a mammoth convention hall. More likely memories of a television set or reading an out-of-town newspaper on a vacation morning. For these words belong to a special hour in American politics when the candidate who has led a victorious coalition in pursuit of his party's nomination must turn and direct his attention toward a quite different goal in November.

In nomination politics, the goal is simple. Fewer people are involved. The point is to get enough groups to join a coalition so that one has a majority of the delegates. The complexities in nomination politics lie in the calendar and legal requirements. Each state selects its delegates at an appointed time, and according to unique laws. Consequently, the focus of attention shifts from a primary election in New Hampshire to precinct caucuses in Washington to district conventions in Iowa to a free-spending primary in California. But the goal remains the same in each case. Get delegates. In a sense, the general election goal is equally simple. Get votes. But a general election takes place in every state the same day. The campaign goes on everywhere simultaneously. Beyond the party activists, the coalition is trying to reach thoughtful independents and less concerned apathetics. To do this, offices must be opened ranging from the several floors of space required for the five hundred to a thousand people at national headquarters to the store front where volunteers meet in a county seat. Tours must be organized and speeches written for the candidates and all the others who will speak in their behalf. In short, organizing a general election campaign on a subcontinental scale is an all-out battle on a thousand fronts at once. More people in more places do more things in a presidential campaign than in any other political task except for running the government itself.

Coalitions and Constraints

Presidential campaigns are carried out by *coalitions,* and in order to think about coalitions, we need to remember they are made up of *groups,* and are aggregated into *institutions.* In other words, we need to use three levels of analysis. This means that the unit on any given level of analysis has *aggregative properties* resulting from the ways in which the smaller units combine, *intrinsic properties* of its own, and *contextual properties* resulting from the constraints of established patterns of behavior on a more inclusive level. Thus, some of the coalition strategy grows out of the behavior of the component groups. Some of the coalition behavior results from the coalition's own attitudes, those to which all of the member groups subscribe. And some of the coalition strategy is due to constraints resulting from the more inclusive institutional pattern.[1] To state this another way, a presidential candidate's behavior should not be judged by asking a naive question such as: "What would a good man tell the American people?" As a spokesman for a coalition, he is not a free agent who can adopt any strategy at will. A candidate's strategy can best be understood by asking such questions as: How would a course of action affect each group in the coalition? Would it hold the coalition together? How would it fit into the larger pattern of behavior resulting from the simultaneous activity of the rival coalitions? Would it be appropriate in view of the accepted norms of American politics? These are the questions that should enable us to make some sense of what has happened in recent presidential campaigns.

Campaign Experience

THE "NORMAL" COALITIONS

The groups in the normal party coalitions have been familiar since the days of Franklin Roosevelt. The Democratic party has been assembled over time as a coalition of minorities. The first two groups were the South and the West, the agrarian supporters of William Jennings Bryan. Another group of urban voters had grown in power, finally winning control of the nomination of Al Smith in 1928. In the 1930s organized labor became important as well, and in the same decade most blacks moved from the party of Lincoln to the party of Roosevelt. Democratic tickets typically had a presidential candidate acceptable to the urban-labor-black wing of the party, and a vice presidential candidate from somewhere in the South or West: Franklin Roosevelt and John Nance Garner, Adlai Stevenson and John Sparkman, John Kennedy and Lyndon Johnson. The Republicans, the erstwhile majority party, were split between moderates and conservatives. The former group had been more successful in nomination politics; the latter was much stronger on Capitol Hill. The Republicans engaged in ticket-balancing, too (witness Thomas Dewey and John

---

[1] For a slightly more extended discussion of this point of view, see my "American Political Parties: An Interpretation with Four Levels of Analysis" in Cornelius P. Cotter, ed., *Political Science Annual*, IV (Indianapolis: Bobbs-Merrill, 1973), pp. 128–131. For a general discussion of the level of analysis question, see Heinz Eulau and Kenneth Prewitt, *Labyrinths of Democracy* (Indianapolis: Bobbs-Merrill, 1973), Ch. 2.

Bricker in 1944), but the balance of power between moderates and conservatives was much more important. In the last of four consecutive nomination contests between New York-based and Ohio-based coalitions, Dwight Eisenhower had 595 votes and Robert Taft had 500 votes before vote switches gave the general the 1952 nomination. At this point (and in this specific context) the moderates were successful, but the crucial fact was that the two wings were of approximately equal size. Both had the potential of leading the party.

STRAIN IN THE FABRIC: THE REPUBLICANS IN 1964

By 1964, the conservatives had grown in power to the point where they could nominate their own candidate, Barry Goldwater. To understand this campaign, it is useful to distinguish among types of conservatives. Four groups could be discerned in the Goldwater coalition. First were the conservative ideologues who had long felt that contests with the Democrats should be fought in terms of liberty vs. socialism, and who favored a much less active role for the government in the management of the economy. Second was a group of foreign policy hard-liners who saw a bipolar world in which there was a total struggle between the free world and the Communists, us against them. The third group was made up of southerners who saw a chance to build a Republican party based on states' rights, and who felt their cause would be advanced by opposition to federal power on many issues, including civil rights. After Goldwater's nomination, these groups were joined by a fourth, the organizational loyalists whose Republican credentials were so impeccable that the Goldwaterites had no doubt about them, and whose party loyalty was so strong that they never had any doubts about supporting the Republican nominee. There was a fair amount of attitudinal overlap between the conservative ideologues and the foreign policy hard-liners (although the government should not simultaneously cut taxes and buy expensive weapons systems), but there was less agreement between these groups and the organizational loyalists or the southerners. The former were less ideological; the latter preferred a more strident conservatism which they thought would help build a party organization in the South. Tensions between these groups were to affect strategy throughout the campaign.[2]

The first phase of the campaign was an attempt, in which the organizational loyalists played a key role, to reunite the moderates and the Goldwaterites. These two factions never had understood one an-

[2] This analysis, and the subsequent analysis of the 1964 Johnson coalition, are developed in much more detail in my book, *The Goldwater Coalition* (Indianapolis: Bobbs-Merrill, 1968).

other very well, and relations had been further strained by the Goldwater references to extremism and moderation quoted at the beginning of this chapter. Richard Nixon sent a letter to the senator:

> I believe it would be helpful to clear the air once and for all . . . and I would appreciate it . . . if you would send me . . . further comments . . . with regard to the intended meaning of these two sentences. . . .

The Goldwater reply came immediately:

> If I were to paraphrase the two sentences in the context in which I uttered them I would do it by saying that whole-hearted devotion to liberty is unassailable and that half-hearted devotion to justice is indefensible. . . .

Further intergroup diplomacy led to a meeting hosted by Dwight Eisenhower at Hershey, Pennsylvania, in mid-August. All Republican governors and gubernatorial candidates were invited, and there was some frank discussion between Senator Goldwater and these moderate leaders. Any hope of bringing an important group of moderates into the Goldwater coalition, though, ended with the senator's first answer at a subsequent press conference when he denied any intent to be conciliatory.

The second phase of Goldwater strategy came with the formal opening of the campaign in early September. The goal then was to win the West and the Midwest, to add these regions to the South, which was assumed to be in favor of Goldwater. The emphasis was to be conservative, and the technique was to give major speeches which would illustrate what the senator meant by his broader themes: a resolute foreign policy with an emphasis on military preparedness and a domestic conservatism stressing free enterprise and law-and-order. Several such speeches were given, one in Los Angeles on programmed tax cuts, another in Chicago criticizing the Supreme Court for infidelity to the principle of limited government, one in Montgomery, Alabama, calling for revenue-sharing with the states, and one in Fargo, North Dakota, advocating reduction of farm supports. The strategists assumed that President Johnson would reply, and that a principled discussion about issues would be joined.

By late September, three things were evident. President Johnson was not going to reply in kind; the existing strategy was not improving Senator Goldwater's standing with the voters; two issues—control of nuclear arms and social security—were in fact doing a good deal of harm to the senator. Each group had its own prescription. Each preferred a new strategy that would shift the emphasis in *its* own direction. Faced with agreement that the strategy needed to be changed, and disagreement as to what the new emphasis should be, the core group decided to respond to the two issues seen as being harmful. So for about two weeks, Republican leaders explained that Senator Goldwater's position on the authority of field commanders (as NATO) did not differ from the practice of the Eisenhower, Kennedy or Johnson administrations, and that the senator had voted several times to increase social security benefits.

The results of this defensive strategy were the same: no change in the survey results and criticism from supporters that Senator Goldwater was conducting an ineffective campaign. Hence, on October 11 the strategy committee shifted again, this time to approve "Operation Home Stretch," a plan drafted by Public Relations Director Lou Guylay. The point was to develop an override strategy, to shift attention away from Johnson's strengths by developing new issues. This fourth plan called for contrasting the moral decay of the Johnson administration (to be tied to rising crime at home and a weakening American posture abroad) with Senator Goldwater's "Hope for a New America." This strategy was given an unexpected boost with the announcement of the arrest of a Johnson aide on a morals charge, but the same fate that smiled briefly on this plan quickly frowned. Within 48 hours, Khrushchev was deposed as the Soviet leader, Harold Wilson led the Labour party to an unexpected victory in Great Britain, and China exploded her first atomic "device." The net of all this was to shift public attention right back to foreign affairs, an area in which voters deemed President Johnson more competent than Senator Goldwater.

By late October, it was clear to the candidate and core group that Goldwater was not going to win. The reaction to this was a final strategy, a reassertion of the correctness of Goldwater beliefs (in *his* heart, the senator knew he was right) and an appeal to the faithful to stay in line so the conservative cause would not be damaged by too overwhelming a defeat. In New York, on Monday, the senator asked plaintively, "I can't help wondering . . . if you think I don't *know* what views would be the most popular." And on Saturday night, he appeared on a platform in Columbia, South Carolina, with a number of prominent southern Democrats, and spoke on a television network confined to the old Confederacy. This was not a case of a general southern strategy (which most observers quite incorrectly alleged had been going on throughout the campaign). Rather, it was end-of-the-campaign fighting for votes which a few weeks earlier had been taken for granted.

THE EXPANDING UMBRELLA: THE DEMOCRATS IN 1964

The Goldwater nomination gave President Johnson considerable flexibility in choosing his strategy. He had been developing a unity appeal since he had entered the White House. He spoke, for example, on the idea of a "Great Society" at the University of Michigan and the need for a "broad national consensus" at the University of Texas on two successive weeks in late May. This strategy was well designed to hold together a coalition of minorities, and the Goldwater nomination gave President Johnson the opportunity to appeal to an even larger set of political groups. The result was the Johnson coalition: moderate Republicans added to the southern-western-urban-labor-black base. Four of the five "normal" Democratic groups were certain to vote for Johnson in 1964; only the loyalty of the South was endangered by the Goldwater nomination. Hence, there were three aspects to the Johnson strategy: a "normal" campaign to remind labor, blacks, urbanites, and westerners that they had been well served by Democratic administrations, a defensive campaign to protect southern support from Republican incursions, and an offensive campaign to convince moderate Republicans that their views lay closer to the Johnson coalition than the Goldwater coalition.

The appeal to normal Democratic groups combined personal empathy, recitation of Democratic accomplishments, and promises in principle to pursue new goals. In Miami Beach, Johnson told machinists that workers' earnings had risen eight times as much since 1961 as they had in a comparable Eisenhower period. In Denver, he promised to put education at the top of America's agenda. In Portland, Oregon, he ticked off a five-point program for a "new conservation." Blacks needed little encouragement since they were convinced that Senator Goldwater had the support of known racists in community after community. But these appeals to labor, urbanites, westerners, and blacks were easy. How often does a presidential candidate get a chance to win votes by promising not to eliminate social security or by reminding voters that his opponent has said it would be well to saw off the eastern seaboard and let it float out to sea?

The southern strategy followed by the Johnson coalition was more interesting. There were four parts to this amalgam. The first was a mobilization of newly registered black voters who were numerous enough to provide the winning margin in many southern states. Second was a reminder of traditional Democratic loyalties, and of the Johnsons' own southern origins. For example, in North Carolina, Mrs. Johnson said that her main reason for coming "was to say to you that to this Democratic candidate, and his wife, the South is a respected, valued, and beloved part of the country." A third element was organizational: local Democrats who had been complaisant in the face of Republican presidential voting were reminded that they were now facing the prospect of Republican candidates for congressman, state senator, and sheriff. The final, and most important, part of the campaign was an economic appeal. When President Johnson met the "Lady Bird Special" campaign train in New Orleans, he quoted an unidentified southern senator:

> I would like to go back there and make them one more Democratic speech. I just feel like I've got one more in me. Poor old state, they haven't heard a Democratic speech in thirty years. All they ever hear is Negro, Negro, Negro! The kind of speech they should have been hearing is about the economy and what a great future we could have in the South if we just met our economic problems, if we just took a look at the resources of the South and developed them.

The South had made considerable economic progress since the Democrats had become the majority party in the 1930s, and President Johnson hoped to remind southerners that they had more to gain by staying with the Democrats than by responding to Senator Goldwater's conservative appeals.

The theme of the campaign for Republican votes was set by Hubert Humphrey in his vice-presidential acceptance speech: Barry Goldwater was not a typical Republican.

> Yes, yes my fellow Americans, it is a fact that the temporary Republican spokesman is not in the mainstream of his party, in fact he has not even touched the shore. . . . I say to those responsible and forward-looking Republicans—and there are thousands of them—we welcome you to the banner of Lyndon B. Johnson. . . .

The President picked up this theme in many of his speeches. In Harrisburg, Pennsylvania, at a Democratic fund-raising dinner, he went out of his way to praise both President Eisenhower and Governor Scranton. Campaigning in Indiana, he acknowledged that Hoosiers had often supported GOP candidates, but declared, "I'm not sure whether there is a real Republican candidate this time." In Rockford, Illinois, four days before the election, Lyndon Johnson pointed out:

> I have always been the kind of Democrat who could work together with my fellow Americans of the party of Lincoln and McKinley, Herbert Hoover and Dwight Eisenhower, Robert Taft, Arthur Vandenberg, and Everett Dirksen.

It had been some time since a Democratic presidential candidate had spoken kindly about William McKinley and Herbert Hoover just before an election, but 1964 gave President Johnson unusual freedom to maneuver. He was not completely free of intraparty criticism, but he was able to make his appeals to Republicans, carry out his defense of Democratic support in the South, and conduct his "normal" campaign for other groups without being subject to the kinds of pressures that would force him to switch from one set of campaign plans to another.

1968 AND THE POSSIBILITY OF A REPUBLICAN VICTORY

If 1964 was a year when an abnormally large coalition could be put together in behalf of a Democratic candidate, 1968 was not. With George Wallace joining those other figures—Theodore Roosevelt in 1912, Robert LaFollette in 1924, and Strom Thurmond in 1948—who had led dissatisfied groups into third-party efforts, it was possible for a normal Republican coalition to win. But for Richard Nixon to hold the coalition together, very delicate balancing was necessary. Mr. Nixon had to remain sufficiently progressive to keep moderate Republicans from supporting Hubert Humphrey if Nixon was to carry enough large states to win. He also had to convince conservatives that he was the authentic antiliberal candidate, that a vote for George Wallace would only be a wasted vote. Doing either of these things by itself would be relatively easy; doing them both at the same time required real political skill. This meant that exactly the right thing had to be said. Richard Nixon had to give voice to attitudes that would be acceptable to all his followers.

This task was begun at the convention in two ways. One was to obtain an acceptable Vietnam plank in the platform by negotiations between Nixon leaders, Rockefeller leaders, and the Platform Committee. The resulting statement began by advocating what later came to be called "Vietnamization."

> We pledge to adopt a strategy relevant to the real problems of the war, concentrating on the security of the population, on developing a greater sense of nationhood, and on strengthening the local forces. It will be a strategy permitting a progressive de-Americanization of the war, both military and civilian.

Then followed words appealing to hawks:

> We will see to it that our gallant American servicemen are fully supported with the highest quality equipment, and will avoid actions that unnecessarily jeopardize their lives.

And to doves:

> We will pursue a course that will enable and induce the South Vietnamese to assume greater responsibility. . . . We will sincerely and vigorously pursue peace negotiations as long as they offer any reasonable prospect for a just peace.

The other important question was the selection of a vice-presidential candidate. Here the party was blessed with a surfeit of possibilities:

Nelson Rockefeller, Charles Percy, Mark Hatfield, Dan Evans among the moderates, John Tower or Howard Baker among the conservatives. But to pick a strong moderate would have produced consternation among the conservatives and to pick a strong conservative would have had a like effect with the moderates. So: "Dick gave us a list. Everybody on the list was unsatisfactory, but Agnew was the *least* unsatisfactory," as a conservative leader allegedly put it. The statement could just as easily have come from a moderate. Neither group was happy with the Agnew nomination, but neither was moved to rebellion. Given a need to hold an unstable coalition together, a vice-presidential candidate whose name was not a household word was a positive virtue.

The Nixon statements on issues during the campaign were similarly calculated to avoid giving offense. On Vietnam:

> We need new leadership that will not only end the war in Vietnam but keep the nation out of other wars for eight years.

On crime:

> I say that when crime has been going up nine times as fast as population, when 43 percent of the people living in American cities are afraid to go out after dark, I say we need a complete housecleaning.

And on welfare:

> Instead of more millions on welfare rolls, let's have more millions on the payrolls.

Richard Nixon did develop an interesting technique of giving more detailed statements on radio, using a low-visibility medium to reach the smaller audience seriously interested in issues. Here he discussed, for example, black capitalism, the alienation of Americans from the governmental process, and the Presidency as a moral and political office. The applause points quoted above, though, were the verbal equivalent of all the balloons released at televised rallies. They took up time with little danger of alienating any support, yet they *sounded* definite.

Mr. Nixon followed a very cautious course throughout September. In spite of a huge lead in the polls (43 percent to 31 percent in the Gallup Poll of September 10), he did not think the election was locked up by any means. He avoided debates, which would have posed high risk to his coalition. By early October, Governor Wallace was still gaining and Vice-President Humphrey was not. Consequently, he moved against the Alabamian. In a speech to a blue-collar audience in Flint, Michigan, on October 8, Nixon addressed three questions to his listeners:

Do you just want to make a point or do you want to make a change? Do you want to get something off your chest, or do you want to get something done? Do you want to get a moment's satisfaction, or do you want to get four years of action?

He continued with direct attacks on Wallace and LeMay:

We cannot threaten to run a presidential car over our people and expect peace in our cities. We cannot put an irresponsible finger on the nuclear trigger and expect to avert the horror of a nuclear war.

The timing of this attack was related to an estimate that Wallace had probably peaked; Nixon's hope was that his move would help reverse this tide and that Wallace strength could be confined to the Deep South. This was what happened. In later October, Wallace faded while Humphrey began to gain rapidly in the large states.

In the face of the threat from the Vice-President, Nixon stepped up attacks on him. Earlier, when Hubert Humphrey had made a speech in Salt Lake City advocating a change in our Vietnamese policy, Nixon charged that what Humphrey brought to foreign policy was "the fastest, loosest tongue in American politics." Now Mr. Humphrey was said to be "the most expensive senator in American history." Further, the Vice-President was accused of taking a "lackadaisical, do-nothing approach to public order." By the end of the campaign (October 30), the race was so close that there was a real chance the election might be thrown into the House of Representatives. At this point, Nixon invited Humphrey to join him in a pledge to support the winner of the popular vote. "I do not fear the voice of the people," Nixon said. "Does Hubert Humphrey?"

THE WALLACE BID FOR NORTHERN SUPPORT

George Wallace's basic problem was that he lacked the support needed to be a viable national candidate. Although the ablest third-party candidate since 1924, he was supported primarily by a single group, southern Democrats. He needed to attract another group, northern blue-collar workers. The governor had to persuade those who were *talking* Wallace to *vote* Wallace, and to do this without losing his base of Dixiecrat support. Therefore Governor Wallace aimed his appeal at "the honest working man," those of average income and education who felt threatened by a rising crime rate, rapid changes in race relations, rising taxes, and a complex world beyond their control. The items Wallace attacked—bureaucrats, briefcases, guidelines—symbolized both federal power and a complex modern society.

Governor Wallace did not have any trouble as long as he stayed with the well-tried applause points in his speeches.

> Turn absolute control of the public schools back to the people of [whatever state he was speaking in].
>
> We're going to see the end of those bureaucrats in Washington who send us guidelines telling us when we can go to sleep at night and when we can get up in the morning.
>
> Militant revolutionary anarchism and communism are the cause of the breakdown of law and order.
>
> You'd better be thankful for the police and firemen, 'cause if it wasn't for them you couldn't walk the streets. The wife of a workingman can't go to the supermarket without the fear of being assaulted.

Wallace certainly did not hurt himself by defining his enemies as "militant revolutionary anarchists" and "Communists" and numbering "police," "firemen," "workingmen," and "wives" among his friends. Nor did he have much exceptionable in his more serious speeches. For example, he delivered an address on foreign policy to the National Press Club that could have been given by almost any American leader since World War II.

Governor Wallace did begin to run into real trouble in early October. He had probably reached his maximum strength by that time, and it was then that he finally selected a vice-presidential candidate, General Curtis LeMay. In the Pittsburgh press conference announcing this choice, the following exchange took place:

> *Question:* If you found it necessary to end the war, you would use nuclear weapons, wouldn't you? *LeMay:* If I found it necessary, I would use anything we could dream up—anything we could dream up—including nuclear weapons, if it was necessary.

Governor Wallace fairly sped to the microphone.

> All General LeMay has said—and I know you fellows better than he does because I've had to deal with you—he said that if the security of our country depended on the use of any weapon in the future he would use it. But he said he prefers not to use any sort of weapon. He prefers to negotiate. I believe that we must defend our country, but I've always said we can win and defend in Vietnam without the use of nuclear weapons. But General LeMay hasn't said anything about the use of nuclear weapons.

Of course, General LeMay had said enough about nuclear weapons to produce a good many headlines. The general was promptly sent to Vietnam on an inspection tour, but the damage had been done.

Wallace strength faded perceptibly after this point. The LeMay remark was by no means the only cause. As we have already seen,

Richard Nixon had attacked him. And labor unions, to whose ability to lead their own members the Wallace candidacy was a threat, had mounted a massive anti-Wallace, pro-Humphrey campaign. They gave wide circulation, for example, to a letter from an Alabama worker detailing unpleasant working conditions in the governor's home state. When national surveys showed that Wallace's support was falling, he attacked the polls as a conspiracy. All of this added up. By the day before the election, he was fighting to retain what had once been ceded to him by campaigning in front of the Georgia Statehouse in the company of Governor Lester Maddox.

THE TRUNCATED COALITION OF HUBERT HUMPHREY

Hubert Humphrey came away from the Chicago convention in serious trouble. He had selected a vice-presidential candidate who would bring strength to the ticket. But with Wallace playing Pied Piper to the southern Democrats, Humphrey had to make do with a truncated Democratic coalition of westerners, urbanites, labor, and blacks. Worse still, the trauma of the convention had created animosities among these groups. Not only was there a prolonged debate over the character of the Vietnam platform plank, but the specter of Chicago police in conflict with young demonstrators disturbed collegians and blacks who thought too much force was being used, *and* union members and urbanites who thought too little force was being used. Moreover, since the convention was not held until the end of August, there were only two months to put the pieces back together.

During September, Vice-President Humphrey worked very hard. He tried talking to the groups in his coalition, concentrating on the issues that would unify them: medicare, the creation of a Department of Housing and Urban Development, the Job Corps, education, Food for Peace, the Peace Corps, disarmament and arms control, and civil rights. But for whatever reason, nothing happened. By the end of September, it seemed that Humphrey's chances depended on some break of which he could take advantage: such as a decision by Hanoi that it would prefer to deal with Johnson rather than waiting for Nixon, a Johnson decision to stop bombing, or a Nixon decision to engage in debates or battle Humphrey on the issues. Instead, the Vice-President made his own break. On September 30, after having the vice-presidential seal removed from the rostrum, he made a speech suggesting the policy a Humphrey administration would follow in Vietnam:

> As President, I would stop the bombing of the North as an acceptable risk for peace because I believe it could lead to success in the negotiations . . . In weighing that risk . . . I would place key importance on evidence . . . of Communist willingness to restore the demilitarized zone between North

and South Vietnam . . . Secondly, I would take the risk that the South
Vietnamese would meet the obligations that they say they are now ready
to assume in their own self-defense . . .

In this speech, Hubert Humphrey departed from the policy then being
followed by the Johnson administration. This did not end all criticism; the Johnsonites were furious. But it did create an environment
that made it a little easier for the groups in the Democratic coalition
to work together.

Shortly thereafter, some state-by-state polls showed the Vice-President
to be in better shape than the national polls. Humphrey was beating
Nixon in Minnesota and Massachusetts, and held a slight edge in
Michigan, Missouri, New York, Connecticut, New Jersey, Pennsylvania, and Texas. To the Humphreyites, this suggested a geographical
emphasis to the campaign. Mr. Humphrey could win by carrying these
larger states by narrow margins even though Richard Nixon was likely
to carry smaller states by very large margins. The results of these surveys were quickly communicated to Democratic leaders who had been
hitherto inactive and to potential donors. The effort and cash flow
thus stimulated helped galvanize the truncated Democratic coalition.

The campaign strategy which had hitherto unified these groups,
especially urbanites, union members, and blacks important in the
large industrial states, was pressed into service once again. Hubert
Humphrey listed Democratic accomplishments: social security, medicare, eight years of prosperity. At one point he asked:

> Imagine what it'll be like if the unemployment rate is up to 7 percent.
> Who's to be unemployed? Which worker is to be laid off? Which family is
> to be without a check?

Memories of the depression of the thirties were further stirred by a
Democratic pamphlet that urged young people to ask their fathers
what things were like during the depression if they could not remember themselves. On civil rights, the Vice-President argued that he was
in the best position to assure racial harmony after the election as he
was the only candidate who was trusted by both whites and blacks.
But at the same time, he made it clear that he was not threatening the
jobs held by white workers.

> I know what the opposition puts out to the blue-collar white worker. He
> says, "Watch out for that Humphrey. He is going to get a black man a job,
> and that means your job." I said, now listen here. I am for jobs. I am for
> an expanded economy in this country. I am for decent jobs and I am for
> jobs and I don't care whether the worker is black, white, green, or purple;
> fat, thin, tall, or short. I am for jobs.

Nixon attacked Hubert Humphrey more sharply as the campaign grew close; Humphrey returned the favor. (In both cases, there was more to this than personal animosity. One way to hold disparate groups together is to remind them of their common dislike for the opposition leader.) Mr. Nixon was characterized as "Richard the Chicken-Hearted." "You want me to tell the truth about this fellow Nixon?" asked Humphrey. "It won't take much time because there isn't much truth." At the same time, campaign chairman Lawrence O'Brien, respected by Democratic groups because of his role in the successful campaigns of 1960 and 1964, was privately telling members of the Democratic coalition they could win, and publicly charging a Nixon–Wallace deal. As we know, all of this *almost* worked. The election was extremely close. It had taken at least a month after Chicago to create the conditions in which Democratic groups could work together. But since the truncated Democratic coalition was about the same size as the normal Republican coalition, and since Democratic leaders were able to use themes which were familiar to Democratic ears from many previous campaigns, the month of October was almost all the time they needed.

REMNANT POLITICS: THE DEMOCRATS IN 1972

George McGovern could have campaigned until November, 1973, and it would not have made any difference in the outcome of that contest. Consider what the McGovern nomination meant to the groups in the normal Democratic coalition. So far as the South was concerned, the situation was best summed up by the comment that McGovern could not carry the South with Robert E. Lee as his running mate and Bear Bryant as his campaign manager. As an authentic inheritor of William Jennings Bryan's moral righteousness, Senator McGovern might have had appeal to westerners. But with major battles seen to be coming in New Jersey, Pennsylvania, Ohio, Michigan, and Illinois, the West was scheduled for relatively little attention in the McGovern campaign. There was some labor support; a National Labor Committee for the Election of McGovern–Shriver was headed by Joseph D. Keenan of the Electrical Workers and Joseph A. Beirne of the Communication Workers. Still, workingmen were not enchanted by McGovern positions on the war and amnesty, nor by his seeming intent to raise welfare payments to a level above what they were earning through their own hard work. Considering this, and the highly advertised neutrality of George Meany, labor support for McGovern was about half of what a Democratic candidate could normally expect. As for the urban vote, the effect of the McGovern nomination was well assessed by Rev. Andrew Greeley of the National Opinion Research Center:

Everybody is noticing the ethnic these days. And it's too late for McGovern. The good Senator has a Catholic problem. The McGovern problem with the Catholic vote starts back in Miami Beach when ethnics, along with other parts of the old Democratic coalition, were clearly excluded, written off, and told we don't need you any more. That's why they are gone this year—that and the McGovern inclination to radicals and hippies and his peculiar behavior since the nomination. The ethnics are just turned off. And they aren't the only ones. You throw out Dick Daley and you throw out a lot of the country. They are gone for 1972. Oh, but they will be back.[3]

Vito Marzullo, Democratic leader in Chicago's Twenty-fifth Ward, put it more bluntly:

I been here since 1920. For all that time now I been seeing these do-gooder boobs come and go, and I'm still here. They come up overnight and think they're going to take over the machine . . . Me and my official family don't believe in the McGovern policies. Those kooks couldn't even be elected street cleaners in Chicago.[4]

Of all the major groups in the normal Democratic coalition, only the blacks were not disenchanted.

The coalition that had dominated American politics since the days of Franklin Roosevelt had been split asunder. And mind-boggling though it be, this was an intentional act. George McGovern had explained his plans to reporter Tom Wicker in 1969:

I've made up my mind. I'm going all the way. I'm going to run for President and the coalition I'm going to put together is going to be built around the poor and the minorities and the young people and the anti-war movement.[5]

Consequently, the McGovern coalition that could be assembled after Miami Beach was made up of young militants, blacks, some labor, and organizational loyalists who stood ready to support any Democratic candidate.

The McGovern plan had called for a "left-centrist" strategy: co-opt the left in order to win the nomination, and then reunite with the Democratic center in order to win the election. The latter part of this plan proved difficult to execute. It might have begun with the selection of a vice-presidential nominee and a national chairman who had good ties to non-McGovern groups in the normal Democratic coalition. In-

[3] Jack Waugh, "Most Catholic Voters Lean toward Nixon," *Christian Science Monitor*, October 12, 1972, p. 12.

[4] Jack Waugh, "A Disaffected Democrat," *Christian Science Monitor*, September 29, 1973, p. 1.

[5] Tom Wicker, "McGovern without Tears," New York *Times Magazine*, November 5, 1972, p. 36.

deed, an immediate postconvention headline read "Eagleton to Woo Labor and Daley." But any centrist strategy based on Senator Eagleton became moot after his departure from the ticket, and his resignation less than a week after George McGovern had said he was "1,000 percent for Tom Eagleton" did not help form a favorable image for the still not well-known South Dakotan. Incumbent National Chairman Lawrence O'Brien had good ties to many groups in the Democratic party, but it turned out that Senator McGovern had promised the national chairmanship to Jean Westwood and to Pierre Salinger as well. So Ms. Westwood became Democratic national chairman, Mr. O'Brien became "national campaign chairman," and Mr. Salinger went off to Paris to contact some North Vietnamese (only to be *again* disavowed by Senator McGovern when he returned). Senator McGovern then tried personal appeals himself in visits to the LBJ Ranch, to Mayor Daley in Chicago, and to Hilton Head, South Carolina, where southern governors were meeting on Labor Day weekend. All for naught. September opened with less chance of bringing other groups into the McGovern coalition than had been the case in July.

As active campaigning began, McGovern was still being urged to concentrate on recapturing lost Democratic votes. But the corruption of those in power was a theme that suited the senator's moral posture, and one that appealed to the nonestablishment groups in the McGovern coalition. As his jet flew from campaign event to campaign event, he was denouncing Watergate, denouncing the war in Vietnam, denouncing special interest groups, and, above all, denouncing Richard Nixon. In Cleveland, he said:

> We didn't have the security chief of our campaign indicted for burglary. We didn't have our campaign manager resigning under strange circumstances.

Speaking to a western conference on water and power on September 25, he declared:

> In growing numbers, the people of this country have become as fed up as I am with the war in Vietnam and the special-interest government here at home. . . . Under the administration of Richard Nixon, the banks, the conglomerate giants, the oil and utility corporations and their coal subsidiaries have received the tender loving care of our government. . . . You have to go back to the time of Warren G. Harding to find an administration so beholden and dominated by big business as the one we have today.

In Pittsburgh, he told a ghetto audience:

> Here in the Hill district, countless children are deprived of a decent chance in life almost before they can walk. But Richard Nixon has vetoed

aid to education, day care centers, and health care assistance. Do you want
four more years of that? . . . Why aren't there better schools here? Because your money has been used to blow up schools in Vietnam. Because
every bomb that is dropped and every bullet that is fired in Southeast
Asia has an echo that is heard in the Hill district. We have paid for the
devastation of another land with the devastation, not just of our conscience, but of our country.

The senator's moralizing continued to build as he campaigned, and
reached a crescendo at the end of September.[6]

With no visible progress, groups in the McGovern coalition were
becoming anxious. Campaign director Gary Hart described the mood
at that point: "[T]here was nothing tangible, nothing concrete, nothing to show movement and progress. At the headquarters, the staff
grasped at straws for encouragement . . . longing for some proof that
victory lay ahead." [7] Shortly after this another shift in strategy became
manifest. The negative tone that had been building during September
was muted. Emphasis was now to be placed on a series of major television addresses. The first of these came on October 10, the anniversary
of a 1968 Nixon statement that "those who have had a chance for four
years and could not produce peace should not be given another
chance." Senator McGovern presented his own "public plan," and
pointed out hopefully:

> This is what I would do to bring America home from a hated war, and it
> is a program that will work. The people of France were once trapped in
> a war in Vietnam—even as we are. But in 1954, they chose a new Presi-
> dent [sic], Pierre Mendes-France, whose highest commitment was to achieve
> peace in Indochina. His program was very similar to mine. And within
> just five weeks, the war was over. Within just three months, every last
> French prisoner had been returned.

This address, together with a policy statement on "The Imperatives of
Environmental Restoration" released the same week, represented the
most positive stance the senator took throughout the campaign.

Two more television addresses followed, but the October television
strategy had no more effect on the polls than the "media events" and
moralizing rhetoric of September. A twenty-point margin remained

[6] I should like to acknowledge the support of the National Science Foundation
for a content analysis of presidential texts that included the 1972 campaign
speeches (Grant GS-35084), and to thank Evelyn Small and Jerry Stacy for their
work on this. It is not possible to discuss this analysis in any detail, but the
analysis of what the 1972 candidates said rests on the efforts of Miss Small and
Mr. Stacy.
[7] Gary Warren Hart, *Right From the Start: A Chronicle of the McGovern Campaign* (New York: Quadrangle, 1973), pp. 299–300.

between Senator McGovern and President Nixon, and the experienced politicians in the McGovern camp knew that time was now too short for the senator to win. The result was a final change of strategy in the last week. Those who had been urging more negative television spots had their way, and the senator's own comments revealed more animosity than at any other time in the campaign. For example he ruled out any postelection effort at unity with Nixon because:

> He's conducted an evil administration. . . . The use of sabotage and espionage and wiretapping, I think those are evil and dangerous practices. I think the exploiting of racial fears is a evil practice. I think the aerial bombardment of Southeast Asia by Richard Nixon is the most evil thing ever done by any American President.

And in comments on the Saturday before the election, Senator McGovern seemed as upset with the voters he had failed to convince as he was with the President:

> It's all right for the people to be fooled once as they were in 1968. If they do it again, if they let this man lead them down the false hope of peace in 1972, then, the people have nobody to blame but themselves. So I make that warning just as clear and sharply as I can here this morning. Don't be fooled by an American President who time after time has put the survival of General Thieu ahead of peace, ahead of the release of our prisoners and ahead of the survival of our young men who are still tied down in this war. I'm going to give one more warning. If Mr. Nixon is elected on Tuesday, we may very well have four more years of war in Southeast Asia. Our prisoners will sit in their cells for another four years. Don't let this man trick you into believing that he stands for peace when he's a man who makes war.

For Senator McGovern, as for Senator Goldwater before him, the general election campaign had been a frustrating experience. Both had begun with the hope of raising fundamental questions about the course of public policy; both had shifted from one strategy to another in the hope of finding success; both had ended their campaigns in an almost completely negative posture.

NIXON TRIUMPHANT: THE REPUBLICANS IN 1972

If George McGovern was perplexed about the reaction of the electorate, Richard Nixon was not. He was confident of his plan for peace in Vietnam, and while final agreement was elusive, he could point out that 90 percent of American troops had been brought home, casualties had been cut by 98 percent, and America's ground combat role had been ended. His generally admired foreign policy included detente with Russia and China along with maintenance of a strong American defense posture. Domestically, President Nixon well understood that the Republicans were vulnerable as long as they remained the minority party, and many of his policies appealed to groups that had been part of the normal Democratic coalition. He had been photographed receiving a hard-hat in his office, and his April, 1972, declaration, "I am irrevocably committed to these propositions: America needs her nonpublic schools; that those nonpublic schools need help; that therefore we must and will find ways to provide that help," did not hurt his standing with Catholics. The McGovern nomination thus provided a real chance for Richard Nixon to continue his courtship of the South and to add urban and labor groups to the normal Republican coalition. The result was what Richard Nixon referred to as the "New Majority."

Southerners had been swelling the ranks of conservative Republicans for some years, and in 1972 the process was facilitated by a sizeable Democrats for Nixon organization. Texan John Connally was the head of this group, and a dinner at the Connally ranch was part of the September campaign. Earlier in the day, the President had stopped at a small Texas high school because, he told the diners, students from that high school had earned their way to Washington in the spring of 1971, and he had spoken to them in the Rose Garden.

> As I came back into the White House that day, one of the members of my staff said, "Isn't it a shame that those poor kids had to work all year in order to make that trip?" . . . and my answer was "Not at all." Because they told us something about the spirit of America. They didn't want something for nothing, and that is the kind of spirit we need in America if we are going to meet the challenges that America faces today.

This tale was quintessential Nixon. He was speaking to an elite audience whose leadership was necessary to create the sinews of organization, but the story praised an important population grouping, spoke positively about the country, and exalted the hard work which he thought important to his own success.

In shaping an appeal to labor, Republican leaders arranged that 1972 would be the first year for some time that a Republican platform did not carry a right-to-work plank which labor leaders found so distasteful. While some labor spokesmen were making their unhappiness with McGovern positions known, workers were also reading that George Meany and Richard Nixon had been golfing together. And of the hundreds of So-and-So for Nixon groups organized, one of the few for whom a White House reception was arranged was "Young Labor for Nixon." The President told them that he had been forced to make some difficult decisions while in office relating to American defense, and that he had always found his staunchest support came from the working men and women of America.

The President did not spend much time in campaigning during September and early October, and his choices of location and audience revealed his desire to add urban voters to the 1972 Nixon coalition. He turned up in Wilkes-Barre, Pennsylvania, to express sympathy to flood victims (and stopped his car to be photographed with a bride and groom), appeared at the Statue of Liberty to celebrate this sight seen by so many immigrants, came to an Italian picnic in suburban Maryland, and took a ride on San Francisco's new Bay Area Rapid Transit. Mr. Nixon spoke of many things, but part of his remarks to a Columbus Day dinner provide a good example of the themes of this bit of 1972 strategy:

> Italian immigrants came to this country by the hundreds of thousands, and then by the millions. They came not asking for something, asking only for the opportunity to work. They have worked and they have built . . . Those of Italian background bring with them a very deep religious faith. . . . The moments that have perhaps touched me most . . . have been those when . . . new citizens have . . . said, "I am so proud to be an American citizen."

Whereas Senator McGovern raised questions about the propriety of American actions, the Nixon strategy was to speak positively about groups of Americans and the country itself.

Mr. Nixon did not neglect the values that held the normal Republican coalition together, nor did he spend all of his time at rallies or other public gatherings. As in 1968, he delivered a series of radio addresses aimed at those who were sufficiently interested in issues to follow them on a low-salience communication medium. In an address on October 21, for example, he identified himself with a series of individualist values:

> The new American majority believes that each person should have more of the say in how he lives his own life . . . in taking better care of those who truly cannot care for themselves . . . in taking whatever action is needed to hold down the cost of living . . . and in a national defense second to none. . . . These are not the beliefs of a selfish people. On the contrary, they are the beliefs of a generous and self-reliant people, a people of intellect and character, whose values deserve respect in every segment of our population.

President Nixon did not begin full-time campaigning until shortly before the election itself. Crisscrossing the country by jet, he ended with a giant rally at Ontario, California. The President reviewed the themes of the campaign: peace that will last . . . the trip to Peking

and the trip to Moscow . . . negotiations to limit arms . . . full
prosperity without war . . . fighting the rise in crime . . . an equal
chance for every American. And then:

> Tonight, as I speak to you in Ontario, I think you should know that this
> . . . is the last time I will speak to a rally as a candidate in my whole life,
> and I want to say to all of you here who worked on this, and to all of you
> who took the time to come, thank you very much for making it probably
> the best rally we have ever had.

A Few Conclusions

COALITION CONSTRAINTS

There have been a number of generalizations about campaign strategy implicit in this recapitulation of particular campaigns. As noted
at the outset of the chapter, coalition dynamics lead a candidate to
appeal to voters in a manner acceptable to the groups already supporting him. Thus we saw Barry Goldwater promising to reduce government expenditures, Lyndon Johnson defending southern support
by stressing Democratic loyalties and economic progress, Richard
Nixon picking a 1968 vice-presidential candidate who was not unacceptable to either moderates or conservatives, George Wallace seeking blue-collar support outside the South, Hubert Humphrey relying
on traditional New Deal–Fair Deal appeals, George McGovern denouncing corruption, and Richard Nixon celebrating the importance
of hard work in the American Way of Life.

But even more important—at least a stronger test of this interpretation of campaign strategy—is what has *not* happened. There were
many other strategies that could have been employed. Barry Goldwater
and George McGovern could have moderated their springtime appeals, and made real efforts to follow paths trod by more traditional
leaders of their parties, but this would have cost Goldwater support of
conservative ideologues and would have disappointed the young militants supporting McGovern. Senator Goldwater could have, in fact,
pursued a vigorous southern strategy, and Senator McGovern could
have become more shrill in his denunciations of corruption. Either
strategy would have made it difficult to retain the support of their
organizational loyalists. President Johnson or President Nixon could
have attacked the opposition party quite openly by telling voters: "For
years, we've been telling you that the Republicans/Democrats were
hidebound reactionaries/wild radicals, and you wouldn't believe us.
Now you have proof! They've nominated Barry Goldwater/George
McGovern!" Such an appeal might well have had a long-term payoff
by causing members of the opposition party to think about the ap-

propriateness of their loyalty, but in 1964, this would have hampered Lyndon Johnson's appeal to moderate Republicans, and in 1972, it would have slowed Richard Nixon's program to get urban Democrats to cast Republican votes. In 1968, Richard Nixon could have told the electorate that better relations with China were needed, and Hubert Humphrey could have admitted that the glut of social legislation passed by the Eighty-ninth Congress meant that there were few resources available for new social programs. Neutral observers were making both points. But many conservatives were dismayed when Richard Nixon went to Peking, and frank talk about the fiscal consequences of Great Society programs was not what the urban/labor/black wing of the Democratic party wanted to hear. Many more examples of plausible strategies that would have been consistent with some campaign goal or a fair reading of the evolution of public policy could be inferred. But the central point is that none of these strategies were used. They were avoided, I would suggest, simply because they would have given offense to some group in the candidate's coalition, and were therefore unavailable.

DISTINCTIONS

The selection of a campaign strategy, however, cannot be explained simply on the basis of avoiding appeals that would give offense to members of your own coalition. There is an election to be won, and voters must be reached. To do this, one must bear some important distinctions in mind. The first distinguishes *the activist* from *the nonactivist*. The activist, who almost by definition has a high interest in politics, will likely have been following the nomination contest for some time. He knows what issues separate the contenders, and how he feels about them. Furthermore, he will have a fairly well-developed set of attitudes concerning the opposition candidate. Given all this, the activist is likely to have made at least a tentative voting decision by convention time. The nonactivist, on the other hand, may know that nominees are being chosen primarily because some of his favorite television programs have been pre-empted for reports on the primary campaigns or for the convention itself. And the policy preferences of the nonactivists may be quite different. Any number of studies have shown that Republican activists are likely to be more conservative than many other Republican voters, and the McGovern nomination, at least, was more acceptable to Democratic activists than to nonactivists. So, ways may have to be found to appeal to nonactivists who want the party to move in a different direction. Even if the policy preferences of the activists and nonactivists correspond, there is still a difference in the sophistication of appeals directed to activists and nonactivists.

The activists must be appealed to, but not in such a way as to alienate the passive, unattentive mass of voters attuned to simplistic appeals—and vice versa.

A second distinction is that between *partisans* and *independents*. This is akin to the party identification scale, a five-magnitude version of which would read: strong partisan, weak partisan, independent, weak opponent, strong opponent. From the viewpoint of the strategists, independents and opponents are treated the same way for different reasons. The independent is uninterested in partisan appeals, and unlikely to be attracted by them. The opponent would resent partisan appeals, and would be likely to return to his own partisan camp if the fact of his leaving his normal partisan home became more salient than policy or candidate-oriented reasons for doing so. These are strong reasons for avoiding a partisan appeal. But if a candidate does so, he may have difficulty with his own partisans who *want* to hear an appeal on these grounds. If the candidate is a member of the majority party, strategists may feel there is more payoff to a partisan appeal than avoiding one. And if he is a member of a minority party, advisors may feel that a favorable year is the time to hold the party's banner high in the hope of increasing their ranks. In either case this is another dilemma facing the strategists.

In the real world of politics, the most fundamental distinction is *us vs. them,* the groups belonging to the coalition vs. everybody else. This distinction does not coincide with the two previous distinctions. Those referred to differences within the electorate to whom the appeals were being directed. The "us" in this case refers to the relatively small groups of partisan activists who have supported the aspirant through his struggle for the nomination, and, usually with a slight augmentation from other party loyalists, constitute his firmest support in the general election campaign. This coalition distinguishes itself not only from the coalition supporting the opposing candidate, but also from other groups within the same party. When coalition members speak in public about fellow partisans who supported other aspirants in the spring, they say, "Of course, we expect all loyal Republicans/Democrats to support the senator." In private, they may express more reservations. Fellow partisans who are not close to the candidate say, "You bet we're working for him! You know who they're going to blame if he doesn't win." With this as a motivation, the extra effort they would put forth for *their* preferred candidate may not be forthcoming. In short, in-group/out-group distinctions are to be found in political campaigns as in all other areas of life.

The reason this distinction is the most fundamental is that it affects the candidate most directly. Whatever the exact nature of the core group with whom the candidate holds his strategy discussions, it is likely to include some leaders of each group in the coalition. Their interpretation of the political situation is the last to reach the candidate before he makes up his mind, and the interpretation presented to the candidate depends on the information each person has received from his own trusted informants. Further, these relationships of trust and confidence have been developed during the preceding months as the members of the core group demonstrated the competence that led the candidate to come to rely on their judgment. Consequently, the candidate is led to adopt a strategy satisfactory to all groups in the coalition for two reasons. First, he wants to retain the loyalty of the inner group and, by extension, the groups they represent. Second, the coalition itself constitutes a communication network that may or may not tell the candidate what the real political situation is, but certainly does lead him to adopt strategies acceptable to coalition members.

CAMPAIGN A TEST FOR OFFICE

What does all of this mean to the candidate? It means he is not a free agent who can choose among strategies at will. It further implies that he is subject to a good many tensions. The course of action that is acceptable to one group in his coalition is opposed by another. The detailed discussion of policy nuances appreciated by the activist will bore the nonactivist, and the simplistic appeal that attracts the apathetic voter may seem unworthy to the attentive elite. The ringing call for partisan support will not produce independent votes, and the less passionate analysis directed to independents may lose the faithful worker who began ringing doorbells in February. The interplay of all these tensions lends dynamism to the campaign, and presents a different challenge to the candidate. He must make his way carefully lest he forfeit vital support, yet at the same time convey those qualities of confidence that win the trust of the people. This is a somewhat different kind of task than those to be confronted in the Oval Office. If elected, mastering the intricacies of international involvement and economic management will take the place of seeking votes. But a President also has to make difficult choices in the face of conflicting evidence. In both settings, leadership requires one to seek some complex goals while maintaining the support of one's coalition. The ability to do this in an electoral setting is no guarantee that the candidate will become an able chief executive, but there are enough similarities for the campaign to serve as one important test.

Fred I. Greenstein

5

What the President Means to Americans:

Presidential "Choice" Between Elections

In matters as sensitive as guarding the integrity of our democratic process, it is essential not only that rigorous legal and ethical standards be
observed but also that the public—you—have total confidence that they
are both being observed and enforced by those in authority, and particularly by the President of the United States. . . . This office is a sacred
trust, and I am determined to be worthy of that trust! . . . We must
maintain the integrity of the White House. . . . There can be no white-
wash at the White House.

> —*Transcript of President Nixon's broadcast address
> to the nation on the Watergate Affair, New York*
> Times, *Wednesday, May 2, 1973 ("Address to the
> Nation," April 30, 1973).*

The President of the United States is a man or a woman or whatever
who is, like, picked by the people to head the country. And they try and
make the person almost perfect. I mean, if he does anything wrong, they
down him . . . because if a person is going to be the head of a country
like the United States for four years, he just has to be just about perfect.

> —*Twelve-year-old American boy interviewed in 1970.*

Leadership as a Relationship

Political leadership is a relationship, not a thing—a relationship
between the leader and the led. The leader's role, like any other, is

---

FRED I. GREENSTEIN *is Henry R. Luce professor of politics, law and society at
Princeton University. He is author of numerous books and articles, including*
The American Party System and the American People, Children and Politics,
Personality and Politics, *and* A Source Book for the Study of Personality and
Politics *(with Michael Lerner).*

made up of the internal elements of the role incumbent's psychological orientations and external elements. The former consist of the leader's own sense of what the job demands of him and what he hopes to make of it. The latter are the expectations of members of the leader's society, and, more generally, their orientations toward leaders and leadership—for example, their assumptions about whether leaders are worthy of respect and about the proper scope of their activities.

During periods of politics-and-government-as-usual, what a political leader such as the President of the United States can or cannot do is largely a function of the expectations of the minority of citizens who are politically active—especially a political leader's most conspicuous counterparts in the leadership stratum. The President is particularly hedged by the expectations of those individuals Richard Neustadt has described as the "Washington Community," which includes other leaders from whom the President must receive respect and cooperation in order to carry out his job effectively—key congressmen, bureaucrats, journalists, columnists, certain interest group representatives, and even certain foreign leaders. But attitudes toward the President held by those Americans who are only intermittently involved in political activities also influence what is and what is not permissible for him to do. Indeed, as Neustadt stresses in his classical attempt to characterize the bases of presidential power, the capacity of the President of the United States to elicit cooperation from his "significant others" in the leadership stratum is to a considerable extent a result of *their* perceptions of *his* standing with the "general public" and with various specialized publics.[1]

The impact of electoral psychology on how the United States empowers its Presidents by means of presidential elections is discussed by Richard Boyd in chapter 7, but presidential choice or "empowering" is also an interelection process resulting from continuities and changes in what the President means to—and how he stands with—the citizens. In other words, underlying the quadrennial debate about issues, candidates, and party performance is a continuing sequence of public response to the President, and to a lesser extent, to the "eligible" alternative presidential contenders described in Donald Matthew's chapter 2. The interelection responses of citizens to the President are in part a function of their responses to issues, events, and the instrumental aspects of how the President handles the tasks of leadership. But in responding to the President, citizens also seem to be seeking to satisfy expressive needs of which they are only vaguely aware—for

1 Richard E. Neustadt, *Presidential Power: The Politics of Leadership* (New York: Wiley, 1960).

example, needs for confidence, security, and pride in citizenship. Meeting these needs is an important, imperfectly understood part of presidential "success." Presidents and presidential contenders who do not fulfill them are likely to be rejected.

The Puzzling Nature of Public Response to the President

In characterizing the meaning of the President to Americans, I shall summarize and bring up to date an assessment I attempted a year after Presidents Kennedy's assassination and six months after Johnson's hyperbolic 1964 election victory.[2] At the time of my original analysis, public respect for the President and the Presidency were extraordinarily high, partly because of the immediate posthumous idealization of Kennedy and his leadership. There was little if any sign that the Johnson administration would terminate at such a nadir of public esteem, and no reason to believe that it would be followed by one in which confidence in the President would almost completely collapse.

My 1965 assessment had taken special note of the great outpouring of intense public feeling in reaction to the death of President Kennedy. This public outburst had a paradoxical aspect. On the one hand, there was and still is evidence of pervasive indifference and inattention by a large portion of the citizenry to the stage on which the President is the principal actor—national political affairs. For example, only a third of the electorate claims to be very interested in presidential campaigns; only a tenth has ever contributed financially to a candidate; and less than a tenth has ever written a letter to the editor. Yet the public grief at the death of an individual from this remote and "uninteresting" environment was both very great and fully genuine.

Perhaps the most detailed of the many empirical documentations of this reaction was the National Opinion Research Center survey conducted immediately after Kennedy's death. It found not only widespread remorse but also reports by many individuals of psychosomatic symptoms that persisted for a number of days after the assassination. These signs of psychophysical stress were even more striking when compared with the finding from an earlier study using the same questions about symptomatology conducted during the Cuban missile crisis: at that seemingly more perilous time Americans had shown no de-

2 Fred I. Greenstein, "Popular Images of the President," paper delivered at the meeting of the American Psychiatric Association, May, 1965; published in *The American Journal of Psychiatry*, 122:5 (November, 1965), pp. 523–529. A slightly updated version appears in Aaron Wildavsky, ed., *The Presidency* (Boston: Little, Brown, 1969).

parture from normal levels in physical indicators of psychic distress (headaches, dizziness, etc.).[3]

The reactions to Kennedy's death were apparently *not* merely to the horror of an assassination or to the youth and attractiveness of the President. Historical accounts make it clear that at least since the death of Lincoln, every presidential death in office—those of Roosevelt, McKinley, Garfield, and even Harding—have produced similar public responses. Something in presidential incumbency itself evidently has been responsible for these reactions since the deaths of other public figures, including *ex*-Presidents, were by no means as emotionally moving to such large numbers of citizens.

Using this apparent paradox as my point of departure, I distilled eight specific empirical observations from the scattered literatures providing data on public orientations to the President, and drew from these a more general set of conclusions about the apparent psychological functions of the Presidency to Americans.

Empirical Propositions About Public and President

How have the post-1965 upheavals in American politics—for example, the draft, Vietnam escalation, widespread urban and campus unrest, the rise of a "counterculture," Watergate, and the resignation of a Vice-President after charges of corruption—affected the meaning of the President and the Presidency to the American people? In the following sections I reexamine the propositions I advanced in 1965 and the conclusions I drew from them, indicating those that appear more or less unchanged by subsequent events and reformulating those that have been substantially altered.

1. *The President is by far the best-known figure on the American political scene* (conclusion unchanged).

On the basis of the only poll data then available on the awareness of national figures, I concluded that "the President is . . . the best-known American political leader. For some people he is the *only* known American political leader, and for others one of the few." To reach this conclusion I relied on a 1945 poll and a scattering of other information, because most pollsters of the 1950s and 1960s had given up asking questions about levels of public political information or the lack of it. More recent data presented in table 1, the results of a national program assessing the educational achievement of children and young adults, provides firm evidence in support of this conclusion.

For the moment, we may note only the portion of the findings which

---

[3] This and other assertions summarized from my earlier discussion are made at greater length in the source cited in the previous note.

TABLE 1. AWARENESS OF POLITICAL LEADERS ON THE PART OF ADULTS AND CHILDREN

	Percent Correct by Age		
	Adult	*17*	*13*
President (Nixon)	98	98	94
Vice President (Agnew)	87	79	60
Secretary of State (Rogers)	16	9	2
Secretary of Defense (Laird)	25	16	6
Speaker of House (McCormack)	32	25	2
Senate Majority Leader (Mansfield)	23	14	4
At least one Senator from Own State	57	44	16
Both Senators from Own State	31	18	6
Congressman from Own District	39	35	11

Source of Data: 1969–70 survey of civic education based on a national sample of 28,000 persons at ages 13 and 17 and 10,000 young adults. The respondents were asked to write the last names of the "persons now holding these offices in the United States" and were not penalized for spelling errors. National Assessment of Educational Progress, *Report 2: Citizenship: National Results—Partial* (Denver and Ann Arbor, July 1970), p. 37.

show that 98 percent of the young adult population was able to name the incumbent President. The majority of young adults were also able to name Vice-President Agnew then at the peak of controversially verbose, public visibility. (In a 1945 survey, only 34 percent of a national sample could identify Henry Wallace, who had been Vice-President only a year earlier.) After the President and the Vice-President, adult recognition of public figures declines very sharply to 57 percent for recognition of at least one senator from the respondent's state, 39 percent for recognition of his congressman, and a third or less for congressional leaders and cabinet members.

2. *The* role *of the President is accorded variable but generally substantial respect in American society* (conclusion changed).

Here my reference is to the Presid*ency* as a job—that unique combination of symbolic head-of-state duties and effective political leadership that inspired its classic description as an "elective monarchy." Obviously reactions to the individual presidential incumbent affect reactions to the presidential role, but both citizens and political analysts seem able to make some distinction between the role and the individual. My 1965 conclusion was that the Presidency was accorded "great respect." I noted that although "Americans tend generally to deprecate and distrust individuals who carry the label 'politician,'" when they are asked to "rank occupations in terms of their importance and respectability, certain high political roles such as Senator or Supreme Court Justice regularly appear at the top of the rankings." At the time, no occupational prestige study had actually included the Presidency, and therefore my statement about respect for the President was an inference from the available data on high political roles in general. The following year, however, the University of Michigan Survey Research Center's midterm election study included a direct question that referred to the role of President of the United States: "We're interested in learning what kinds of work Americans respect highly. Which of these occupations do you respect most?" Respondents were handed a card that included such terms as "famous doctor," "president of a large corporation like General Motors," "bishop or other church official," and various state and national political roles including governor, Supreme Court justice, senator, and (tucked away in the middle of the list) "President of the United States." Analysis of these unpublished Michigan findings shows that the presidential job was the hands-down winner, receiving 52 percent of the first-choice references; the runner-up roles, cleric and physician, garnered slightly more than 10 percent and no other role more than 3 percent.

Unfortunately, this question was not asked during the time of President Johnson's troubles. A somewhat different question *was* asked of a national sample during the "low-profile" first year of Mr. Nixon's first term. The context was a series of questions about leaders and institutions worded in such a way as partly to elicit response to the officials themselves and partly to their roles. The question was: "The President can be trusted to do what is good for the people (Agree/Disagree/Don't Know/Not Sure)," and 75 percent of the respondents opted for "agree" with only 11 percent disagreeing. Between 8 and 15 percent more chose "agree" for the President than for governors, senators, local judges, or Supreme Court justices. Furthermore, when respondents were asked to list specific acts of the President, governor, and Supreme Court they approved or disapproved of, the ratio of positive to negative was more than two-to-one for the President, but there were more negative than positive references for the governor and the Supreme Court.[4]

Unfortunately, no national survey appears to have been conducted during the post-Watergate Presidency on attitudes toward the Presidency as an institution. Just as the implications of Watergate began to unfold and shortly after the speech by President Nixon quoted as an epigraph to this chapter, the Gallup organization did conduct interviews on confidence in various national political institutions, but

[4] Robert G. Lehnen, "Public Views of State Governors," in Thad Beyle and J. Oliver Williams, eds., *The American Governor in Behavioral Perspective* (New York: Harper & Row, 1972), pp. 258–269.

they did not include the Presidency on their list. During the same month, however, a statewide California survey asked about confidence in the "President of the United States," using an item worded so as to focus attention more on the institution than on the individual. The phrase "President of the United States" was listed with a series of institutions (rather than individuals) and prefaced by the following introductory question:

> Now I would like to find out how you feel about some of our governmental, business and social institutions. . . . For each group listed on this card, I'd like you to tell me how much confidence you, personally, have in it.

As table 2 makes clear, in this post-Watergate California rating, the Presidency ranked third among the three branches of government, al-

TABLE 2. CALIFORNIANS' EVALUATIONS OF AMERICAN NATIONAL GOVERN-
MENTAL INSTITUTIONS DURING POST-WATERGATE REVELATIONS PERIOD

	Total Ex-pressing Confidence	Level of Confidence			
		A Lot of Confidence	Some Confidence	Not Much Confidence	No Opinion
The President of the United States	68%	34%	34%	31%	1%
Congress	83	30	53	15	2
The Supreme Court	76	31	45	21	3

Source of Data: The California Poll, May 7–17, 1973, Field Research Corporation (state adult sample of 541), as reported in *Current Opinion: A Monthly Digest of The Public's Views on Contemporary Issues,* 1:8 (August, 1973), p. 79.

though only a minority of the respondents placed it in the lowest evaluative category. (The California interviews were conducted between May 7 and May 17, 1973.) It should be noted that the lower rating of the Presidency resulted mainly from a larger number of "not much confidence" responses and a lesser number of "some confidence" responses than the other two branches of American national government. The President was slightly *more* likely to be mentioned in the "lot of confidence" category. Thus early in the period of the Watergate controversy and at a time when Mr. Nixon's personal popularity had already been deflated sharply, the Presidency itself had not been completely repudiated, even if it had declined in esteem from earlier periods. From the standpoint of political attitudes, Californians appear to be reasonably typical of the nation, and contrary to popular mythology, not distinctively conservative.[5]

So visible and prestigious has the American Presidency been from time to time that surveys in other countries as well as in the United States point to the popular esteem of the President. In November 1972 British Gallup asked, "What man that you have heard of or read about living in any part of the world today do you admire most?" President Nixon tied Prince Philip for first place (9 percent: responses are invariably scattered to this open-ended Gallup item), and was slightly although not significantly ahead of the only two English elected poli-

[5] Raymond C. Wolfinger and Fred I. Greenstein, "The Repeal of Fair Housing in California: An Analysis of Referendum Voting," *American Political Science Review,* 62 (September, 1968), 753–769.

The following fragments of other survey data are relevant to assessing trends in citizen views of the presidential role:

1. Fall, 1964, and June, 1972, national Gallup surveys asking citizens how much "trust and confidence" they had in "the executive branch, headed by the President," and the judicial and legislative branches showed predominantly positive evaluations of all three branches and somewhat more favorable evaluations of the executive than the two other branches. (Lloyd A. Free and Hadley Cantril, *The Political Beliefs of Americans,* New Brunswick, New Jersey: Rutgers University Press, 1967, p. 193; and William Watts and Lloyd A. Free, *State of the Nation,* New York: Universe Books, 1973, p. 323.)

2. A September, 1973, Louis Harris and Associates survey, which asked about confidence in the "executive branch of the federal government" but unfortunately did not use the cue "President," showed a slight decline in confidence in the executive and an increase in confidence in Congress over pre-Watergate Harris pollings (percent expressing "a great deal of confidence"):

	1966	*1972*	*September 1973*
Executive Branch	41%	27%	19%
Congress	42	21	30
Supreme Court	51	28	33

(Subcommittee on Intergovernmental Relations of the Committee on Government Operations, United States Senate, *Confidence and Concern: Citizens View Their Government: A Survey of Public Attitudes,* Part I, Washington, D.C.: U.S. Government Printing Office, 1973, p. 33.)

3. It should be noted that when citizens (apart from very young children) are asked who "should" or who "does" make governmental policy in the United States and are given fixed-choice response alternatives among the governmental branches, they refer to Congress. My own view is that these are conventional civics-book responses, and that in fact citizens of all ages take their main political cues from the President and are ordinarily barely aware of congressmen and congressional activity. Compare the data on verbal responses to Congress vs. the President in Donald J. Devin, *The Political Culture of the United States* (Boston: Little, Brown, 1973), pp. 155–63, with the pattern of findings summarized in Fred I. Greenstein, *Children and Politics* (New Haven: Yale University Press, 1965), pp. 61–63.

ticians—the Prime Minister and Mr. Enoch Powell—who were mentioned by more than 3 percent of the respondents.[6] Similar results would certainly not have emerged during Mr. Nixon's period of precipitously declining domestic popularity a few months later, but these findings hint at the psychological functions the American President can perform even for citizens of other nations.

3. *The President is ordinarily the first public official to come to the attention of young children* (conclusion unchanged).

At the time of my summary, more was known about young children's images of the President than about adults' conceptions of him. Children's images of leaders are of interest because some of the more elusive adult needs to be reassured and made to feel secure by leaders seem to arise from the process of psychic development in childhood. Furthermore, much of the mystique of the American President as a national hero has been transmitted over the years through messages directed to children about the virtues of various Presidents. By the age of nine and probably earlier, virtually every American child has some awareness of the Presidency and can name the incumbent President. Very young children, like the least informed members of the adult population, typically have no sense of any other roles or institutions in the political system (apart from the police). Most of them have not heard of Congress, for example.

Looking back at table 1, we see that even by the end of the elementary school years (age thirteen), the almost universal pre-adult ability to name the President and reasonably widespread ability to name the then highly publicized Vice-President (60 percent) is accompanied by virtually *no* awareness of other fixtures of national politics.

As I have already mentioned for adults, cognizance of the American President also reaches beyond national boundaries at the pre-adult level. Surveys of children in Australia and Canada have shown greater awareness of the name of the President of the United States than of the name of the prime ministers of their own countries.[7]

4. *Even before children are substantively informed about the President's functions, they believe (a) that he is exceptionally important, and (b) that he is benign* (conclusion unchanged but with important qualification).

In 1965 support for the first assertion was that when children as

[6] London *Daily Telegraph*, November 27, 1972.

[7] R. W. Connell, *The Child's Construction of Politics* (Melbourne: Melbourne University Press, 1971), p. 125; and Jon H. Pammett, "The Development of Political Orientations in Canadian School Children," *Canadian Journal of Political Science*, 4 (March, 1971), pp. 132–141.

young as nine were asked to rank occupations in terms of importance, the President was regularly placed at the top of their rankings, ahead of such roles as physician, school teacher, and clergyman. For the second assertion that the President is viewed as benign, two kinds of evidence were adduced. The first was children's answers to fixed-choice questionnaires in which they were asked to check whether the President was doing a good job, whether the President was more important or more kindly than other people, and so forth. In general, children's responses to these items appeared to be highly, sometimes extravagantly, positive, with the more extreme and unrealistic assertions diminishing during the course of pre-adolescence. Furthermore, children were far less likely than adults to use negative alternatives in response to questionnaire items calling for evaluation of the President. The second piece of evidence—data on images of the President that relied on the children's own spontaneous response categories—was important because of the danger that children's responses to a check-list questionnaire may be unthinking or may reflect a desire to check the "right" answer. My 1960 article entitled "The Benevolent Leader" drew on the fortuitous finding that, when I asked children to write descriptions of the President's job, I elicited many positively-toned assertions about the kindly, helpful qualities of the President.[8] These statements had the aura of authentically held perceptions and did not seem to be mere attempts to say the "right" thing.

These highly positive pre-adult views of the President seemed to result from a combination of adult tendencies to cushion children from the more negative aspects of adult perceptions of the political world, and from pre-adult tendencies to perceive selectively the kindly, supportive aspects of a central figure in the wider environment. One common speculative interpretation of these early findings was that the citizen who as a child had learned to idealize the President might as an adult be disposed to back up and rely upon the President in the ways I shall note below. Even though the adult had more balanced, less idealized views of the President than the child, there might remain as a legacy of juvenile learning, basic assumptions about presidential benevolence and a respect for the Presidency that could redound to the President's advantage, for example, under circumstances of presidential conflict with other political actors.

Interesting and important subsequent questions have been raised about the applicability of the "benevolent leader" literature to the

---

8 Fred I. Greenstein, "The Benevolent Leader: Children's Images of Political Authority," *American Political Science Review*, 54 (December, 1960), pp. 934–943.

roiled political circumstances of the United States after the mid-1960s. One data report of the mid-1960s was instructively titled "The Malevolent Leader." [9] This study of children from an impoverished Appalachian subculture, in which deep negativism toward political authority and outsiders in general had long been endemic, helped to draw attention to the failure of earlier studies to focus on subcultural differences in political socialization, including the political socialization of the nation's most persistently deprived and sizable minority group—blacks. The first studies of black children's political orientations did *not* show distinctly negative views toward public officials and the political process, but as black militancy increased during the 1960s, evidence grew that black children were no longer acquiring the benevolent leader political orientations of the Eisenhower–Kennedy years.[10]

More generally, as the 1960s unfolded into a period of ghetto rebellions, antiwar protests, and college and to a lesser extent high school student activism, it seemed impossible to believe that children would exhibit positive images of the President. The early reports themselves seemed suspect to some commentators who wondered how it could be the case that late-1950s, early-1960s children had had positive orientations to their nation's leaders, when many of these same children were later active as protestors against "the system," or at least against particular policies. (I shall suggest a reason for this seeming paradox in the concluding paragraphs of this chapter.)

In 1969 and 1970 I collaborated in a cross-national political socialization study of British, French, and American children, which included detailed tape-recorded interviews with a small but varied sample of children from a number of localities in the eastern United States. By asking these children to describe their national leaders and to imagine the outcomes of incomplete stories such as one in which the President is driving his car above the speed limit and is stopped by a traffic policeman, we sought to establish their abstract conception of the nation's leaders and their perception of how the leaders would act in concrete situations. I was surprised at the exceptionally *positive* tone of the 1969–70 responses of the one-hundred-odd American children with whom the interviewers had conversations. Both in their general descriptions of the President and in their story completions, the

9 Dean Jaros, Herbert Hirsch, Frederic J. Fleron, Jr., "The Malevolent Leader: Political Socialization in an American Subculture," *American Political Science Review*, 62 (June, 1968), pp. 564–575.

10 Paul R. Abramson, "Political Efficacy and Political Trust Among Black School Children: Two Explanations," *Journal of Politics*, 34 (November, 1972), pp. 1243–1264.

respondents frequently volunteered statements about the favorable characteristics of the President—statements that were not merely conventional and that clearly were not planted in their minds by the interviewers.

We found important racial differences within our small sample, however. The American white children were consistently more likely to interject a positive evaluation of the President in response to the question asking for a description of his duties than were the British and French children, when asked about their nations' heads. In contrast, the black respondents (who were interviewed by a black) were the least positive and most negative of any of the four groups, although even the black children had more favorable than unfavorable statements to make about the President in their description of his role. For all groups the story-completion items asking for a reaction to the President as a speed-law violator showed a more balanced mixture of negative and positive evaluations.

Here are some examples of children's positively toned, general descriptions of the President recorded early in Nixon's first term.

> Well, he's the person that helps guide the people. He doesn't, like, rule but he helps people. Well, he makes decisions for what he thinks is best for the country. . . . And [he tries] to keep peace among, like, so there won't be any fighting and stuff around.
>
> —(*White American girl, twelve years old.*)

> He answers the questions and he tries to make America a better place to live in ways, like, he tries his best to keep the war in Vietnam calm . . . he's trying to calm it and he's . . . and he's making sure that everybody he's sending, he doesn't always care about his country himself, too. Like, he, he is already conducted a Biafra fund . . . in New York.
>
> —(*White American boy, eleven years old.*)

> Well, you're talking about the President of the United States? My opinion of him? Well, Nixon, I guess he's all right. Yes, he's all right. I mean, he gives everybody a fair chance to do things. You wouldn't exactly say he's prejudiced 'cause he isn't. . . . His job is to keep mainly law and order in all the states and mostly supply the people what they really need and help everybody; I mean every possible way he can.
>
> —(*Black American girl, thirteen years old.*)

In response to the traffic violation story-completion episode, a variety of outcomes such as the following were adjudged to evince positive images of the President:

> Well, and then the policeman sees he's the President. He wants to forget about it, but the President doesn't want him to forget about it because he knows that he was doing wrong, and it's the policeman's job to stop people that are doing wrong.

As noted, however, this hypothetical episode also evoked negative imagery as in the following example of a brusque, peremptory, imagined response of the President to the traffic policeman:

> [The President says] "I'm the President of the United States. I was in a hurry and I wanted to get to the meeting fast. I know I went through . . . disobeyed the speed limit . . . and don't give me a ticket." [11]

The black children were much less likely than the white children to perceive democratic norms and values in connection with the interchange between the President and the policeman. Furthermore, a number of the black children did not even need the stimulus of a hypothetical presidential law infraction to exhibit attitudes more in tune with the end than the beginning of the 1960s. This is evident in the following exchange in which an interviewer asked a thirteen-year-old black boy how he would describe the President of the United States to a foreign child:

> *Interviewer:* Suppose a foreign child asks you, 'What is the President of the United States?'
> *Respondent:* A rat.
> *Interviewer:* Okay, try to give the foreign child an idea of what he does. What does he do?
> *Respondent:* I can name a lot of things. . . . He prejudiced. . . . He lousy. He pick the . . . Spiro Agnew. Spiro Agnew stinks, and he ain't no good, none of them.
> *Interviewer:* What is the President's job?
> *Respondent:* To try to make people happy, but he's making them miserable.

In the early part of June, 1973, during the first phase of the televised Watergate hearings, we returned to some of the Connecticut schools in our sample and conducted tape-recorded interviews asking the same questions about the President with a sample of approximately 50 white children roughly comparable to our 1969–70, President-idealizing white comparison group. Although the interviewers made a point not to introduce references to Watergate in any of the questions, about half of the children spontaneously referred in some way to Watergate, but often to express puzzlement rather than criticism of the President. For example:

11 Compare Tolley's study of children's reactions to presidential leadership in the Vietnam conflict, in which children show willingness not to support the President in specific contingencies where his behavior is perceived as wrong. Howard Tolley, Jr., *Children and War: Political Socialization to International Conflict* (New York: Teachers College Press, 1973), pp. 35, 129–131.

Interviewer: OK. What does [Mr. Nixon] do?

Respondent: He, uh, he's the President. He signs papers and, like, helps turn out the laws, and stuff like that.

Interviewer: Anything else?

Respondent: Well . . . he gets in trouble a lot.

Interviewer: What kind of trouble?

Respondent: I don't know. The Watergate and everything like that now.
                                        —(*Twelve-year-old white boy.*)

At the time of these June interviews, the President's popularity among adults had dropped to the lowest point in his term of office, but was still not at its ebb state. To our surprise even this group of children interviewed during a period of presidential unpopularity made numerous idealized references to the President. But there were interesting and possibly highly significant differences between the statements made by the June 1973 interviewees and their Nixon first-term predecessors. During the Watergate period children idealized the President more by referring to his power than to his benign and helpful qualities. When asked to imagine what would happen if the President broke the law (the traffic violation story), the Watergate interviewees were much more likely to imagine that the President was above the law. ("I'm the President, I'm not going to pay *any* traffic ticket.") They were also, however, somewhat more likely to invoke the theme that the President *should* be treated as equal to others. ("You're the man who makes the laws, you should enforce them.") If our 1973 interviews had been held after Cox's dismissal and serious impeachment discussion, it is possible that the climate of the wider political environment would have eroded the juvenile tendency to idealize the President. But the June, 1973, interviews show both the tenacity of juvenile idealization of the President, and that idealization itself is not a unitary phenomenon, in that it can vary in its concrete content depending on whether the child is describing the presidential role in general or evaluating the President in specific situational contexts.

5. *Adults' assessments of incumbent Presidents are considerably more variable than their assessments of the presidential role. Half of the modern (since FDR) Presidents have been consistently favored by more adults than disapproved of them, even though these adult views of the President are not so automatically favorable as those held by children. But the other half (Truman, Johnson, and Nixon) have fallen into substantial disapproval, following initial periods of positive ratings* (conclusion changed).

This proposition has undergone the most drastic reconsideration as a result of events since 1965. My indicator of presidential popularity was the regular Gallup Poll question asked monthly of national cross sections of the American population (except during presidential election campaigns) since the beginning of Franklin Roosevelt's third term: "Do you approve or disapprove of the way President X is handling his job?" [12] At the time I delivered these remarks in May, 1965, Johnson's Gallup Poll popularity was 64 percent with only 22 percent disapproving—a respectable support level, not much below the averages of Kennedy and Eisenhower over their terms in office, but 16 percentage points below Johnson's own peak just after his overwhelming election victory in 1964. Two years later Johnson's popularity rating had dropped a further 20 percentage points, and in the latter part of 1967 and much of 1968, he became the second President (Truman being the first and post-Watergate Nixon the third) to register more disapproval than approval ratings. The percentage of the Gallup national cross section approving of Johnson's handling of the Presidency was down to 36 percent just before his announcement that he would not run for the second full term in office he was constitutionally entitled to seek.

In figure 1, which is the Gallup organization's summary chart on Johnson's period in office, we see the steep decline from his initial peaks of support to the unpopularity of his final two-and-a-half years in office. During the latter period we rarely see a peak rising above the boldface line I have imposed at the 50 percent mark on the Gallup chart.[13]

In his decline to a point at which negative assessments exceeded the positive, Johnson resembled his only predecessor since the advent of national cross-section polling who did not owe his initial accession to office to the nominating process—Harry S. Truman. Truman's Gallup ratings went through *two* declines. Truman's high popularity after FDR's death collapsed within a year. The glow following Truman's unexpected reelection had an equally short life, and after a brief

[12] There are limitations to this poll question as a way of measuring true public feeling toward the President. It does not distinguish depth of feeling. Although other indexes are used in polls on leaders, there is a surprising lack of attention to the subtleties of assessing candidate images. There has been an uncritical reification of polls as an object of politicians' attention beginning in the early Johnson years. Johnson, as was often reported, carried poll results in his pocket and doted on them—until they became unfavorable to him.

[13] The reciprocal of "disapprove" is never "approve" in that "no opinion" responses range from about 25 percent, just after first-term election, to 10 to 20 percent during the President's second term. Thus it is not until popularity sinks to 45 percent that "disapprove" ever exceeds "approve."

Fig. 1. LBJ's Approval Rating—1963–1968

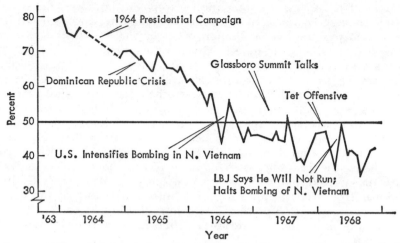

Source: Gallup Opinion Index, December 1968. (Reproduced courtesy of the American Institute of Public Opinion.)

upward spurt on the occasion of the decision to fight in Korea, Truman regularly registered the lowest figures in the history of the Gallup time-series on presidential popularity.

My 1965 conclusion that the public usually views Presidents favorably was based on the poll results for Roosevelt, Eisenhower, Kennedy, and Johnson up to the time of my assessment. FDR's popularity was regularly over 50 percent during the period for which polls were available—his third and brief fourth terms—as was Kennedy's for his sadly truncated first term. Figure 2, charting Eisenhower's popularity, which in eight years was consistently above the 50 percent bar, suggests what in 1965 looked like the "norm" for presidential support. Truman's negative assessments seemed to have been abnormalities. By 1973, however, the Gallup statistics had recorded not only the steady decline in esteem of President Johnson but also the drastic post-Watergate deflation of President Nixon's support—from 68 percent approval in January, 1973, shortly after the second-term inauguration, to 31 percent approval in early October, 1973.

During both his terms in office, Eisenhower showed a midterm trough following the postelection honeymoon. Roosevelt and Kennedy showed regular declines of support within high overall levels of popularity, as Nixon did in his first term—up until his fourth year of globe-trotting diplomacy in China and the Soviet Union, which was accompanied by popularity increases. John E. Mueller, in his fascinating study of fluctuations in presidential support, attributes much of the regular decline in presidential support to a "coalition of minorities effect." [14] Mueller's proposition is that it is easier for the President to make enemies by antagonizing small, well-organized groups than to make or keep friends as a result of his domestic actions, which are designed to be in the interests of nonminorities. The other and more dramatic causes of collapsing presidential popularity were the post-World War II reconversion strains in Truman's first term, the prolonged unpopular military actions in Truman's second term and under Johnson, and the Nixon administration Watergate revelations and their aftermath.

President Nixon's spurt in popularity at the end of his first term was closely associated with his skillful use of the resources of office in a way that enhanced his public stock. An incumbent President has at his disposal, in principle—and often in practice—two kinds of resources: the highly endowed physical and logistical infrastructure of the modern Presidency (the capacity to make news by traveling, presenting himself to the media on his own terms, etc.), and the reservoir of public esteem and respect for the presidential role itself, even when the individual role incumbent is unpopular. Perhaps the most beguiling example of reliance on respect for the role to achieve support for the individual was the 1972 Republican campaign slogan, which was "Reelect the President," rather than "Reelect Richard M. Nixon." As Russell Baker put it in a column entitled, "Nobody Here But Us Presidents," in the New York *Times*, August 15, 1972:

> Mr. McGovern wants to run against Richard M. Nixon. Of course, he believes Mr. Nixon would be easier to beat than the President, and he's probably right.
>
> Americans tend to like the President and dislike the people who oppose him. The President is one of those universally revered modern American institutions like Mother, Friday night, the flag, burgers, progress, and plenty of free parking which everybody assumes that all decent, right-thinking citizens approve of and support. Other countries have the cult of personality; we have the cult of the Presidency. "I may not like the man or anything he does," we say, "but I respect the office."

It would have been considerably more difficult to write so whimsically about the national love for Presidents fourteen months later when members of Congress were seriously exploring the possibility of the procedure that constitutional scholars have traditionally described as

14 John E. Mueller, *War, Presidents and Public Opinion* (New York: Wiley, 1973).

Fig. 2.   Eisenhower's Approval Rating: 1953–1961

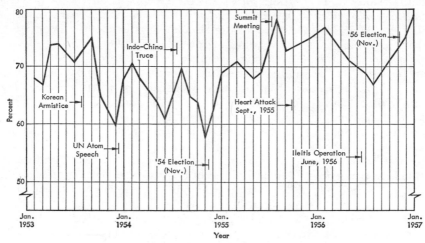

Source: Public Opinion News Service (Gallup) release, January 17, 1961. (Reproduced courtesy of the American Institute of Public Opinion.)

a "rusty blunderbuss"—impeachment. Nevertheless, even during some of Mr. Nixon's most beleaguered—and distrusted—periods there was an obvious psychological brake on public disposition to attack the President. In June, 1973, when presidential approval was down to 45 percent approve, 45 percent disapprove, and 71 percent of a national sample asserted that they thought he had been involved in some way in the illegal Watergate activities or their cover-up, only 18 percent agreed that he should be removed from office. Immediately following Cox's dismissal a telephone poll, which registered a 22 percent approve/75 percent disapprove ratio comparable to Truman's record low during the Korean War, still elicited less than a clear majority in favor of impeachment (44 percent in favor, 43 percent opposed, 13 percent no opinion).[15]

15 For a report of this NBC poll see the New York *Times,* October 23, 1973, p. 33. The NBC poll showed a remarkably low 3 percent "no opinion" response, whereas when Truman's popularity reached the previous low for a President (23 percent approve), the incidence of disapproval was 58 percent with 19 percent expressing no opinion. For the Gallup statistics on monthly presidential popularity over the years, see the *Gallup Opinion Index* (February, 1970). A Gallup Poll was conducted on October 19–22 with the interviews overlapping the Cox ouster. Interviews conducted before announcement of the ouster were about 31 percent approve; after announcement of the ouster, 17 percent approve. *Gallup Opinion Index,* November, 1973, pp. 4–9.

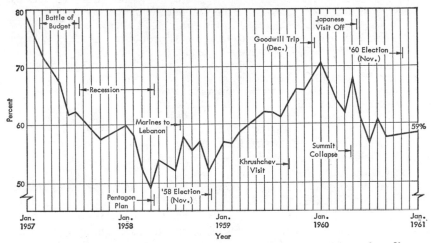

At this point the discrepancy between the 75 percent who disapproved of the President and the 44 percent who favored impeachment may have resulted less from respect for the presidential role than from fear of the consequences of impeachment. The man who said, "If you're in a plane and have only one pilot, you don't shoot him through the head" (New York *Times,* October 26, 1973), pinpointed a source of presidential leverage over citizens that rests more on fear of instability than on positive views of the President's virtues or those of this office.

Taking stock of the ups and downs of presidential popularity through 1968, Burns Roper makes the following instructive observations, which also seem to be applicable to Mr. Nixon's first term in office:

> The most obvious pattern the trend data reveal is that when a President takes office he has nowhere to go but down. A winning candidate has been successful in building voter support and starts his term with something approaching a consensus. As he takes office, he is the focus of the nation's hopes. Since he hasn't done anything yet, there is nothing to criticize for, and those hopes can become pretty expansive. In a sense, presidential elections are quadrennial myth-builders which every four years make voters believe some man is better than they later conclude he really is. The President takes office with most of the nation on his side, but this artificial "unity" soon begins to evaporate . . .
> The lowest ebb of approval is within a year of the end of the term. In the last few months of a term, a President's approval rating tends to start

back upward again. There are several reasons for this final upward turn. In mid-term a President is judged against the earlier inflated hopes as well as against the deficiencies of the state of the nation. As the next election approaches, he is compared to flesh and blood alternatives. The "anyone but him" sentiment tends to fade out as people realize who the "anyone buts" are. Then, if he is running again, he has already started his new campaign and is consensus-building once more the last months of his term. If, on the other hand, he is not running, there tends to be a mellowing towards him, a forgiveness for his mistakes or inadequacies, a nostalgic sense that he is perhaps "not so bad after all." [16]

6. *There is a significant tendency for citizens to rally in support of the President, when he acts at times of international crisis, and at certain other times when he symbolizes national solidarity* (conclusion slightly changed).

It is well known that poll support of the President increases under such circumstances as Truman's decision to resist the Communist invasion of South Korea (but not the prolonged aftermath thereof), Eisenhower's actions during the Suez crisis and after sending Marines to Lebanon, and even after those international actions viewed by informed observers as fiascos. For example, Eisenhower experienced a six-point increase after the U-2 incident and the collapse of the summit meetings, and Kennedy a ten-point increase after the abortive Bay of Pigs invasion.

The original wording of this proposition had stressed international crisis events, but Mueller notes as "rallying points" various noncrisis occasions when the President acts as symbolic leader and defender of international order (e.g., by taking part in summit conferences), plus the occasion of the President's taking office, another regular point at which popularity ratings move to especially high levels for reasons that can only be connected with the symbolism associated with assumption of office. Mueller has presented a detailed catalog of such "rally-round-the-President" incidents in the Truman through Johnson administrations.[17] Similar effects were evident in the Nixon years—for example —a twelve percentage point increase after Nixon's October, 1969, "Vietnamization" speech and a seven-point increase after an inter-*cosmic* event with which the President involved himself—the first moon landing. Nixon's aggregate popularity also increased following an event that evoked widespread protest on college campuses—the 1970 Cambodian intervention—and, as noted, after his 1972 travels to China and the Soviet Union.

[16] Burns Roper, "The Public Looks at Presidents: Thirty Years of Polls," *The Public Pulse*, 28 (January, 1968).
[17] Mueller, op. cit., p. 211.

An instructive, if grim, example of the effect of the presidential "mantle" is the spurt of support that goes to the Vice-President succeeding a President who has died in office, as evinced by the following quotation from a set of interviews with college students just after Johnson acceded to office in the wake of Kennedy's assassination:

> Getting to Johnson. . . . This strikes me again . . . the fact that we immediately began to think of Johnson in slightly better terms than we have before. . . . I at least began to think things like, well, he's the man who put the two civil rights bill through the Senate, the first time this had been done since the Civil War. He was a Roosevelt New Dealer, and so forth.[18]

7. *Citizens perceive and evaluate the President (and presidential candidates) in terms of their stand on issues, party connections, leadership qualities (record and experience), and personal qualities. A persistent minority of citizens appear to evaluate the President in purely personal terms* (conclusion changed).

My 1965 proposition, based largely on Hyman and Sheatsley's classical analysis of Eisenhower's appeal [19] and the University of Michigan Survey Research Center analysis of why people said they favored or opposed the candidates of the 1950s,[20] stressed the predominance of voter references to the purely personal aspects of presidential image—for example, "his sincerity and integrity, his conscientiousness, his warmth or coolness, his physical vigor." In 1960 it was difficult to classify the controversy over Kennedy's religion as either a personal or an issue conflict, and in 1964 a similar problem existed with the image of Goldwater as impulsive and therefore militarily dangerous. In both instances, personal images and issues were intertwined. Analysis of the Michigan data on images of candidates in the post-1950s elections suggests that people are more disposed now than in the 1950s to describe Presidents and presidential candidates in terms of their capabilities or positions on issues, although the assessments by roughly one-fourth to two-fifths of the respondents are still expressed in terms of their personal qualities.[21]

Doris A. Graber, who has analyzed images of presidential candidates available in the press during election campaigns, argues that citizens,

18 Fred I. Greenstein, "College Student Reactions to the Assassination of President Kennedy," in B. Greenberg and E. Parker, eds., *Communication in Crisis* (Stanford: Stanford University Press, 1965).

19 Herbert H. Hyman and Paul B. Sheatsley, "The Political Appeal of President Eisenhower," *The Public Opinion Quarterly*, 17 (Winter, 1953–54), pp. 443–60.

20 Angus Campbell et al., *The American Voter* (New York: Wiley, 1960).

21 I am indebted to Richard Kroenick for the secondary analysis of University of Michigan Survey data that led to this conclusion.

presumably motivated by expressive needs like those referred to in the introduction to this chapter, tend to perceive news about the President selectively, and extract from it a higher component of information about the President's personal image than is in fact evident from the media content.[22]

This allusion to the diffuse, underlying public needs that may be met through the Presidency leads to the final point in my 1965 assessment, which had been prepared for an audience of psychiatrists who were interested in the emotional concomitants of Kennedy's assassination—both the psychology of assassination and the sources of the massive public emotional response to the President's death.

8. *There is some scattered clinical evidence that, at least for a portion of the population, the President provides an outlet for expression of deep, often unconscious personality needs and conflicts* (conclusion slightly changed).

Under this heading I reviewed two kinds of writings: (1) speculative discussions by psychoanalytic theorists arguing that the deep positive or negative feelings children form about the authority figures in their primary environment become unconsciously extended in later years to figures in the wider, public environment, thus charging attachments to public figures with special force; and (2) the surprisingly large number of case reports by psychotherapists who, at the time of the deaths in office of Presidents Kennedy and Roosevelt, were struck by the emotional force of their patients' responses, as well as by the spontaneous references by many patients to their parents in reacting to the presidential deaths. I noted the possibility that for these individuals the President serves as an "unconscious symbolic surrogate of childhood authority figures." Such an hypothesis needs qualification however:

> although we have had a number of such clinical reports of patients who symbolically link the President with parental authority, there is no evidence as to the frequency with which this linkage occurs among psychiatric patients, much less in the general population. Nor do we have a clear indication of the variation in form that such linkages might take from individual to individual. As Lasswell has pointed out, if images of objects in the secondary environment (such as the world of politics) acquire meaning from experiences in the primary environment (such as the family), it does not follow that the former will be simple extensions of the latter. Generalization may be compensatory, taking the shape, for example, of reaction formation. To complicate matters, both types of generalization may be at work. For some people, orientations toward secondary environment authorities may be extensions of primary environment orientations; for others the generalization may take a compensatory form. (This may

22 Doris A. Graber, "Personal Qualities in Presidential Images: The Contribution of the Press," *Midwest Journal of Political Science,* 16 (February, 1972), pp. 46–76.

account for the lack of significant correlation between attitudes toward different authorities in the quantitative research on this topic.) Moreover, linkages between primary environment experience and orientations toward the President may differ from President to President. Thus, for example, it is difficult to believe that many adults would treat a youthful President such as Kennedy as a father surrogate, even though there is some evidence that for children he may have unconsciously been perceived in these terms.[23]

The clinical findings do indicate that at least for some individuals there is empirical validity to Lasswell's famous formula that private needs become displaced onto public objects and rationalized in terms of general political principles.[24] In reviewing the same evidence today I am inclined to place less emphasis on the capacity of public figures to become surrogates of childhood authority figures. Instead I would stress the great variety of perceptual, cognitive, and emotional mechanisms that can lead a citizen to invest positive and negative psychic energies in the most conspicuous figure of the remote environment— the President.

In the area of psychodynamic connections between the President and some citizens, a literature of post hoc psychodiagnosis of actual and would-be assassins of Presidents and presidential candidates has arisen since 1965. For example, Weisz and Taylor review information on the individuals held responsible for the assassinations of Presidents Lincoln, Garfield, McKinley, and Kennedy and for the attempted assassinations of Jackson, Theodore Roosevelt (in the 1912 campaign), Franklin Roosevelt (as President-elect), and Truman. Of these, only the ideologically motivated Puerto Rican nationalists who tried to kill Truman were without substantial psychopathology.[25] The two assaults on presidential candidates since Weisz and Taylor published their work—the assassination of Robert Kennedy and the shooting of Alabama Governor George Wallace—also reflect the psychopathological pattern, but in neither case does the fragmentary available data suggest that an adequate explanation would be provided by a mechanical Freudian formula—e.g., of deflected patricidal impulses.

[23] For a much fuller discussion of these points, see Fred I. Greenstein, "Private Disorder and the Public Order: A Proposal for Collaboration Between Psychoanalysts and Political Scientists," *Psychoanalytic Quarterly*, 37 (April, 1968), pp. 261–281.

[24] Harold D. Lasswell, *Psychopathology and Politics* (Chicago: University of Chicago Press, 1930).

[25] Alfred C. Weisz and Robert L. Taylor, "American Presidential Assassinations," *Diseases of the Nervous System*, 30 (October, 1969), pp. 659–68. Also see Murray Edelman and Rita James Simon, "Presidential Assassinations: Their Meaning and Impact on American Society," *Ethics*, 79 (April, 1969), pp. 199–221.

Psychological "Uses" of the President

Partly on the basis of the foregoing empirical propositions, and partly on more speculative grounds, a number of general observations can be distilled on how Presidents and the Presidency figure in the psyches of citizens. The first five generalizations about "functions of Presidents for citizens" were in my 1965 discussion. The sixth generalization is strongly suggested by the post-1965 experience.

To varying degrees, citizens appear to draw on

1. *The President as a cognitive aid,* and
2. *The President as an outlet for feelings*

These two complementary general functions subsume the more specific ones. The presence of a single, highly publicized national leader, combining political leadership with symbolic head-of-state functions, undoubtedly simplifies perceptions of politics and government for citizens at all levels of the political system. Within the leadership stratum, even when "The Myth of the Strong Presidency" is challenged, the President's program is the single most important influence on the content of the agenda of political discourse and decision-making. Hence the ubiquity of "President-watching" on the part of "the Washington Community." The further down one moves in the citizenry in terms of political information and attention, the more one finds that the President is virtually the *only* cognitive link to government and politics. Similarly if we look at the political awareness at successively younger ages, we reach a point where the President is a tall, lone tree on a plateau of stumps.

The President serves obvious emotion-venting functions for his intense following and for the vehement antagonists of "that man in the White House" in addition to the "more general—and more diffuse— emotional functions" for other members of the population. The detailed preoccupation of the media with the President's hobbies and social activities has become an American equivalent of the more ceremonial displays of symbolic activity associated elsewhere with monarchs. Since the President is so publicized and since it is so simple for citizens to personify the government and even the nation via their perceptions of him, he inevitably serves cognitive and emotional functions such as the following three, which I described in 1965 and which are qualified by the mordant, bracketed after-thoughts based on subsequent events.

3. *The President as a means of vicarious participation*

By personifying the complex process of government and politics, the President becomes a potential object of identification. To the degree that the President's actions are effective, citizens who identify themselves with him may experience heightened feelings of potency—of being in a world in which one is not completely dependent upon external circumstances and events. In addition to whatever attachments there may be to the President at the deeper motivational levels, it seems quite likely that, under some circumstances, a variety of people "identify" themselves with the President at least in the superficial fashion of our "identifications" with the heroes in novels and films. This probably occurs especially during international crises, such as the bombing of Pearl Harbor, when the President provides a ready outlet for patriotic feelings.

[But the identification can be negative—and the vicarious participation can be with the President's real or perceived opponents—for example, Watergate investigators.]

4. *The President as a symbol of national unity*

The survey of reactions to President Kennedy's death continues to offer an excellent illustration of this function in that it shows a high degree of consensus in response to the Presidency on the part of groups that normally are severely polarized. To take the most extreme examples, anti-Kennedy southern whites and pro-Kennedy northern blacks, while the furthest apart of all population groups in the *intensity* of their distress at Kennedy's death were uniform in their regret that he had been assassinated.[26]

[But the President *can*, if he "chooses," use his great public saliency to divide and polarize the nation.]

5. *The President as a symbol of stability and predictability*

We may assume that the Presidency normally helps to signify social stability since for so many people one of the most disturbing aspects of President Kennedy's assassination was that it carried implications of domestic and international disorder. Again, the ease with which even the most apolitical citizen can personify the government in the President is probably significant. Our own lack of interest in the details of how the nation is governed becomes more acceptable if we feel that *someone* is attending to such matters. The assumption is that events are being controlled, that life is not whimsical and dangerous.

[Conversely, a President who is perceived as being vindictive, unstable, or erratic may exacerbate public feelings of uncertainty and insecurity, although we may assume that many citizens are as resistant to perceiving their President in these terms as young children are to perceiving him in a negative light at all.]

[26] Paul B. Sheatsley and Jacob J. Feldman, "The Assassination of President Kennedy: A Preliminary Report on Public Reactions and Behaviour," *Public Opinion Quarterly*, 28 (Summer, 1964), pp. 189–215.

6. *The President as a "lightning rod" or object of displacement*

Commenting on the repeated research findings in the early political socialization literature that children idealize political leaders, and notably the President, David Sears[27] makes a point that is no less important for being definitionally true: *idealized attitudes are unrealistic.* Two traits that have long been seen by foreign observers as reciprocal parts of "the character and values of Americans" are a kind of soaring optimism about human potentialities and a censorious moralism about the actual elements of the political process, since these can never achieve the full purity called for by the moral norms. The area of campaign finances and management in general (and not merely particular episodes like those of the political espionage scandals in the 1972 presidential campaign) provide excellent examples of how unrealistic Sunday School standards foster unsatisfactory workaday behavior.

In the case of the central, energizing institution in the modern American political system, the Presidency, the very strength that accrues to the President by his singular visibility and his capacity to become the receptacle of widespread personal hopes and aspirations carries with it, in the clarity of post-1965 hindsight, an obvious weakness: if things go wrong, who else is there to blame? The depression becomes "Hoover's depression"; the "mess in Washington" becomes Truman's or Nixon's, even before a proper assessment of responsibility has taken place. Precisely *because* children of the 1950s acquired glowing images of the President, they were likely to be drastically repelled by the spectacle of 1960s and 1970s Presidents pursuing policies they found highly repugnant.[28]

One indicator of the President as lightning rod may be the flow of protest communications to Washington on occasions such as the Cox ouster, at which time Western Union reported in the New York *Times* (October 24, 1973) "the heaviest concentrated volume [of telegrams] on record," and all indications were that the overwhelming bulk of these had opposed his action.

It is tempting as well as true to American traditions to assume that for every problem there ought to be an obvious remedy. Hence the occasional and highly impractical suggestion that the American Presidency be Anglicized, devolving the figurehead functions to a decorative office-holder. In fact, there is no simple foolproof way for a nation

27 David O. Sears, "Political Behavior," in Gardner Lindzey and Eliot Aronson, eds., *The Handbook of Social Psychology*, V (Reading, Mass.: Addison-Wesley, 1969), p. 443.
28 For a discussion of "The President as a National Symbol" at various times in American history, see Wilfred Binkley in *The Annals*, 283 (September, 1952), pp. 86–93.

of the size and complexity of the United States to carve out a chief executive that permits sufficient empowering for the policy-making process to come to productive issue from time to time, as well as encouraging citizens to feel secure and productive.

The most probable source of change in the tendency for the President *either* to be unrealistically idealized *or* to assume the status of handy scapegoat would appear to be in the formal and informal political socialization process, including learning from peers and from one's own thought and experience as well as from "authorities," and involving the learning of nonconformity and autonomy as well as conformity. Much of the standard public discourse on the Presidency (the images of the loneliness of the Oval Office and so forth) are as romanticized in a twentieth-century way as the apocryphal stories about George Washington and the cherry tree. As Barber puts it, there needs to be recognition that "the President, while *primus*, is also *inter pares*, that we elect men, not gods, and that the President is not the Wizard of Oz." [29]

[29] James D. Barber, "Resources: Presidential Style and Public Mood," paper delivered at the Annual Meeting of the American Psychiatric Association, May, 1971.

Murray Edelman

6

The Politics of Persuasion

Social Conditions

MEANING OF ELECTIONS

Campaign strategists can be effective only when they take account of what presidential elections mean to voters. That meaning is complex. It is not the same for all voters, nor is it stable or consistent for the same voter. If it were simple, effective tactics would be self-evident, campaigns would be less problematic, and strategists would have less leeway to devise original plans and to make mistakes.

We know a good deal of what presidential elections symbolize to Americans: the beliefs, hopes, and fears they evoke and the limits within which they are important to all. First, politics is just not very salient most of the time to a large part of the electorate when compared to their private concerns. Asked in one study to tell their "fondest hopes," only 2 percent mentioned political affairs and 10 percent international events; 5 percent cited political affairs in listing their "worst fears," and 24 percent feared international developments.[1] There is both considera-

---

MURRAY EDELMAN *is George Herbert Mead professor of political science at the University of Wisconsin, where he is also affiliated with the Institute for Research on Poverty. His books include* American Politics: Public Policy, Conflict, and Change *(with Kenneth Dolbeare) and* Politics as Symbolic Action: Mass Arousal and Quiescence. *He is also the author of several other volumes and many articles.*

Professor Edelman wishes to acknowledge that Ruth Greenspan and Anne Machung provided invaluable criticism of an early draft of this chapter.

[1] David O. Sears and Richard E. Whitney, *Political Persuasion* (Morristown, New Jersey: General Learning Press, 1973), p. 6.

ble support for elections and considerable skepticism about their effectiveness in giving the people a voice, though very high proportions of the population, including many of the skeptics, believe they have a duty to vote.[2] The skepticism is continuously reinforced, for many realize that elections typically do little to get them what they want even when their preferred party or candidate wins. Voters without high economic and social status have good reason to doubt that it is worth their while to devote much attention to elections or spend time or money seeking information about the candidates and issues.[3] This widely prevalent attitude makes it all the more crucial for campaign managers to win the attention and support of potential voters.

Elections evoke other attitudes as well. Feeling that voting is an obligation, many rely upon long-standing identification with a major party to guide them, though the proportion who do so declined markedly in the late sixties. Particular issues do become important to a high proportion of voters on occasion. Sometimes, as in major depressions, the issues are manifestly based upon objective conditions. Often they are contrived or spurious, playing upon the anxieties of large numbers of people and made potent by the capacities and limitations of the mass media.

Elections carry still another meaning: one that helps explain the curious fact that many who are skeptical about the effectiveness of voting think it their civic duty to vote anyway. Voting constitutes a ritualistic expression of involvement, a chance to vent personal hopes and anxieties, an affirmation of the obligation to conform to legitimate public policies and laws. In voting a person expresses confidence in the legitimacy of the political system, and some refuse to vote to express lack of confidence.

For practically all of the electorate presidential elections also evoke deep-seated feelings about the Presidency as a symbol of the state, the national interest, and the protection of the citizen.[4] This probably does less to make people attentive to campaigns than to instil support for incumbents and to determine which attributes of candidates voters see as important.

SUSCEPTIBILITY TO PERSUASION

These various influences upon voters in presidential elections are overlapping, partly contradictory, and often experienced by the voter

2 Jack Dennis, "Support for the Institution of Elections by the Mass Public," *American Political Science Review*, LXIV (September, 1970), pp. 819–835. See chapter 7 for data on increasing public skepticism and mistrust of government.

3 This position is trenchantly expounded in Anthony Downs, *An Economic Theory of Democracy* (New York: Harper & Row, 1957).

4 Cf. chapter 5.

as ambivalence. They make it possible to influence voters. People who lack stable and gratifying roles in life arising out of their work, their social ties, or their political beliefs are especially susceptible to persuasion and especially likely to seek roots and stability through support of the incumbent President.

To the degree that men and women maintain ties with a political party and let those ties determine their presidential votes, efforts at persuasion are manifestly pointless. Similarly, ethnic, regional, economic, or other identifications that consistently influence voting choice reduce the effect of persuasive strategies in particular campaigns. But after this is said, the influence of persuasive efforts remains decisive; for elections are won by relatively small margins. The most telling evidence lies in the comparatively wide swings in the proportion of the popular vote gained by the major parties in different presidential election years: from 49.6 percent for the Democratic candidate in 1948 to 44.4 percent four years later, for example; from 49.5 percent for the Republican candidate in 1960 to 38.5 percent in the next election. In the elections from 1948 to 1968 about a third of the voters decided for whom they would vote during the nominating conventions and roughly another third did so during the campaign. Deliberate efforts to sway voters through the mass media during the campaign account for only a part of this fluctuation, but appeals for attention and for support that vary from one campaign to another are critical.

Such appeals are very likely growing *more* crucial. Network radio has been available for nationwide campaigning since the early thirties and television since the late forties. These electronic media have brought drastic changes in strategies, in financing, in the treatment of issues, and in the components of the voter's psyche upon which politicians and campaign planners focus. When news of candidates and political events came chiefly from local newspapers and from opinion leaders dependent on the local newspapers, voters were more exposed to diverse regional, ethnic, party, and other relatively stable influences that segmented the electorate; and they could more easily insulate themselves from more transitory appeals. Franklin Roosevelt demonstrated that through radio a President could bypass local newspapers and local opinion leaders and instil his own perspective about the issues facing the country and about his own competence in a high proportion of his listeners. More than that, he could force the press to help him do so, in their news columns if not on their editorial pages. Presidents had always been able to do that to some degree, but the electronic media have magnified their power to capture popular attention and direct it. The opportunities, the challenges, and the pitfalls facing campaign decision-makers and citizens are therefore different from what they have been through most of American history.

The media that reach a national audience carry political information (accurate or inaccurate), appeals for support, and interpretations of current developments and alleged developments on the national and world scenes. What kinds of messages reach which kinds of people, what difference do they make, and what strategies can campaign planners employ to take advantage of the psychological tendencies of their target audiences? People can fail to expose themselves to messages, ignore or reinterpret what they see and hear, and forget what they once accepted; or they can be quite susceptible to persuasion—through exposure to facts, through the subtle and unintended meanings conveyed by governmental actions, and through the deliberate contriving of events ("pseudoevents"). The range of manipulatory strategies and of reactions is wide; but we do know something about the conditions that determine which forms of response are probable and therefore which strategies are likely to work.

VOTERS WITH ENDURING COMMITMENTS

Whether people have strong and stable social ties is critical to persuasibility. Voters with roots in a profession, ethnic group, union, religion, or craft are more likely than the rootless to identify with a political party. Such enduring commitments carry with them a set of political predispositions that substantially limits the power of the mass media or campaign strategies to change attitudes, perceptions, and voting behavior.[5] People enjoying high income and social status are more likely to have roots and enduring commitments in the social and economic structure than are the poor and the lower middle class. Here is one reason the effects of mass persuasion techniques in the electoral process generally differ according to socioeconomic level. Enduring commitments are usually acquired early in life. For change to occur there must be a marked alteration in the climate of opinion and continuing support for new commitments from people with whom an individual has close emotional links.

Roots and rootlessness are of course matters of degree, and the same person is likely to fluctuate in his feelings of alienation with changing circumstances. The striking increase in the 1960s and early 1970s in voters not identified with a party suggests that the number of voters who feel alienated a large part of the time may be growing.

Enduring social roots help define people's self-concepts and so are vitally important to them. They create and give meaning to a person's work, including his political work. People expose themselves disproportionately to news bearing on their organizational and personal ties

⁵ Dan D. Nimmo, *The Political Persuaders* (Englewood Cliffs: Prentice-Hall, 1970), pp. 35–36; Sears and Whitney, op. cit., p. 9.

and to interpretations consistent with their interests. Campaign appeals are designed in part to tap such enduring interests and to suggest that the party and candidate are responsive to them. But rhetoric can rarely change the long-standing party identifications of racial, religious, and economic groups; it mainly reinforces and activates predispositions.

People seek out, perceive, or remember messages consistent with their interests, but this is less important than their penchant for *interpreting* communications to make them consistent with their existing attitudes.[6] This finding is crucially important in an age in which television and radio can achieve high rates of exposure and reception. For people with strong commitments neither the "balance" of stories in newspapers and other media nor their slant is very important. They remain impressed with the news that fits their commitments and discount or reinterpret what does not, a tendency reinforced by their friends and colleagues who do the same thing. Contributing money, time, or public support to a candidate strengthens both the predispositions and the bias toward consistency with them. Voters with organizational roots are the most likely to make such contributions. Even for the committed, the penchant for interpreting news to suit their interests is not total. Facts make a difference, and change occurs; but it is slower.

Socially rooted people, then, are insulated from the possibility of easy conversion through campaign appeals, though communications and campaigns do affect the intensity of their attitudes. The insulation extends to developments that are real as much as to alleged events that are contrived for campaign purposes. The strong supporters of an incumbent regime can easily see rising unemployment as the fault of the unemployed or of the political opposition, just as opponents of the regime see it as bad planning by the administration in power.

A rather small group of voters with stable social roots has a special kind of stake in politics, based upon an expectation of substantial economic benefits from governmental action through subsidies, contracts, or tax benefits. Businessmen, farmers, and professionals with such an interest regard pertinent political developments as part of their business affairs, which means they have an overriding interest in evaluating the news realistically and in supporting the opposition party when that serves their interests. The large number of businessmen fearful of Goldwater's adventurism who switched to Lyndon Johnson in 1964 and the movement of traditionally Republican farmers to support for Roosevelt in 1936 illustrate the point. For the issues that are most important

[6] Research suggesting the relative unimportance of selectivity and the crucial importance in consistency biases is reviewed in Sears and Whitney, op. cit., pp. 4–6.

to these interest-oriented voters, psychological consistency and selectivity are minimal and economic realism is crucial. With respect to these issues, though not necessarily others, such voters are relatively immune to vacuous rhetoric and pseudoevents.

Some others also realistically assess their interests, sometimes at considerable effort. In the late sixties and early seventies a growing number of educated people, largely young, have maintained substantial independence from the political parties. Like the material beneficiaries of public policies, these people typically seek out information bearing on their interests, which may not concern material gains for themselves.[7] They, too, are relatively insulated from campaign appeals and are more impressed with the similarities in the major parties and candidates than with vacuous rhetoric or symbolic acts designed to show they are different.

ROOTLESS VOTERS

One of the most confident conclusions we can reach from communications experiments and electoral studies is that people without enduring commitments are the most susceptible to persuasion, both by mass communications and by personal influence. For such potential voters communications cannot serve chiefly to reinforce pre-existing attitudes. Those who are low in socioeconomic status are most likely to lack the close organizational ties that carry political commitments with them, and they are also most likely to be weak party identifiers. Obviously, voters who are unemployed lack significant ties to the world of work; but even those with jobs may suffer anomie.

A 1972 governmental study of *Work in America* demonstrates that people at all but the top levels of the American social and economic structure feel little or no gratification or self-respect from their work, though they would like to have meaningful work.[8] Among the many pathologies to which this condition gives rise is susceptibility to facile appeals and contrived developments. Both psychological experiments and a major electoral study[9] suggest that some people are highly susceptible to persuasion on all issues and that such "topic-free persuasibility" is not related to intelligence. It stems from low self-esteem and feelings of inadequacy, precisely the conditions found prevalent

7 Cf. Robert D. McClure and Thomas E. Patterson, "Media Influences in the 1972 Election: Preliminary Findings and Speculation" (mimeo), pp. 10–11.

8 Cf. United States Department of Health, Education and Welfare, *Work in America* (Washington: Government Printing Office, 1972).

9 Nimmo, op. cit., p. 72; Paul F. Lazarsfeld, Bernard Berelson, and Hazel Gaudet, *The People's Choice* (New York: Columbia University Press, third ed., 1968), p. 70; Carl Hovland, Irving Janis, and Harold H. Kelley, *Communication and Persuasion* (New Haven: Yale University Press), 1963.

through much of the social structure in the 1972 study of working conditions.

With the appearance of the electronic media able to reach national audiences it has become possible to appeal powerfully to the needs of such people for meaning, for guidance as to what will help and hurt them, and for understanding of the confusing political world, a world that threatens them more than it satisfies them.

Not that the ordinary forms of politics are salient for most of the voters. As already noted, they are not. The citizens without social roots vote in significantly lower proportions than those with larger stakes in existing social and economic institutions. Nor are they eager to expose themselves to political communications; often the problem for campaign decision-makers is to reach them at all. They are unlikely to read political news, and their attention to news and political advertising on television is limited, though one study concludes that they do gain some information from political television commercials.[10]

The combination in relatively anomic voters of a general absence of interest in elections and susceptibility to arousal and manipulation calls for explanation. While these voters are skeptical that they can gain much through politics and do not normally find elections and representative institutions especially relevant to their lives, they are aware that public policy can severely disrupt and even destroy their lives. Taxes, military drafts, foreign enemies, crime, immorality, unemployment, inflation, and other dangers—real and imagined, actual and potential—are threats that evoke anxiety. The anxiety is sometimes conscious and very likely continuously subconscious. There always is a great deal of ambiguity about how real such threats are, what their causes are, and what can be done about them. The person without social roots finds little intrinsic interest or chance of direct gain in politics, but knows that he or she can be hurt through incompetence or malfeasance in those who direct the affairs of state, and especially the President. The concern therefore is not for personal involvement but for supporting a President who seems to know how to cope and how to assuage public fears. The incentive is for personal disinvolvement through trust in a benevolent leader.

Campaign Mechanisms

SYMBOLIC POLITICS

Such ambivalent attention to the political scene offers an opportunity to campaign decision-makers and public officials. When attention to

[10] Thomas E. Patterson and Robert D. McClure, "Political Advertising on Television: Spot Commercials in the 1972 Presidential Election," *Maxwell Review* (1973), pp. 57–69.

politics hinges upon the menacing or reassuring nature of the political
world the ability to shape the contours of that world means control
over public attention and response. "For the lesser involved of our
citizens," Nimmo observes, "a campaign is effective to the degree that
it gratifies inner needs rather than converts basic beliefs." [11] Through
their actions, speeches, and use of the mass media, officials and campaign managers play upon the need for reassurance against threats,
evoking dangers and then conveying the belief that they can keep the
threats under control.

Audiences who are neither well informed about the issues nor motivated to become so are susceptible to ambiguous cues into which they
can read their anxieties and their hopes. In this situation campaign
decision-makers can often attract attention and change perceptions
more effectively through contrived impressions than through serious
and exhaustive discussion of the issues. *People for whom politics is not
important want symbols and not information:* dramatic in outline, de-
void of detail and of the realistic recognition of uncertainties and of
opposing considerations.

Television is especially well suited to meet such inner needs. Both
time constraints and the difficulty of reconsidering the information
that is presented assure that discussion will be brief and uncomplicated.
At the same time the medium effectively presents vivid impressions,
especially impressions of the style and personality of candidates. Television can structure the political world of people for whom that world
is inchoate, evoking stark impressions of benevolence and hostility, of
competence and confusion, respecting candidates and parties. It does so
to some degree for everyone but only slowly for the involved and
already motivated and much more quickly for the less involved.[12]

Even when "involvement" is selective, it can be effective in protecting
people against pseudoevents. Some who do not find politics very interesting or worth large investments of time or money are nonetheless sensitive to the dangers of simplistic messages. Persuasion and attention
are complex processes in which symbols, myths, and reality-testing are
all components; but for the uninvolved, reality is less intrusive. People
interpret communications to make them compatible with enduring
commitments, with the beliefs evoked by contrived events, and with
demonstrable "reality" to the extent that that is known. It is as if the
voter converts whatever information comes through to him to reassure
himself that his strongest inclinations are correct. In the 1952 Nixon
slush-fund incident, "many persons, Republicans and Democrats alike,

11 Nimmo, op. cit., p. 183.
12 Kurt Lang and Glady Engel Lang, *Politics and Television* (Chicago: Quadrangle Books, 1968), pp. 300–310.

did not want to see the general [Eisenhower] embarrassed politically and hence were ready to exonerate Nixon as long as he offered them a rationale for doing so." [13] This tendency limits markedly the effects the media can have through the prominence and the slant they give to news stories.

This view of the function of campaigns explains the fact that campaigns change the intensity of attitudes, but much less often change their direction and convert voters to a different position.[14] It also explains the absence of any significant relationship between the amount of program time on television and radio used in each state to promote presidential candidacies and the direction of either the national popular vote for President or the vote in the state. There is evidence, moreover, that people do expose themselves to the appeals of the party and candidate they do not favor. In a predominantly Republican area Republicans outnumbered Democrats "among those who viewed over 70 percent of Stevenson's speeches" in 1952.[15]

The appearance of television has enormously expanded the opportunity for influence and manipulation. Increased social malaise and disorganization reinforce this effect. In consequence, campaign management has become an increasingly technical and an increasingly profitable profession, dominated more and more by people whose paramount commitments are neither to political parties and candidates nor to particular public policies, though these were the allegiances of campaign managers through all of American history until about the middle of the twentieth century. Instead, contemporary campaign managers are technical specialists, knowledgeable in campaign organization, public relations, polling, fund-raising, mass mailing, speech writing, television direction and production, and in some cases, spying and the devising of fraudulent documents and news releases. Their services typically are for sale. As the power of these techniques becomes more widely appreciated, the campaign management firms gain increasing influence, not only over how the campaign is conducted, but even over the selection of candidates. The party organizations have increasing reason to consider whether an aspirant is marketable; and because their reputations depend upon winning, the management firms refuse to work for candidates who are sure losers. A professional campaign manager first recruited Richard Nixon to run for office.

13 Ibid., p. 31.

14 Lazarsfeld, et al., op. cit.; William A. Glaser, "TV Turnout," *Public Opinion Quarterly*, XXIX (Spring, 1965), pp. 61-86; Angus Campbell, "Has TV Reshaped Politics?" *Columbia Journalism Review*, I (Fall, 1962), pp. 10–13.

15 Based upon a study by Fred Siebert, reported in Joseph T. Klapper, *The Effects of Mass Communication* (New York: The Free Press, 1960), p. 64.

DELIBERATE MANIPULATION IN CAMPAIGNS

The voter is not a conditioned reflex responding automatically to the siren call of political pitchmen who know how to orchestrate the media and evoke whatever effects they like. Nor do campaign decision-makers know a great deal about the precise effectiveness of campaign strategies based upon large-scale media use. There is still a large element of un-certainty, manifestly qualified by sufficient hope and anxiety to induce campaigners to spend impressive amounts of money on the media even if they are not sure what they are buying.

We do know that neither the printed media nor the electronic ones are omnipotent. Voters have other sources of information; they often have strong resistances based upon real or imagined interests; and they cannot be counted on either to pay attention or to interpret messages as intended. Communications are most influential with people who have not had earlier opinions on the issue.[16] Opinions may be based upon knowledge of fact and careful reasoning or upon less solid founda-tions; they limit the effects of new communications in either case. With respect to the candidates and issues in presidential campaigns a large part of the electorate is opinionated in some degree through the media-tion of group norms, colleagues, opinion leaders, party identification, and status consciousness. People with such predispositions can absorb facts without being converted to the positions the facts are expected to suggest.[17] Though sources of information with high credibility can make some headway in overcoming predispositions, even the advantage of high credibility disappears over time.[18]

Although these conclusions are largely based upon laboratory experi-ments, studies of persuasibility in campaigns seem to bear them out. Those who expose themselves *most* to the media are *least* likely to shift voting intentions during the campaign, for this group is composed dis-proportionately of people with enduring commitments. In the 1960 campaign many Democrats voted for Nixon because of anti-Catholi-cism. Studies of the effects of short-term propaganda campaigns or of a single media program conclude quite uniformly that they have little persuasive impact, serving chiefly to reinforce pre-existing attitudes, as the 1960 Kennedy–Nixon debates did.

The frequent willingness of aspirants for the Presidency to let their poll standings dictate their availability suggests that candidates also

16 A number of experimental studies reaching this conclusion are discussed in Klapper, op. cit., pp. 53–57.

17 Ibid., p. 58.

18 Arthur Cohen, *Attitude Change and Social Influence* (New York: Basic Books, 1964), pp. 23–26.

recognize that there is little possibility of effecting major change in the voters' intentions. Gallup and Harris polls showing that any of the leading Republican aspirants would defeat Lyndon Johnson and private polls suggesting the same thing were major considerations in Johnson's withdrawal from the 1968 race. Romney withdrew from the 1968 New Hampshire primary as a result of discouraging private polls, and Robert Kennedy relied heavily on polls to assess his chance of winning the 1968 nomination.

Election night broadcasts have no detectable effect on voting intentions.[19] Even dramatic and vivid television presentations apparently change few people's attitudes toward controversial public issues. Television depictions of the brutalities of the war in Southeast Asia did not reduce support for the war below the levels of support for the Korean War, which was fought without nightly television coverage; and the networks' favorable depictions of the demonstrators at the 1968 Democratic convention did not generate popular sympathy for their cause.[20]

All these indications of the limits of effectiveness of the media are based, however, upon *short-term* effects or upon people's own perceptions of how much they have been influenced. The most profound effects of mass communications are certainly long-term, subtle and subconscious and therefore very likely not tapped or inadequately tapped by the observations just reviewed.

Intentionally and unintentionally, directly and indirectly, the mass media play a major part in shaping the perceptions of the candidates' abilities and weaknesses, the issues and nonissues, the threats to people's welfare or security, the ability of the incumbent administration to cope with its problems, the experience of the campaign as a sporting contest. The media and their messages influence some more quickly and more completely than they do others, and the media differ in the groups they most readily reach; but it is doubtful that anyone is wholly immune to their influence, for no one can directly verify all of his beliefs about the candidates, the issues, and the future, or take cues from others who are themselves immune to media influence.

But with most voters chiefly interested in matters other than politics, with political events and issues neither clear nor easily clarified, with underlying anxiety about the impact of politics upon people's welfare and security often intense, conditions are ideal for response to symbolic

[19] Sam Tuchman and Thomas E. Coffin, "Influence of Election Night Broadcasts on Television in a Close Election," *Public Opinion Quarterly*, 35 (Fall, 1971), pp. 315–326.

[20] John E. Mueller, *War, Presidents and Public Opinion* (New York: Wiley, 1973), p. 167.

cues rather than to facts. Campaign managers and the media are growing more effective in supplying the cues.

SYMBOLIC MEDIA PRODUCTS

The impressions and beliefs campaign planners create are typically
neither true nor false, but "ambiguous truths" [21] that rely upon their
true component to be convincing and upon their subtle distortions to
produce the desired response. Their success in doing so depends upon
the special stance of the electorate. When people are not called upon
to participate in government but only to grant or withhold moral support and votes on the basis of issues that are unconnected with everyday life and work, issues that are often unintelligible, it is tempting to
deal with them as we do with a dramatic performance, suspending
disbelief and finding gratification in experiencing fear and triumph.
In elections, as in any art form, the world that is evoked is composed
partly of semblance; and belief in the semblance itself creates a new
kind of fact. Obviously, few potential voters respond completely in this
way. Response is to a mix of symbol and reality; and the symbolic
component is more crucial to the degree that people lack meaningful
social commitments that provide a benchmark for evaluation. By the
same token, politicians and campaign planners are effective at persuasion in the measure that they are able to take the role of the political
spectator while working at their craft.

In governmental policy-making, symbolism is only one component,
and most potent when not deliberately planned; but in presidential
elections symbolism is increasingly both the most powerful component
and meticulously planned. The seduction of the public is most deliberate in precisely that part of the political process that symbolizes
popular participation.

Contrived events can be more vivid, more credible, and more persuasive than the normal flow of life, for they are simpler, less ambiguous, and so focus attention more sharply. When well done, they tap
strong personal needs. Because the message comes partly from the
spectator himself, he can be counted on to cooperate in seeing it as a
valid clue. Daniel Boorstin, who coined the term "pseudoevent" for the
contriving of reality, recognized that "strictly speaking, there is no way
to unmask an image. An image, like any other pseudoevent, becomes
all the more interesting with every effort to debunk it." [22]

Threats—Pseudoevents create beliefs about threats to the country,
beliefs about the accomplishments, skills, competence, and public po-

---

[21] Daniel Boorstin, *The Image* (New York: Harper & Row, 1964), p. 34.
[22] Ibid., p. 194.

sitions of the candidates, and beliefs about the concerns and attitudes of the public. In the 1960 campaign the Democrats created a widespread belief in a "missile gap," through repeated use of the phrase and through statistical revelations about the size of the gap. In a cold war atmosphere this issue apparently convinced many voters that the previous Republican administration had been lax in protecting national security; but after Kennedy's election it became clear that there had never been a gap and that the issue was a nonissue. Both candidates in that same campaign cooperated in creating another threat by debating vigorously just how to counter allegedly imminent Chinese attacks on the Pacific islands of Quemoy and Matsu, a nonproblem that was not heard from again after election day. Throughout the fifties and early sixties, the political parties similarly cooperated in creating the belief that a world Communist conspiracy was assiduously pushing over dominoes reaching ever closer to American shores, with each party proposing more vigorous and militant plans to stop the threat to national security.

Those pseudoevents that take the form of nonexistent or highly dubious threats seem to occur largely in the field of international relations because foreign policy issues evoke shared fears in a very substantial part of the electorate. Both candidates can then try to channel the anxieties to their own advantage. On issues on which there is less public consensus this kind of contriving of reality is less feasible because there is strong motivation in many to face facts and considerable ambivalence in many others. Though trends in unemployment, wages, and prices become campaign issues, they cannot be built upon contrived reports or fantasy in the degree, or for as long, as is typical of national security issues. There are periods, however, in which security from *internal* threat has evoked sufficiently wide concern that pseudoevents become politically feasible, as in Nixon's use of the internal communism issue when he was the vice-presidential candidate in the 1952 campaign.

Personal Traits—Very likely the most effective contriving of events occurs in presidential campaigns as a strategy for creating beliefs about the traits and talents of the candidates. In both his 1968 and his 1972 campaigns Nixon remained largely aloof from the public infighting of the campaign, giving brief and infrequent press interviews. In this way he evoked an image of a calm, low-key, and efficient man too busy with momentous events and crises to indulge in campaign rhetoric or base political maneuvers. The tactic helped him overcome the public's memories of his vehement attacks on opponents in earlier campaigns and of an emotional outburst against the press after his loss in the 1962 California gubernatorial race.

The qualities a candidate displays in contrived events and on bill-
boards and in his television commercials are a fairly good indicator of
the desirable traits his private polls tell him he lacks in the public mind. He can also reinforce prevalent perceptions he wants to
strengthen and create an impression that his opponent has undesirable
qualities. In 1972, pro-Nixon television commercials graphically depicted a McGovern who flip-flopped on such major issues as welfare
policy and his choice of a running mate. This pitch had a basis in fact,
but of course said nothing about the major issues on which McGovern
had been consistent or those on which Nixon had switched positions.

The spectator who witnesses an event on television or radio finds it
hard to be skeptical, for he then has to deny that seeing is believing.
The question is not what happened but what it means, and it often
means only that campaign planners have been hard at work. It is routine in contemporary campaigns to arrange for ticker tape to fall like
snow on the candidate's car, for television cameras to record outpour-
ings of people at a busy spot in a city whether or not the turnout is
impressive, and even for contrived stealing of the candidate's cuff links,
ties, or handkerchiefs. The hope, and often the result, is that the acting out of a little play about popularity and charisma will induce
popularity and charisma when the drama appears on the nightly television news shows.

Play acting can have other themes. When a candidate answers even
a few questions at a press conference or from an audience in a way
that shows he is well informed and has a plan for dealing with a problem, he creates an impression of general knowledgeability and competence; but because questions are both predictable and easily planted,
knowledgeability may also be a pseudoevent. In his 1968 campaign
Nixon made especially effective use of this kind of scene, answering
spontaneous questions at televised meetings of small groups of people
carefully selected both to look representative of the range of ethnic
and social groups and to avoid embarrassing questions or remarks.

The Eisenhower administration arranged to televise several "Cabinet meetings" that were planned and rehearsed to look spontaneous, a
device for creating pseudopeople engaging in a pseudoevent, but doubtless useful in building an impression of knowledgeable officials pursuing the public interest. The very setting of televised press conferences
similarly creates episodes and beliefs that would otherwise not exist.
Because questions are highly predictable and those not asked can be
planted, impression management is easy. At presidential press conferences the norms of decorum, the difficulty of asking follow-up questions, and the President's control over whom he recognizes gives the
reporters something close to the role of straight man, while the im-

pression conveyed is that of a well-informed official fearlessly taking on all comers.

Sometimes it is reporters who create pseudoevents—by asking whether a candidate agrees with a reporter's statement, for example, and then asking the opposing candidate to respond to a position that would not have been taken if the reporter had not forced it.[23]

Public Responses and Attitude—Opinion polls have become major pseudoevents, though this contriving of reality is not intentionally deceptive in the case of the honest polls. On the basis of responses that are very largely evoked by passing cues, including the appearance of a pollster with pencil poised, the poll provides a picture of a solid and stable public opinion that can in fact be unstable, ambivalent, or non-existent. One thoughtful study describes the poll interview as "a rather primitive stimulus-response social situation in which poorly thought-out answers are casually fitted to questions that often are overly ingenuous";[24] and another concludes that many responses are "non-attitudes."[25] But candidates devote a great deal of attention to emphasizing polls or belittling them, depending on what the polls show, thereby focusing attention on an artifact and supplying voters with a clear benchmark, though its clarity and simplicity is contrived. It is true that surveys of voting intentions are better predictors than surveys of other attitudes because elections tap the same symbolically induced attitudes that polls do. Neither of them forces the voter to make his response in the course of coping with real economic or other problems that directly affect his welfare. This similarity very likely helps publicized poll results to crystallize attitudes that are not based on enduring commitments.

Means and Ends—As campaign decision-makers recognize that they *can* induce responses that do not reflect real issues or interests, many come to believe that they *should* do so. With the electoral process so largely insulated from resolution of issues that affect the course and the quality of most people's lives, those with a high stake in the outcome are tempted to see it as a competition in which any tactic that brings votes and victory is justified. Tactics that go beyond evoking misleading impressions to outright illegality and fraud have always played some part in elections, and the resources and the willingness of

[23] Douglass Cater, *The Fourth Branch of Government* (Boston: Houghton Mifflin, 1959).

[24] Mueller, op. cit., p. 265.

[25] Philip E. Converse, "Attitudes and Non-attitudes: Continuation of a Dialogue," in E. R. Tufte, ed., *The Quantitative Analysis of Social Problems* (New York: Addison-Wesley, 1970), pp. 168–169.

high officials to engage in them have grown, culminating in "Watergate" in 1972. Resort to burglary; illegal espionage; forgery of disparaging documents; encouragement, and perhaps payment, of militant demonstrators against one's own candidacy in order to portray the opposition as violent and radical; deliberate violations of the campaign finance laws; and solicitation of large campaign contributions through thinly veiled threats or the promise of governmental favors were apparently all part of the strategy of the Committee to Reelect the President and of high White House officials. All these tactics helped to create false beliefs among the voters about the candidates and the issues.

THE MASS MEDIA AND THEIR SPECIAL TARGETS

In the efforts of campaign planners to shape the issues, the interests, and the candidate images to which voters respond, what help can they draw from the communications media? The various media reach rather different audiences, making it possible to vary the form of appeal to maximize its impact on specific target audiences. People with only a high school education and incomes below or just above the poverty line are the most voracious watchers of television; and those who have the greatest trust in television as a news source have a relatively low level of education, little interest in politics, and do not identify with a political party. Those who rely on the printed media are likely to be better educated, members of organized interest groups, feel moderate to strong party loyalties, and decide for whom to vote early in a campaign. While increasing proportions of the electorate have been getting most of their news from television, those who read newspapers and journals are also likely to use other media, while those relying heavily on television are unlikely to get information from other media.[26]

Television, with its special capacity for creating pseudoevents, pseudocandidates, and pseudoissues, is also the medium which most effectively reaches people who lack party ties and enduring social commitments. Spot commercials offer an especially potent means of creating a vivid image, with a minimum of information and verification. A Democratic spot in 1964 linked Barry Goldwater to the extermination of a little girl's beautiful world by an atomic bomb. A Republican spot in 1968 left the impression Hubert Humphrey was responsible

[26] Nimmo, op. cit., pp. 114–119; Bradley Greenberg and Hiduya Kumata, "National Sample Predictors of Mass Media Use," *Journalism Quarterly*, XLV (Winter, 1968), pp. 641–644; Bruce H. Westley and Werner J. Severin, "A Profile of the Daily Newspaper Non-Reader," *Journalism Quarterly*, XLI (Winter, 1964), pp. 45–50.

for the urban riots. In both cases protests about the spots led to *more* eager mass viewing of future spot commercials. Many see election campaigns as a form of sporting competition and admire aggressive tactics, at least ambivalently. Tough onslaughts, even when they are patently contrived or unbelievable as statements of issues, seem to evoke a certain amount of approval of the candidate as a forceful person. A study of spot commercials in the 1972 campaign concluded that they "appear to penetrate where other communications channels are ineffective" and "carry the candidate's message to low-interest and opposition voters with minimal information distortion or loss," though the study did not find that they were persuasive.[27] None of this suggests, of course, that television cannot also provide accurate information to many who would otherwise remain without it.

Like television, radio reaches voters directly. While Roosevelt found it useful as a way to bypass hostile editorial pages, Nixon has relied on both radio and television to bypass what he regards as unfriendly news reporting in papers that usually support him editorially. It was chiefly through radio that Wendell Willkie became nationally known within a few months after he emerged as a dark horse in the 1940 Republican convention. In the elections of the sixties and early seventies radio achieved renewed importance, for it reaches an audience newspapers and television often miss, including old people, young people, commuters, and housewives who listen while working; and it does so comparatively inexpensively. In his 1968 campaign Nixon broadcast detailed radio speeches that made him sound well informed. In his 1960 debates with Kennedy he sounded better to most listeners on radio than Kennedy did, though television viewers had the opposite reaction, suggesting that the voice evokes different responses than appearance and demeanor. Radio can also create pseudoevents through such devices as staged calls on talk shows.

It is clear, then, that the mass communications media not only report what happens, but play upon fears and hopes to shape the meanings of events and the contours of the political world in which the events occur. People see success or failure, threat or hope, competence or incompetence in the light of cues that can as easily be misleading as accurate.

COSTS OF CAMPAIGN ADVERTISING

It is a commonplace that the costs of electoral advertising are steep and rising, a trend that systematically benefits Republican candidates, incumbents, and candidates who espouse the issue positions of affluent

[27] Patterson and McClure, op. cit., pp. 57–69.

groups. High costs also encourage candidates to evade campaign finance laws.

An hour on prime-time network television costs more than $100,000 (plus production charges), but because at least 95 percent of American households have a television set and watch it an average of 45 hours every week, campaign planners pay the price necessary to reach that audience. Expensive private polls further escalate costs.

Nimmo calls attention to a "vicious cycle" effect in modern campaign techniques: ". . . media exposure affects poll results, poll results affect fund-raising, fund-raising affects media exposure." [28] In several ways this cycle hurts candidates who offend large potential donors, and it also hurts challengers of incumbents. Because funds hinge so largely upon immediate success in the polls, they are withheld from candidates who might be able to educate or persuade voters in the future, discouraging education and encouraging manipulation. Because incumbents always do well and those who promote the interests of corporations and large unions have money, they benefit from the vicious cycle.

By forcing aspirants for the nomination of the party out of power to attack each other as strongly as possible in the primaries, the cycle weakens the successful aspirant of the minority party, as Goldwater was weakened by the efforts of other Republicans to portray him as trigger-happy and McGovern was weakened by Humphrey's charges that he would scuttle the country's defenses and increase welfare costs astronomically.

Adding to these effects is the fact that it is important to get money early, not only to get large amounts eventually. Television time at the end of the campaign must be reserved long in advance if the time is not to be preempted by the other party; and television is more likely to be effective early in the campaign, before opinions are fixed.

Without question the chief impact of the very high costs of campaigns is the link they establish between politics and wealth: the fact that contributions come chiefly from the wealthy; the expectation that donors will get favorable policies in return for their money; fear of governmental discrimination against noncontributors; and the consequent emphasis on winning no matter what tactics are required to carry it off. The tactics have come to include both deliberate deception through public relations techniques and illegal interference with opponents' campaigns. Behind the deception and the illegality are the high stakes, both for large contributors of funds and for the politicians who receive them and whose status and power depend upon them.

28 Nimmo, op. cit., p. 105.

A large proportion of the electorate, by contrast, see little at stake for themselves, rendering them more susceptible to manipulative information and leaving the highly interested all the more leeway to treat elections as though they were private business rivalries or tribal battles.

Candidate Strategies

The attention-getting and persuasive possibilities gain no votes unless campaign planners find strategies for taking advantage of them. In the last analysis strategies and the psychological needs upon which they play are the critical factors, though the electronic media make more effective strategies possible.

Some of the most successful strategies take advantage of problems that affect the lives of the voters in a real and direct way. Regardless of impression management, unemployment hurts those who suffer from it or fear it, and so challengers can usefully call attention to its prevalence. At the same time many people are not directly affected, and so attempts are made to shape impressions of its seriousness. Incumbents promise future downward trends. During a period of steeply rising unemployment, the Nixon administration ended traditional monthly briefings on trends by Labor Department economists, a tactic that reminds us that some of the most effective strategies, especially those available to incumbents, occur before campaigns begin. Economic problems are probably less susceptible to impression management than most influences on the voter.

Far more manipulative are perceptions of threats to the public security and hopes for the solution of pressing problems. Roosevelt's attack upon "economic royalists" at a time of severe anxiety about economic collapse, the Republican attacks in 1952 upon Democratic policies respecting "corruption, communism, and Korea" at a time of severe anxiety about Communist conspiracies at home and abroad, and Nixon's attacks on protestors, street crime, and welfare fraud in 1968 and 1972 illustrate the strategy of focusing upon threats. It takes advantage of already prevalent fears of a kind that cannot be either verified or inhibited through direct observation, enhancing the opportunity to shape beliefs about remote enemies. At the same time real threats may be widely ignored, as the failure of Watergate to become an effective issue against Nixon in 1972 and of an Asian war to become one against Johnson in 1964 illustrate. In 1972 distrust of McGovern apparently detracted from the credibility of his Watergate charges. In 1964 Goldwater's militant stance apparently enhanced the credibility of Johnson's protestations that he would not fight an Asian land war.

In the same way candidates can arouse false hopes that they will solve pressing problems. To launch a widely publicized "War on Poverty," set up a cancer research agency "under presidential guidance," or reorganize health care services tells voters what they want to believe even if it does not make a substantial dent on poverty or sickness.

While widespread unemployment, steep inflation, and foreign and domestic enemies threaten a large part of the population, and so it is safe to be against them, most controversial issues must be handled carefully and ambiguously, for they are divisive by definition. On these issues a candidate may seem to be forthright while encouraging diverse groups to read their own meanings into his words. The favorite device for accomplishing this is to be forthright in tone and style and vague in content: to introduce a banality, a tautology, or an ambiguity, for example, with a stern warning that the candidate wants to make things perfectly clear.

Still another strategy is designed to convey an impression of the candidate's great popularity. Rallies, demonstrations, and polls can help do so even if they have to be rigged or carefully interpreted to make the point. A large turnout of volunteer workers does so for the occasional candidate who attracts them. Endorsements from celebrities also make the point to particular audiences.

People who trust a candidate to act competently can be counted on to interpret his words as serving their interests, a phenomenon that clouds the distinction between issues and candidate images. But there is strong reason to believe that the large group of people without stable social ties are critically influenced by their view of the candidates' abilities to cope with complex, anxiety-producing public affairs. This consideration explains both the virtual certainty that incumbents will be reelected and the occasional landslides in presidential elections.

Doris Graber's study of twenty newspapers during the last four weeks of the 1968 campaign found that 97 percent of all presidential qualities mentioned dealt with personality traits rather than the President's professional abilities or specific elements of his political philosophy.[29] Another study, based on the presidential elections from 1952 through 1964, concluded that fluctuations in electoral attitudes depended "to a remarkable degree" on differences in candidate image, with this factor substantially more important than party image.[30] Wide and apparently growing ticket splitting in the elections of the late sixties and seventies seems to confirm this view.

29 Doris A. Graber, "Personal Qualities in Presidential Images: The Contribution of the Press," *Midwest Journal of Political Science*, 16 (February, 1972), pp. 46–76.
30 Donald E. Stokes, "Some Dynamic Elements of Contests for the Presidency," *American Political Science Review*, LX (March, 1966), pp. 19–28.

The qualities people want in one kind of celebrity are different from what they look for in others. Manifestly, different qualities make for satisfaction with a beauty queen, a congressman, and an FBI director. In the case of the President, there is strong ground for the conclusion that he need not be personally likable. The crucial thing is that he seem to know how to cope effectively with domestic problems and with national enemies.

The very ruthlessness that raised questions in people's minds about Nixon's earlier political career was apparently an asset when he ran for President, especially against McGovern, who did not seem to be either ruthless or tough. "In matters of style," Graber found, "the public seemed concerned primarily with elements of strength. . . . Compassion was hardly mentioned." [31] A good military record has helped elect seven Presidents. One of these, William Henry Harrison, had been the hero of Tippecanoe 30 years before the election, was 68 years old, and was to die within a month of his inauguration; but the virile image Whig newspapers conveyed of him enabled him to defeat an incumbent, Martin Van Buren.

The Advantages of Incumbency

In general, however, incumbency is by far the most potent device to give a candidate the image of ability to cope and doubtless more potent than ever in the age of the electronic media. An incumbent benefits from people's belief, learned early, that the President is a benevolent leader and from their eagerness to trust him to manage the affairs of state. For an incumbent the crucial image building occurs before the campaign starts; much of it occurs during the childhood of the voters.

Chapter 5 discusses the psychological basis of these beliefs. The modern President builds upon them by using the whole executive branch of government to convey an impression of competence and success. Regardless of his record in actually solving problems, and even in the face of manifest fiascoes, such as the Bay of Pigs, a President benefits from a continuous stream of publicized gestures proclaiming that he can handle problems and threats. He also benefits from his ability to create benchmarks of success that may depend upon dubious statistics, grandiose rhetoric, or dramatic procedural steps that often fail to bring eventual payoffs.

The Office of Management and Budget estimated that in the first Nixon administration there were 6,144 people engaged in public re-

---

31 Graber, op. cit., pp. 54–55.

lations, at a cost of $161,000,000 a year. Approximately 60 people on the White House staff itself were engaged in public relations, including about 12 people under Herbert Klein, 14 working for Ronald Zeigler, and a third group directed by Charles Colson. On Saturday mornings an "Image Committee" consisting of Klein, Colson, and Dwight Chapin met to plan tactics.[32]

The dependence of journalists upon official sources complements such administration planning, especially because a reporter comes in time to adopt the perspective of the officials he regularly covers, partly to insure their future cooperation but also because of his constant exposure to the same information as the officials. Congressmen have declined in importance as news sources as executive officials have grown more important. For reporters inclined to become mavericks, there are crude and subtle pressures to stay in line: trading of notes among reporters and group pressures from peers that subtly build individual values from group judgments and define these as the professional stance. There is also widespread use of the New York *Times* and the

TABLE 1.   SOURCES OF INFORMATION IN THE *Times* AND THE *Post*—ALL STORIES
(N = 2,850)

	% of Total Sources
U.S. officials, agencies	46.5
Foreign, international officials, agencies	27.5
American state, local government officials	4.1
Other news organizations	3.2
Nongovernmental foreigners	2.1
Nongovernmental Americans	14.4
Not ascertainable*	2.4

Source: The table, reprinted by permission of the publisher, is taken from Leon Sigal, *Reporters and Officials* (Lexington: D. C. Heath, 1973), pp. 47 and 124–129. It is based on a count of a sample of stories in the two newspapers over the years 1949 to 1969.

* Not Ascertainable includes stories in which the channel was a spontaneous event of the reporter's own analysis.

Washington *Post* as models. Though often critical of the administration editorially, these papers are heavily dependent on official sources, as table 1 shows.

32 David Wise, *The Politics of Lying* (New York: Random House, 1973), pp. 188–213.

One result of psychological needs and governmental domination of news is trust in incumbents that may be ambivalent in some of the electorate but is crucial in a decisive segment of it. No matter how low his popularity, the incumbent President always is high, and usually at the top, of the annual popularity referendum posed by Gallup: "What man that you have heard or read about living today in any part of the world do you admire the most?" No matter what he does on specific issues, a sizable group can be counted on to rally to support him. Public issues fade from attention after a period in the limelight even when they are not "solved" because they cannot remain dramatic and exciting for long, and the media then have economic and psychological reasons to softpedal them. The attribution of benevolence and competence to the President therefore provides a sense of continuity and progress as well as reassurance.

To trust in the President's competence is to accept him as a symbol that problems can be solved without a basic restructuring of social institutions and without the threat a radical reordering poses both to the contented and to the anxious. A superficial bemusement with personalities substitutes for tough-minded analysis of problems and social structures. Little wonder that incumbents almost never lose. In view of the reelection record of incumbents in the twentieth century (two defeats in twelve opportunities), a presidential election involving an incumbent is more like a midterm confidence ritual than a true contest.

A comparison of those elections in the 40-year period since 1932 that have been sweeps with those that have been very close offers further insight and confirmation of this view of the functions served for uncommitted voters by the images of the candidates and the expectations people hold of the presidential office. There were landslides in 1936, 1956, 1964, and 1972. In every sweep there was an incumbent who had dramatically handled major threats either with success or with apparent success, and in every case he was the winner. In every instance, the challenger was widely regarded either as a vacillating and indecisive type, impractical and unsure how to cope with problems (Landon, Stevenson, McGovern), or wild, trigger-happy, and too likely to bring disaster through impulsive action (Goldwater). In this same period, the elections of 1960 and 1968 had hairbreadth outcomes. In neither case was there an incumbent or a clear-cut case for choosing between the candidates on the basis of the decisiveness or the clarity of their stands on the major issues.

The effective candidate strategies, then, would seem to be those that emphasize competence and strength. Incumbency is especially useful in conveying these impressions, largely because citizens want to believe their leaders are capable.

What Can Be Done

Deceptive and illegal manipulative practices change the idea of "government by the people" from an imperfectly realized ideal to a manipulative symbol in itself.

Desirable changes are not hard to identify, though the most fundamental ones call for a drastic restructuring of our institutions and so are the least likely to be adopted. The problem plainly goes well beyond electoral institutions. It lies in the norm of rewarding those who manipulate public attitudes while real social, economic, and international problems remain unsolved. In business, in foreign policy, in domestic policy, and in parts of the burgeoning mental health movement the view has become prevalent that inducing people to accept a product, a policy, or a set of conforming attitudes, regardless of the means or the effects upon their lives and welfare, is the test of competence and of the right to power and high status. Some such tendency has always been present, but the new communications media, new techniques for psychological manipulation, and the consequent elevation of manipulation over ethics and concern for the welfare of the manipulated has created a qualitative difference, which Watergate epitomizes. If business, the CIA, and behavioral psychologists subscribe to a norm that sanctions manipulation or dirty tricks, so will the institutions of government, for they reflect prevailing norms. Only a drastic restructuring of the functions, the objectives, and the rewards of our major economic and political institutions can cure the blight.

Less fundamental but nonetheless important are changes in the character of the presidential office to make it less potent as a symbol of the public welfare, built-in benevolence, and competence to lead. To accomplish this we need some device to make removal of the President possible when he loses the confidence of the country and of Congress. Calendar elections and socialization into the belief that any President is a benevolent leader and his impeachment virtually unthinkable instil uncritical acceptance of presidential leadership into people without adequate benchmarks for evaluating him, and so encourage insulation of the President from information and from criticism. The treatment of the President in elementary school curricula might also portray him less as a symbol and more as a politician.

Some widely discussed changes in electoral processes would be helpful, though they are not likely to be effective without more drastic reforms as well. Public financing of presidential elections and the prohibition of spot announcements would be moves in the right direction. So long as business fortunes depend heavily upon public policy, some of the profits are likely to find their way into campaign activities, but public financing might inhibit the imbalance a little. Spot announcements epitomize the noninformative and manipulative uses of the media and certainly do no more to raise the quality of life than the cigarette advertising that has already been banned.

The media and the campaign decision-makers are not autonomous institutions. They reflect prevailing norms, social achievements, and social pathologies, and must be understood and evaluated in that perspective.

Richard W. Boyd

7

Electoral Trends in Postwar Politics

The actors featured in previous chapters are the political elite in America—presidential candidates, convention delegates, the congressional, presidential and state wings of the major parties, professional campaign experts, among others. This emphasis on elites is justifiable. As Ranney notes in chapter 3, the most important phase of the process of choosing the President is the nomination battle, when the alternatives facing the electorate are reduced to only two candidates who have any chance of winning. Though the American electorate has a greater voice in the nomination process than citizens in any other country,[1] the nomination decision is still strongly influenced by these political leaders.

In contrast, the general election campaign brings in millions more actors. Independents and members of the opposition party become an important part of the campaign calculus. Perhaps more importantly the participating electorate takes on a very different character. The electorate in the primaries is usually small, partisan, and politically involved. In a general election the participants increase severalfold in number and represent a more accurate cross section of the public. The perspective of this chapter is to consider the motive impulses of this

RICHARD W. BOYD *is assistant professor of government at Wesleyan University. He has written several articles on voting behavior, including "Popular Control of Government. A Normal Vote Analysis of the 1968 Election,"* (American Political Science Review, *June, 1972*), and is at work on a study of the causes and consequences of legislative role orientations.

[1] James W. Davis, *Presidential Primaries: Road to the White House* (New York: Crowell, 1967), p. 15.

larger voting public and to place the analysis of voters in the context of more general postwar political trends.

Images of Voters

We owe our images of voters in postwar politics principally to a notable series of national sample surveys, which the University of Michigan Survey Research Center has conducted in the presidential and congressional elections since 1948. These studies are now so well known and authoritative that I will refer to them, as most scholars do, simply as SRC elections surveys.

Prior to the 1964 survey, the studies presented a consistent picture of the American voter.[2]

The most important factor in voting decisions was party identification. Most voters had acquired a deep-seated allegiance to one of the parties prior to voting age, many even prior to adolescence. Partisanship tended to strengthen as they grew older, and they rarely switched their allegiance to the opposition. With individual party loyalties so strong and stable, the proportion of self-identified Republicans, Independents, and Democrats scarcely changed from election to election. Democrats consistently outnumbered the Republicans by a ratio of 3:2 and monopolized electoral victories in Congress and in the states.

In the voting booths, party loyalties and evaluations of the candidates decided people's choices. Neither was greatly influenced by opinions people might have held on major public issues. Indeed, political information and interest in public issues were fairly low, and there were few discernible differences in the beliefs of ordinary Republicans and Democrats on government policy. Though information and interest were low, people's confidence in the political system remained fairly high. Voters believed that they significantly affected the course of politics, and they had moderate faith in the integrity of elected officials. This was, of course, the reason why issues seemed unimportant to people. Issues do not become salient when people's information is low and their confidence in the elected is high. Few candidates made issues a focus of their campaigns. Typically, candidates left issues in slogan form—for example, John Kennedy's appeal to "get the country moving again."

---

2 The bibliography is too voluminous to be cited. The two most influential interpretations of the electorate of this period are Angus Campbell, Philip E. Converse, Warren E. Miller, and Donald E. Stokes, *The American Voter* (New York: Wiley, 1960), and, by the same authors, *Elections and the Political Order* (New York: Wiley, 1966).

Since the 1964 election, the electoral landscape has changed. Voters are more interested in public policies and less confident that political leaders have the capacity, or even the will, to cope with social problems. Most of these discussions of current political trends possess one of two underlying themes.

1. *One theme is that the electorate is increasingly dominated by disaffection, cynicism, and powerlessness.* Voters are disaffected because they question their own influence on elections and policy. They have also come to believe that candidates are self-interested and their methods corrupt. A notable example of this cynicism is the apparent willingness of the voters to dismiss the Watergate incidents during the '72 campaign as simply what one should expect in politics. One consequence of this disaffection is the erosion of the effectiveness of parties, both as psychological bonds for voters and as organizations efficiently pursuing election victories.

2. *The second theme* contrasts with the first. It *is that voters have become more interested and informed about issues and politics, and more willing to make personal sacrifices to campaign actively in support of preferred candidates.* Thus, their allegiances are less to parties as organizations, and more to candidates whose issue positions they share. If traditional party organizations are in disarray, this is an unlamented recognition that the strong party loyalties of the 1950s were rooted more in family ties or historical conflicts than in the knowledge of contemporary party differences.

The rub about presenting these themes as alternative perspectives on current politics is that underneath their obvious exaggerations both have a ring of truth. Certainly, there is enough evidence for each that we are faced with the puzzle of reconciling why a public that feels powerless and cynical should at the same time be interested in political issues and active on behalf of candidates they admire. First, I will discuss the evidence for each theme and then explore whether the two themes are consistent with one another.

The Theme of Voter Disaffection and Party Disarray

VOTER DISAFFECTION

1. *Feelings of Political Powerlessness*—A familiar and well-tested measure of people's sense of their influence on the federal government is the "index of political efficacy." First constructed by the Survey Research Center in 1952, the questions making up the index have been repeated in each of the SRC election surveys. Philip E. Converse has

traced popular responses to the questions and has found three of the original four to be reliable measures over time.[3] These are the items:

1. I don't think public officials care much what people like me think.
2. People like me don't have any say about what the government does.
3. Sometimes politics and government are so complicated that a person like me can't really understand what's going on.

Fig. 1.   Trends in Responses to Political Efficacy Items, 1952–1972

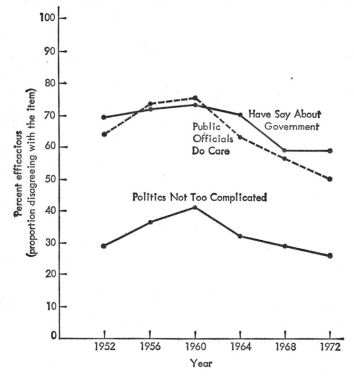

Sources: Based on a figure in Philip E. Converse, "Change in the American Electorate," in Angus Campbell and Philip E. Converse, eds., *The Human Meaning of Social Change* (New York: Russell Sage Foundation, © 1972), p. 328, and the 1972 Election Survey, Survey Research Center, The University of Michigan.

Figure 1 displays the public's responses in each election year since 1952. One need not ponder long why people have more confidence in

[3] Philip E. Converse, "Change in the American Electorate," in Angus Campbell and Philip E. Converse, eds., *The Human Meaning of Social Change* (New York: Russell Sage, 1972), pp. 328–329.

the concern of public officials than they have in their own ability to understand politics. Subtle changes in the wordings of the items could easily reverse those results. The important point is the trend in each item itself. Throughout the '50s, self-confidence in political competence rose, reaching a peak in the election year of 1960. Since then this confidence has been systematically eroded, with 1972 representing a new low on two of the three items.

Converse points out that people's confidence in their political influence has declined in the face of an important counter trend, an increasingly educated electorate. Education is related to feelings of political influence for two reasons. First, education provides personal skills that are as useful in political life as in professional life. Second, confidence in understanding and influencing political events is one of the normative values emphasized in formal education. Looking only at increasing levels of education within the American electorate, one would predict that each of the efficacy measures would have *risen* five or six percentage points between 1952 and 1968.[4] Thus, the actual decline in feelings of political efficacy becomes more striking and significant.

2. *Mistrust of Government and Leaders*—A sense of political powerlessness has been accompanied by a growing cynicism about the responsiveness of government and the integrity of its leaders. With the following series of items, the Survey Research Center has documented the intensification of mistrust. (Mistrustful responses are italicized.)

1. How much of the time do you think you can trust the government in Washington to do what is right—just about always, most of the time, or *only some of the time?*

2. Would you say the government is pretty much run by a *few big interests* looking out for themselves or that it is run for the benefit of all the people? [5]

3. Do you think that people in the government *waste a lot* of the money we pay in taxes, waste some of it or don't waste very much of it?

4. Do you feel that almost all of the people running the government are smart people who usually know what they are doing, or do you think that quite a few of them *don't seem to know what they are doing?*

5. Do you think that quite a few of the people running the government *are a little crooked,* not very many are, or do you think hardly any of them are crooked at all?

4 Ibid., p. 327.
5 In 1958 the wording of this item is different: it then read, "Do you think that the high-up people in government give everyone a fair break whether they are big shots or just ordinary people, or do you think they pay more attention to what big interests want?"

Fig. 2. *Trends in Responses to Political Cynicism Items*
1958–1972

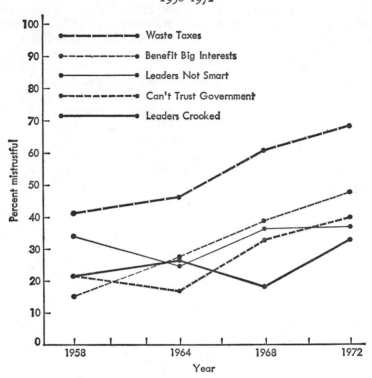

Source: Arthur H. Miller, Thad A. Brown, Alden S. Raine, "Social Conflict and Political Estrangement, 1958–1972" (paper presented at the 1973 Midwest Political Science Association Meetings, Chicago, May 3–5), p. 7.

As the work of Arthur H. Miller shows (figure 2), mistrust in our federal government and its leaders has increased significantly since 1960. That mistrust peaked in 1972 is all the more significant because these questions were asked before Watergate became an important issue in the public's mind. This did not occur until the spring of 1973, when the Ervin Committee began its hearings and President Nixon acknowledged the possible complicity of White House and campaign officials in the scandal.

The depth of the public's mistrust is evident in almost any question one asks about the integrity of officials, the quality of our institutions, or the influence of our citizens. Miller's analysis shows a similar growth of cynicism in regard to feelings about the responsiveness of congressmen, the importance of elections, and the contributions of political parties.

3. *Faith in the Nation's Achievements*—A third example of public disaffection is the declining faith in the nation's achievements. Revealing evidence of this trend is the "self-anchoring striving scale," developed by Hadley Cantril and Lloyd A. Free in a series of studies in eighteen countries between 1958 and 1964.[6] The ingenuity of the technique is that each person evaluates the nation's achievements in relation to his own hopes and fears for it. Each person is first asked to describe "the best possible situation for our country," followed by "the worst." He is then shown a ladder, with the explanation that the tenth or top rung represents the ideal state of the nation as he has just defined it and that the bottom rung represents the worst. Having judged his own aspirations and fears for the nation, he then indicates where the nation stands on the ladder at present, where he believes it stood five years ago, and where he expects it to stand five years in the future. A person thus anchors his evaluations to his own expectations of the nation's achievements.

Typically, people are optimistic about a nation's future. They judge the present better than the past and expect the future to be better still. In the many countries in which the self-anchoring ladder technique has been used, only once (the Philippines in 1959) did a nation judge its present condition to be worse than it had been five years before. There is now a second exception, the United States in 1971.[7]

Figure 3 presents another perspective on these ladder ratings of national achievements. Americans evaluated the nation five times between 1959 and 1972. The trend is clear. The nation falls lower and lower in relation to people's expressed aspirations. The same is true with people's retrospective evaluation of the nation's past, and their expectations for the future are similarly pessimistic. This catalogue of national disappointment is not simply a reflection of the negative evaluations of disgruntled groups in the population such as the young and the blacks. Among nearly all occupational, racial, income, and age groups, the gap is widening between Americans' best hopes for the nation and their sense of its actual achievements.

4. *Declining Voter Turnout*—For harder evidence of voter disaffection, one only needs to look at the pattern of turnout in recent presi-

[6] Albert H. Cantril and Charles W. Roll, Jr., *Hopes and Fears of the American People* (New York: Universe Books, 1971), pp. 15ff.

[7] Ibid., pp. 25–26. In a 1972 survey, Americans again rated the present worse than the past, but in this case the difference was not large enough to be statistically significant. See William Watts and Lloyd A. Free, *State of the Nation* (New York: Universe Books, 1973), pp. 27–28.

Fig. 3.   Trends in People's Judgments of the Nation's Past, Present, and Future, as Measured by Self-Anchoring Scales

1954–1977.

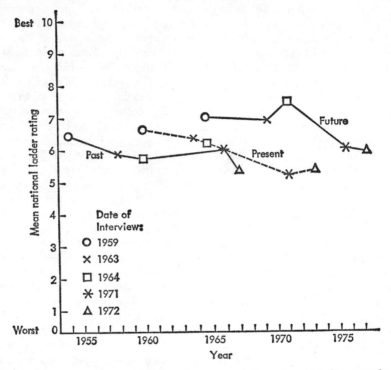

Judgments of the past and the future are recorded on the chart five years backward and forward from the actual date of the interview. E.g., the first set of interviews took place in 1959. Thus, the first judgment of the past is recorded for 1954, and the first projection of the future is recorded for 1964.

Sources: Based on tables by William Watts and Lloyd A. Free, *State of the Nation* (New York: Universe Books, 1973), p. 304; Albert H. Cantril and Charles W. Roll, Jr., *Hopes and Fears of the American People* (New York: Universe Books, 1971), p. 26; Lloyd A. Free and Hadley Cantril, *The Political Beliefs of Americans* (New York: Simon and Schuster, 1968), p. 231; and Hadley Cantril, *The Pattern of Human Concerns* (New Brunswick: Rutgers University Press, 1965), p. 43.

dential elections. From 1920 to 1960, the proportion of the electorate going to the polls steadily increased, from 43.4 percent in 1920 to 63.1 percent in 1960.

After 1960, however, turnout begins an uninterrupted decline. In 1972 only 55.6 percent of the electorate voted, the second smallest turnout since 1932. Quite literally, the decline represents millions of potential votes lost to the candidates. If the 1972 electorate had simply gone to the polls at the 1968 rate of 60.7 percent, over seven million additional people would have voted.

It is tempting to explain away the 1972 decline by noting that eighteen-year-olds were eligible to vote for the first time in 1972. It must have been, one might argue, the typically low turnout of young voters rather than general voter disaffection that caused the five percentage point decline in 1972. This is simply not the case. The newly enfranchised eighteen-to-twenty age group represented only 8 percent of the eligible electorate in 1972, and the turnout rate of these new voters was only fifteen percentage points less than the national average.[8] At most, the eighteen-year-old vote accounted for less than two percentage points of the decline from 1968 to 1972.

One might suggest other legal explanations for the decline of turnout since 1960. The Twenty-fourth Amendment (ratified in 1964) abolished the poll tax for federal elections. The Voting Rights Act of 1965 suspended the use of literacy tests in states and counties where fewer than 50 percent of the voting age residents were registered to vote or actually voted in the 1964 election. The Voting Rights Amendments of 1970, in addition to lowering the voting age to eighteen, abolished residency requirements over 30 days (which enfranchised about ten million citizens in 1972) and suspended literacy tests in all states for five years (enfranchising one million new voters). Such changes have greatly expanded the eligible electorate, but they have enfranchised those who are least likely to vote—the very poor, the illiterate, the mobile, the young. By this argument a decline in the *percentage* of voters was to be expected simply because of these legal changes in registration laws.

On closer analysis, these amendments and statutes also fail to explain the decline in turnout since 1960. The reason lies in the crudeness of United States voting statistics. These statistics nearly always state the eligible electorate as the total number of residents of voting age, rather than the number who are legally eligible to vote. As we have just seen millions of residents were legally barred from voting until the above limitations were removed. Thus, prior to these acts, the real turnout rate was actually higher than official statistics show, and the decline in turnout since 1969 has even been greater than the official statistics imply.[9] We are thrown back to the original suggestion. Millions of people

8 Bureau of the Census, "Voter Participation in November 1972," *Current Population Reports*, Series P-20, No. 224 (December, 1972), p. 1.

9 Official figures continue to count as nonvoters millions of residents who are legally barred from registering. The largest remaining categories are aliens and

are staying away from the polls because they see little to be gained from participation.

The suggestion that disaffection is the cause of low turnout has an undeniable plausibility. The 1952 SRC election survey first established that people who feel politically powerless do not usually vote.[10] (The items are those in figure 1.) Numerous studies since then have given this finding a status about as close to a law as any generalization in social science. Thus, the explanation remains persuasive that feelings of political powerlessness have contributed to high ratios of vote abstention.

PARTY DISARRAY

1. *Weakening of Voters' Long-term Party Ties*—It is often argued that a major consequence of voter disaffection is the enfeebling of long-term party allegiances. Until recently most voters identified with the same party for most of their adult life and only infrequently cast votes for opposition candidates. Now, voters are increasingly detached from these loyalties. The proportion of the electorate who call themselves Independents is rapidly growing. In the 1972 SRC election survey, Independents outnumber Republicans. Among voters under 30, Independents outnumber both parties together. The old pattern of party loyalties may reestablish itself in time, but there is no such evidence at present.

Those who still identify themselves as party members now vote for opposition candidates with alacrity. The fate of McGovern in '72 is perhaps the most striking example; 44 percent of the Democrats voted against him. This trend is quite general. Converse has accumulated reported votes in the SRC samples for all congressional, senatorial,

---

inmates of correctional and mental institutions. Excluding just these residents from the eligible list, plus those who then failed to meet residency requirements, the Bureau of the Census raised the extimated turnout in 1964 from 62.1 to 67.0 percent. (Bureau of the Census, "Estimates of the Population of Voting Age, for States: November 1, 1968," *Current Population Reports*, Series P-25, No. 406, October 4, 1968, p. 6.) If one also excludes from the eligible electorate persons who face other legal barriers to voting (e.g., many states bar persons who have ever been convicted of serious crimes) and those who face substantial obstacles to voting (e.g., members of the armed forces, the hospitalized, the institutionalized aged, and persons who must vote absentee), the turnout rate is actually higher still. At whatever level one estimates the *absolute* rate, however, the downward trend in turnout remains. (See Meyer Zitter and Donald E. Starsinic, "Estimates of 'Eligible' Voters in Small Areas: Some First Approximations," *American Statistical Association: Proceedings of the Social Statistics Section,* 1966, pp. 368–378.)

[10] Angus Campbell, Gerald Gurin, Warren E. Miller, *The Voter Decides* (Evanston, Ill.: Row, Peterson, 1954), pp. 187–193.

gubernatorial, and presidential offices since 1952, and his analysis shows
a significant decline of party fidelity in the late '60s.[11]

Fig. 4. *Trends in Split Ticket Voting for President and Congressmen*
1920–1972

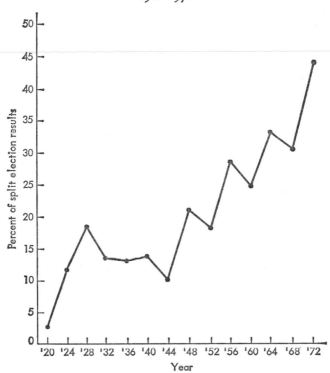

The figure is the percentage of congressional districts carried by presidential and
congressional candidates of different parties in each election year.

Sources: For 1920–1964, Milton C. Cummings, Jr., *Congressmen and the Electorate*
(New York: Free Press, 1966), p. 32. For 1968, Walter DeVries and V. Lance Tar-
rance, Jr., *The Ticket-Splitter* (Grand Rapids: Eerdmans, 1972), p. 30. For 1972,
the data are provided by Pierre M. Purves, director of statistical research, National
Republican Congressional Committee, Washington, D.C., and by Michael Barone,
Washington, D.C.

A result of this decline in party loyalty is a major increase in ticket-
splitting. Figure 4 documents historical highs in recent years in the
percentage of congressional districts carried by presidential and con-

11 Converse, "Change in the American Electorate," p. 321.

gressional candidates of opposite parties. Projecting the present increase into the future, straight-ticket voters may have to petition for public protection.

2. *The Staying Power of Incumbents*—In general ticket-splitting has favored the incumbents. This is particularly true in postwar elections to the House of Representatives, where over 75 percent of the 435 House seats are generally regarded as safe seats.[12] Indeed, even if we combine the mortality rate in primaries and general elections, 90 percent of incumbent congressmen are regularly reelected.[13]

Incumbent senators are only slightly more vulnerable than congressmen. They won 80 percent of their reelection bids from 1946 to 1970. An analysis of Senate elections from 1966–1970 shows that incumbency was worth 12 percent of the two-party vote for the average senator seeking reelection.[14] As seats have become more safe for the incumbent, they have become less safe for the party. Oftentimes, a retiring incumbent is replaced by a candidate from the opposite party, who then enjoys a similarly long tenure.

Finally, one of the safest incumbents is the President himself. Since the Civil War only Cleveland, Taft, and Hoover have lost reelection bids. Each was defeated in the most exceptional of circumstances. Cleveland won the popular vote but lost in the Electoral College; Taft was victimized by the split of his party that yielded the Progressive candidacy of Theodore Roosevelt; and Hoover stands as a constant reminder to the elected that depressions are depressing. We can safely conclude that had McGovern run the most astute of campaigns, he would probably have succeeded only in losing less badly.

3. *Withering of the Surge-Decline Cycle*—An important consequence of the strength of incumbency is the withering of the surge-decline cycle connecting presidential and congressional elections.

The surge-decline cycle is a gain in seats in Congress by the party capturing the Presidency, followed by that party's loss of seats in the succeeding off-year, congressional election. The regularity of this sequence is impressive. Only four times in this century—1908, 1916,

---

12 H. Douglas Price, "The Electoral Arena," in The American Assembly (David B. Truman, ed.), *The Congress and America's Future* (second ed.; Englewood Cliffs: Prentice-Hall, 1973), p. 50.

13 Charles O. Jones, *Every Second Year* (Washington, D.C.: Brookings Institution, 1967), p. 68. See also Barbara Hinckley, *Stability and Change in Congress* (New York: Harper & Row, 1971), Ch. 2.

14 Warren Lee Kostroski, "Form and Substance in Theory Construction: Electoral Behavior in Postwar Senate Elections" (paper presented at the 1972 American Political Science Association Meetings, Washington, D.C., Sept. 5–9), p. 11.

1956, and 1960—has the party winning the Presidency failed to gain seats in the following off-year elections. Only once, in 1934, did the presidential party not lose seats in the following off-year.

Angus Campbell has explained this regularity by noting the different character of the electorate in presidential and congressional elections.[15] In a presidential year, the relative excitement of the election brings voters to the polls who do not ordinarily turn out in off-year elections. Campbell calls those who vote only in presidential elections "peripheral voters," in contrast to the "core voters" who turn out in congressional and presidential elections alike. Fewer of the peripheral voters have long-term party loyalties than do the more highly committed core voters. Lacking long-term party loyalties, most of these peripheral voters cast ballots for the presidential winner, who has been blessed by the short-term events in the campaign years. Enough of them cast straight tickets that a number of congressmen in competitive districts are elected who would not have won without the participation of these less partisan, peripheral voters. The result is a surge of congressional seats won by the party capturing the Presidency. In the following off-year election, the less interested peripheral voters stay home, and the congressmen elected in the presidential year surge must struggle for reelection without them. The presidential party thus suffers the off-year loss of the congressmen elected on the wave of the presidential year surge. This explains why a President nearly always enjoys a more sympathetic Congress after a presidential election than after an off-year election. His party is numerically larger, and it contains a number of congressmen who feel they owe their election to his drawing power.

Now, however, the surge-decline cycle is breaking down. Because incumbents are more secure in their seats, the congressional races have become increasingly insulated from the presidential contest.[16] Fewer seats are gained in the presidential year; fewer are lost in the following off-year. The evidence is in figure 5, which details the average gains or losses by the Democratic party in the House of Representatives by decade. In the five elections of the 1930s, for example, the average Democratic gain or loss was over 48 seats. In recent elections the surge-de-

[15] Angus Campbell, "Surge and Decline: A Study of Electoral Change," in Angus Campbell, *Elections and the Political Order*, Ch. 3.

[16] This insulation of congressional races from the presidential contest is closely related to the process Nelson W. Polsby has described as the "institutionalization of the House of Representatives." See in particular his evidence on the differentiation of the House from other organizations, the stabilization of its membership, and the growth of careers specialized to House leadership. (Nelson W. Polsby, "The Institutionalization of the U.S. House of Representatives," *American Political Science Review*, 62, March, 1968, pp. 114–168.)

Fig. 5.   *Trends in the Average Seat Swing in the House of Representatives*
       by Decade

1900–1972

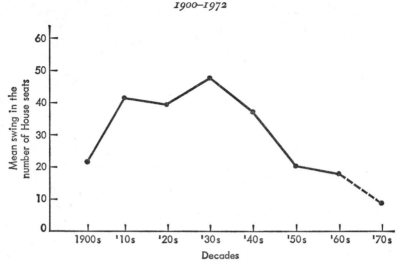

The figure is a plot of the mean number of Democratic seats gained or lost in the House of Representatives in the five elections each decade. The figure for the '70s is for 1970 and 1972.

Source: Based on a table by Robert A. Diamond, ed., *Politics in America* (Ed. IV; Washington, D.C.: Congressional Quarterly, n.d.)

cline pattern is much less important. In 1968 Nixon gained only 4 seats in the House. In 1970 he lost only 12. In 1972 he gained back only 11, leaving the composition of the House almost unchanged in partisan strength across three elections, including Nixon's landslide victory in '72.

INFERENCES

If we pause to consider the theme we have just discussed—the disaffection of voters, the increase in ticket-splitting, the security of incumbents, and the insulation of the presidential from the congressional races—we are led to three conclusions.

Landslide presidential victories will be commonplace.

Four of the six elections since 1952 have been of landslide proportions. Eisenhower polled 55 percent of the vote in '52 and 57 percent in '56. Johnson and Nixon both captured over 60 percent of the vote in '64 and '72. This trend toward landslide victories has two causes. One is the loosening of long-term party ties. Not bound by stable partisan loyalties, voters are responding to the short-term events and issues of the campaign year. When these short-term factors uniformly favor one of the candidates, he will likely swamp his opponent. A second cause is the nationalization of electoral politics.[17] Before World War II both parties had their bastions, which they could expect to hold even in the face of national tides against them. Now, electoral swings are increasingly uniform across the nation. To underline the historical contrast, with a popular vote share similar to Nixon's in '72, Harding in 1920 lost eleven states. In 1952, Ike lost nine; in '56, only six. Johnson lost only six in 1964, and Nixon, of course, failed only in Massachusetts and the District of Columbia in '72. Typically, the battle of the electoral college is now a massacre.

It is increasingly likely that the Presidency and the Congress will be controlled by different parties.

In the postwar period, the Republican party has controlled Congress only four years, from 1946–48 and from 1952–54. In view of the electoral security of congressional incumbents, this pattern is not likely to change. Yet, a Republican President has governed more than half of the postwar years. One can sometimes find solace in the divided control of the government, but what it has most often meant is that there is neither control of the President in foreign affairs or effective policy in domestic affairs.

Federal elective offices have become more insulated from public moods.

If we ponder the forces that lead governments to be responsive to public opinion, we would surely conclude that responsiveness is encouraged if people feel they can affect the system, if candidates believe their own electoral fortunes are linked to those of other elected leaders, and if incumbents feel electorally vulnerable. As we have seen, the political trends in the '60s and '70s have tended to undercut all of these conditions. First, an increasing number of people feel they have little impact on politics, and they resent their leaders as a consequence. Second, candidates for President and for Congress have good reason to doubt that their electoral fortunes are closely linked. The emphasis on personalistic rather than party campaigns is the new wave, encouraged by the growth of ticket-splitting. Divided control of the federal government has become accepted as a quite ordinary state of affairs. Third, the incumbent who feels electorally vulnerable today should, by any objective criteria, be the exception. If congressmen work their districts as much as they appear to, it is probably because most con-

17 Graham K. Wilson and Philip M. Williams, "Mr. Nixon's Triumph," *Parliamentary Affairs,* 26 (Spring, 1973), p. 197.

gressmen see their office as a life career. When one's career is at stake, even small dangers loom important. The fact remains that postwar electoral trends have created the pattern in which the potential for conflict and stalemate between the President and Congress is high and in which neither enjoys the confidence of the public. If this is the new politics, we might find new virtues in the old.

4. *Conclusion*—We have now followed this first theme to its pessimistic end. There is little doubt that the theme is accurate in its details. Turnout has declined. Elections to Congress have become more insulated from the presidential race. The increase of ticket-splitting, along with many other indicators, does show that the level of allegiance to political parties has fallen. To the degree that we adequately measure attitudes toward politics with public opinion polls, the evidence is clearly that people feel less politically potent than they did in the recent past and that they mistrust public officials as well.

Many will disagree, however, that the most appropriate evidence has been presented and will deny the explanation that connects voter disaffection with party disarray. For example, they will point to other evidence that voters are not disaffected from politics, such as the large numbers of volunteers that have sustained the ideological candidacies of Goldwater, Wallace, McCarthy, and McGovern. They will also deny that the disarray in the party system can be blamed on an electorate that avoids political activity and commitment. They would argue, rather, that the parties have failed the voters, failed to present clear choices of issues and attractive candidates, and failed to provide means for interested citizens to participate actively in party affairs. Such voters have not left politics. They have just left the establishment party candidates in favor of maverick challenges by issue candidates on the right and the left.

The Theme of a More Informed and Activist Electorate

There is an impressive body of evidence that the present electorate is more ideological and activist than its counterpart of the '50s. Issues, in contrast to party loyalties and candidate preferences, have a more central role in people's beliefs and behavior. In addition, citizens are increasingly active in political campaigns. The SRC election surveys provide extensive data on these points.

THE CENTRAL ROLE OF ISSUES IN POLITICAL BELIEFS

1. *Consistency in People's Issue Beliefs*—One of the major myths deflated by the election surveys of the '50s was that people's attitudes

on specific issues conform to more general patterns of liberal and conservative beliefs. Contrary to the commonplace use of such labels by academics and journalists alike, relatively few Americans were consistently liberal or conservative across a range of beliefs such as civil rights, civil liberties, social welfare, and anticommunism. People with liberal attitudes on one topic were as likely as not to hold conservative beliefs about others, and few people seemed to have sets of political beliefs organized around abstract ideologies regarding the proper role of the state in social and economic affairs.

As is the perverse tendency in scholarly matters, just as the revisionist position became the conventional wisdom, new studies began to support the old "myth." For example, using the SRC election surveys of 1952 through 1968, Norman H. Nie analyzed patterns of beliefs regarding the role of the federal government in five important areas: general social welfare, welfare measures specifically for blacks, the size of the federal government, racial integration in public schools, and the cold war. Nie's analysis of studies before 1964 confirmed that patterns of beliefs were not then consistent across the population, and that a person's attitudes on one issue could not be predicted from knowledge of his position on another. But the election of 1964 proved to be a major turning point. In both the 1964 and 1968 elections, Nie found that voters held consistent political beliefs, strikingly so.[18]

In all likelihood, people are now more consistent in their political attitudes as a response to the events of the 1960s. Protests over racial discrimination and the Vietnam war made many Americans rethink positions on race and military issues. Beginning with Goldwater a series of candidates staked campaigns on popular reactions to issue-based appeals. Whatever judgments one makes about the success of these campaigns (though Goldwater, Wallace, and McGovern failed to win the Presidency, clearly ideological appeals were necessary to their nominations), their programs served to crystallize beliefs across a range of issues among supporters and opponents alike.

2. *Issue Beliefs and Partisan Loyalties*—A second aspect of the new importance of issues in political behavior is the changing relationship of issues to party loyalties. Studies of elections of the '50s viewed party loyalties in a rather anomalous light. Most people developed partisan

18 Norman H. Nie, "Mass Belief Systems Revisited: Political Change and Attitude Structure," *The Journal of Politics,* 36 (August, 1974). Miller, et al., confirm the continued consistency of political beliefs in the 1972 election survey. (Arthur H. Miller, Warren E. Miller, Thad A. Brown, and Alden S. Raine, "A Majority Party in Disarray: Social and Political Conflict in the 1972 Election," paper presented at the 1973 American Political Science Association Meetings, New Orleans, Sept. 4–8.)

allegiances prior to voting age, and most maintained that allegiance all their lives. Moreover, on the best evidence party loyalties were the most important factor in voting choices, strongly influencing judgments of the merits of candidates.

Yet, in spite of the influence of partisan attachments on vote decisions, these same studies usually failed to find any consistent relationship between party loyalties and policy beliefs. Except for a few bread and butter issues such as labor-management conflict, the average Democrat of the '50s was not more liberal on any given issue than the average Republican. Only among political activists, such as congressmen or convention delegates, were Democrats consistently more liberal than Republicans.

Since 1964, however, Republicans and Democrats in the electorate have become increasingly polarized on a series of important issues. Figure 6 presents the relationship of people's party identification and their policy beliefs on the proper role of the federal government on four representative issues: publicly financed medical care programs, forced school integration, federal job guarantees, and federal aid to public education. On all four issues the average Democrat in 1968 is substantially more liberal than the average Republican. Taking federal medical care programs as an example, the principle is supported by over 81 percent of Strong Democrats. In contrast, only 43 percent of Strong Republicans supported the principle, a difference of almost 2:1.

The most significant change in issue differences since the '50s is the newly partisan character of racial attitudes. Before 1964 there was little difference between Republicans and Democrats in their support of civil rights legislation. Goldwater's Southern strategy changed that, linking the Republican party to the conservative position on federal civil rights legislation. Despite stereotypes of the racially prejudiced, blue-collar Democrat, the average Democrat in both the North and the South is more liberal on race attitudes than his Republican counterpart. Figure 6 presents supporting evidence on the issue of school integration. The same is true for a range of other race and civil rights beliefs as well.[19]

3. *Issue Beliefs and Voting Decisions*—A third aspect of the changing importance of issues is that policy beliefs are now more highly related to people's voting choices than in the '50s. Then, people cast votes on the basis of their evaluations of the candidates and/or their long-term party attachments, but rarely on the basis of major controversies over public policy. Generalizing from the elections of the '50s,

[19] Richard W. Boyd, "Popular Control of Public Policy: A Normal Vote Analysis of the 1968 Election," *American Political Science Review*, 66 (June, 1972), p. 435.

Fig. 6. Party Identification and Policy Beliefs

1968

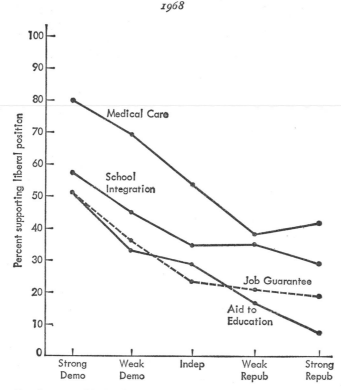

Source: Based on a table by Gerald M. Pomper, "From Confusion to Clarity: Issues and American Voters, 1956–1968," *American Political Science Review,* 66 (June, 1972), p. 417.

voting studies commonly assert that knowledge of a person's party identification is the most accurate predictor of his vote.

Despite its currency, the generalization is no longer valid. Nie has systematically compared the relative ability of issues and party identification to predict votes from the elections of 1956 through 1968.[20] In '56 and '60 a person's party identification proved to be three to four times better in predicting his vote than his issue beliefs. In both '64 and '68, however, the relationship is reversed. *Issue stands are now a significantly more accurate predictor of votes than party identification.*

20 Nie, "Mass Belief Systems Revisited . . . ," pp. 40–41.

Goldwater's ideological challenge to the country set the tone for the issue-based campaigns of '64, '68, and '72. In 1964, the power of the federal government, medicare, racial segregation, the government's handling of foreign affairs, and the Vietnam policy—all were significantly related to voters' preferences between Goldwater and Johnson.[21] In 1968 these same issues continued to be important, each reinforcing Humphrey's major burden, the disposition of the electorate to vote against him if they thought poorly of Johnson's performance as President.[22] In 1972 the Vietnam war and the familiar social and economic controversies remained important voting issues, and a new category of cultural or lifestyle issues (equal rights for women, abortion, legalization of marijuana) cleaved the existing voting coalitions. That the public should have identified a man of such conventional background and values as McGovern's with strong support for these lifestyle issues is one of the many ironies of this election. Nonetheless, these and related issues clearly distinguished McGovern's supporters from his opponents in both the primaries and the general election.[23]

In sum we have noted three trends toward a greater importance of issues in the '60s and '70s. (1) There is more consistency, liberal or conservative, in people's attitudes. (2) For the declining number of people who identify with one of the parties, issue stands are more highly related to partisan allegiances. (3) Issues more strongly influence voting decisions.

These trends are not always complementary. As issues proliferate, it becomes increasingly likely that policy disagreements will emerge within party coalitions. Despite the tendency of voters to be consistent in their beliefs, persons attracted to the Democratic party on one issue will incline toward the Republican or a third-party candidate on another. The strains within the Democratic party are greatest between those who support the party on the basis of social welfare and labor issues and those who want the party to pursue new goals on foreign policy, race, and lifestyle issues.

This disagreement on policy goals within the Democratic party is at the crux of the debate on whether the party system is presently in the process of a major realignment. In terms of presidential elections, that realignment is a present fact. The deep South has left the Democratic party in presidential politics. Not a single deep South state has voted

[21] John H. Kessel, *The Goldwater Coalition: Republican Strategies in 1964* (Indianapolis: Bobbs-Merrill, 1968), ch. 9.

[22] Boyd, "Popular Control of Public Policy . . . ," pp. 429–441.

[23] Miller, "The Majority Party in Disarray . . . ," and Peter B. Natchez, "The Unlikely Landslide: Issues and Voters in the 1972 Election" (paper presented at the 1973 New England Political Science Association Meetings, Boston, April 27–28).

Democratic since 1960, and it is difficult to project a Democratic candidate who is both acceptable to the northern, reformist wing of the party and who could also carry the South against a moderate Republican or a third-party candidate such as Wallace. Without the South as a solid sectional base for the Democratic party, the party will continue to run a high risk of defeat in each presidential contest, maintaining the postwar pattern of Republican Presidents and Democratic congresses.

The pivotal role of the '64 election in this realignment of presidential politics suggests an interesting comparison between the elections of 1928 and 1968. In 1928 the majority Republican party continued its dominance with Hoover's landslide victory over Al Smith. Yet, the foundation of what was to become the Democratic majority of the '30s was already set in the defeat of '28. As Key has demonstrated, the working-class, industrial communities of the Northeast began their shift to the Democratic party in 1928.[24] Moreover, Smith's Catholic candidacy, as unsuccessful at that time as Goldwater's nomination appeared later, established the ethnic character for the coalition that was to become the Democratic majority.

Similarly, Goldwater's defeat in 1964 seemed at the time no more than an aberrant footnote to history, a reminder that ideological politics is losing politics. But certain issues Goldwater raised, most fundamentally his opposition to federal civil rights and social welfare programs for blacks and his attack on liberal assumptions about urban crime and disorder, struck a sympathetic cord with a great many voters. Recognizing this, Nixon made these themes the basis of his subsequent victories in '68 and '72. Goldwater's nomination was not essential to the Republican victories that followed, but he raised controversial issues and identified the Republican party with what is surely the present majority position in the country on race, crime, and welfare. It is in this sense that the 1928 and the 1964 are both critical elections. Each involved the initial defeat of election strategies that subsequently proved the foundation for realignments of historical voting patterns.

CITIZEN PARTICIPATION IN POLITICAL CAMPAIGNS

As we have seen the '60s and '70s have witnessed a trend in which people's beliefs are more internally consistent and more related to their party attachments and voting choices. The consistency of people's beliefs and the accuracy with which they can identify candidates' posi-

24 V. O. Key, Jr., "A Theory of Critical Elections," *Journal of Politics,* 17 (Feb., 1955), pp. 3–18.

tions on issues suggest a public that is both attentive and informed about politics. While people may be disaffected from the parties, they are not disinterested in politics generally. Hundreds of thousands have contributed both time and money to their favored candidates. In fact, the proportion of citizens actively involved in campaigns is probably higher than at any previous time in American history, though we lack the hard data to be certain. These volunteer efforts have changed the character of fund-raising and grass roots organization.

1. *Campaign Contributions*—If modern campaigns are notable for integrating grass roots participation with computer-based fund-raising, market research, and mass communications techniques, Goldwater ran the first of the modern campaigns. As is usual in American politics, the party out of office had the incentive to adopt new strategies. Throughout the '60s, Democratic presidential candidates raised money in the old style, depending predominately on contributions from labor unions and a small number of large contributors. Kennedy, Johnson, and Humphrey all relied on versions of a President's club, the price of entry being a thousand dollars.[25] Such a scheme only works for winners. The Republican party and Goldwater exploited the potential of a systematic appeal to small givers instead, utilizing direct mail solicitation.

The Republican emphasis on soliciting contributions from a large number of small givers began in 1962, when the party inaugurated the first successful drive for small contributions in American politics.[26] Expanding the program in 1964, the party raised $5.7 million from 410,000 individual responses to its direct mail campaign.[27] To underline the contrast with Democratic fund raising in 1964, only 28 percent of the total individual contributions to the Republican campaign came from donations larger than $500, compared to 69 percent of Johnson's total.[28] In 1968 the Republican direct mail campaign was even more successful, raising $6.6 million from 450,000 contributors.[29] Even these figures, however, are dwarfed by the Republican small gifts campaign of 1972. The Republican National Committee and the Nixon reelection committee together persuaded at least 500,000 to contribute more than $13 million through direct mail appeals.[30]

25 Herbert E. Alexander, *Financing the 1968 Election* (Lexington: Heath, 1971), pp. 151–152.

26 Kessel, *The Goldwater Coalition* . . . , p. 147.

27 Herbert E. Alexander, *Financing the 1964 Election* (Princeton: Citizens Research Foundation, 1966), p. 70.

28 Ibid., p. 84.

29 Alexander, *Financing the 1968 Election*, p. 147.

30 The Republican figures for 1972 and the 1972 Democratic totals below are preliminary estimates, kindly provided by Herbert E. Alexander of the Citzens Research Foundation in a personal communication, October 5, 1973.

Nixon's success among small givers proves that it is not just the ideological candidate of the left or right who can profit from small gifts campaigns. However, the success of McCarthy, Wallace, and McGovern in persuading hundreds of thousands to contribute money to their campaigns suggests the special advantage of candidates who stimulate loyal personal followings through issue-based appeals. In 1968 McCarthy spent about $11 million in his quest for the nomination, most of which came from a large number of small givers, aided, to be sure, by a small number of large givers.[31] Until superseded by the McGovern effort in '72, Wallace's '68 campaign was unprecedented in grass roots fundraising. Conservatively, 750,000 people contributed over $6 million to the Wallace campaign with over 80 percent of the contributions being less than $100.[32]

In '72 the McGovern campaign eclipsed all previous successes among small givers. His direct mail campaign helped raise more than $15 million from small gifts. An estimated 530,000 contributed to the campaign. McGovern did not lose the '72 election for want of funds. His expenditures more than doubled those of Humphrey in '68.

In short, despite the recent attention paid to the sugar daddies of both the Nixon and the McGovern campaigns, the more important trend in fund-raising is the increasing courtship of small contributors. The success of grass roots responses to direct mail appeals does not evoke an image of an electorate so cynical that it does not believe it makes a difference who wins. Though the number of contributors to a presidential campaign is a small proportion of the electorate, the raw numbers of those willing to support political convictions with money is impressive. It is particularly so when we also take note of the number of volunteers who donate their time as well as their money to the modern campaign.

2. *Volunteer Work in Campaigns*—There are no hard data on trends in volunteer work in political campaigns. In the 1972 SRC election survey, 5 percent of the persons interviewed said that they "worked for one of the parties or candidates." However, the question does not specify either the political office or the type of work, so we are thrown back on impressionistic judgments about campaign activity in the 1960s and 1970s.

Each of the recent campaigns has relied significantly on volunteer work. In 1964 Goldwater coordinated a large voter canvass program around a vote quota system for each of 185,000 precincts across the country. At least 3.4 million voters were contacted by his workers, an

31 Alexander, *Financing the 1968 Election*, pp. 43–44.
32 Ibid., p. 159.

effort which, when integrated with an election day get-out-the-vote drive, added substantially to the Goldwater vote.[33]

More familiar are the grass roots canvassing efforts of the McCarthy and the McGovern campaigns. Because both were relatively unknown when they announced for office, their canvasses were designed to introduce their names and programs to the voters. A second purpose was to exploit the low turnout that typifies primary elections. When turnout is low, great dividends accrue to a candidate who can get his own supporters to the polls. Their canvasses, plus election day mobilization work, proved particularly effective in many primaries.

Finally we should not overlook the Wallace campaign of '68. The drive that successfully placed his name on the ballots of all 50 states required a nationwide organizational effort, relying primarily on volunteers. Some states had minimal requisites to appear on the ballot. At the other extreme California law demanded that 66,059 residents formally register as members of Wallace's American Independent Party. In all states more than 1.6 million signatures were legally filed, and many more than this were collected. One set of observers judged the Wallace ballot drive "perhaps the most remarkable triumph of participatory democracy at the grass roots in the campaign of 1968, not excluding the McCarthy campaign." [34]

If we reflect on the total number of volunteers who have contributed time and money to the campaigns of issue candidates—Goldwater, McCarthy, Wallace, and McGovern—we surely must question assertions that voters are so disaffected from politics that they refuse to make sacrifices for their political beliefs. Moreover, not only the maverick challengers attract volunteers. We do not know how many people worked in the Nixon campaigns of '68 and '72, but the number is probably as great as for any of the more issue-based candidates. In short, across the spectrum, left to right, there remains a large number of canvassers and contributors who are quite literally voting with their feet and their checkbooks for their preferred candidates. Their commitment to politics is sufficiently great that many candidates have the resources to compete for presidential nominations.

Conclusion

There remains a certain inconsistency between the two major themes about trends in postwar politics. The first emphasizes that the electorate is politically disaffected—distrustful of the integrity and

[33] Kessel, *The Goldwater Coalition* . . . , pp. 162, 167–169, and 286–289.

[34] Lewis Chester, Godfrey Hodgson, and Bruce Page, *An American Melodrama: The Presidential Campaign of 1968* (New York: Viking Press, 1969), p. 284.

ability of government officials and pessimistic about its influence on the course of government policy. These trends in beliefs are supported by the harder evidence of voting patterns: during the '6os, turnout declined, as did fidelity to the parties with which people identify.

In contrast, the second theme argues that the public has become more issue-oriented in its voting decisions and more willing to contribute time and money to campaigns.

The two themes do not directly contradict one another. Though politically active voters have usually been partisan voters, it is not surprising that people who are highly interested in political issues are now quite willing to vote against their parties' candidates. It is plausible as well that a public highly concerned with certain issues could become politically disaffected. Nonetheless, the two themes do evoke inconsistent images of the public. If turnout has declined, why has participation in campaigns appeared to have increased? If people are cynical about politicians, how can candidates as different as Nixon and McGovern both draw great numbers of volunteer workers to their campaigns? We will conclude with some observations, if not definitive answers, on reconciling the two themes.

I have spoken of general movements within an undifferentiated public: growing issue awareness and campaign activity, yet growing disaffection. But these two trends may occur among very different groups in the population. Studies of people who say they participate in campaigns nearly always conclude that activists have a high sense of political competence, are informed about politics, and feel a civic duty to participate.[35] Such characteristics are not ones we usually associate with people who are cynical about the political system or its leaders.

Yet, accepting this explanation that the activists of recent campaigns may not be politically disaffected requires at least three critical leaps of faith. One, it assumes that people who report in national surveys that they participate in campaigns accurately represent the true population of campaign activists, and we know, quite the contrary, that many people exaggerate their political activity in such interviews. Two, the explanation assumes that political knowledge and feelings of political efficacy and civic duty go hand in hand with trust in the political system, when in fact the correlation is fairly weak. Three, and most importantly, the explanation assumes that our research on campaign activists of the '5os and early '6os equally applies to activists of '68 and '72. This seems most implausible. The maverick candidacies of McGovern, McCarthy, and Wallace all emphasized the theme that

35 Sidney Verba and Norman H. Nie, *Participation in America* (New York: Harper & Row, 1972), pp. 91–93, and Lester W. Milbrath, *Political Participation* (Chicago: Rand McNally, 1965), pp. 56–62.

government leaders had violated their public trust by pursuing policies on Vietnam and on race that the average American opposed. Surely
it is likely that the volunteers who peopled these campaigns shared
their candidates' disaffection with public officials. The activists of '68
and '72 may have ranked high in political skills and felt political competence, but they likely also ranked among those who were highly
cynical about the integrity of most office holders. In short, though we
can reconcile the increase of cynicism and of volunteer campaign participation by asserting that the two trends are based in different
groups in the population, the explanation rests on a series of tenuous
assumptions.

How then may trends toward activism and disaffection be recon-
ciled? William A. Gamson and Philip E. Converse argue that what is
new about popular attitudes in the '60s and '70s is the number of people who feel politically competent and influential but who also mistrust the officials in office.[36] Such people provide, as Converse says,
"prime setting for the effective mobilization of discontent."

Converse suggests that the politically cynical are composed of two
very different groups. One consists of people who have less than average
education and minimal confidence in their own political skills. These
people have responded to what they have perceived as a lack of public
integrity with acquiescence and resignation. The second group, better
educated and more confident of their political skills and their potential to induce political change, have acted on their belief that one can
do more to influence policy than simply vote. In all likelihood it is
these people who have been active in the movements for civil rights,
Vietnam disengagement, and maverick presidential candidates. When
people trust their political effectiveness, then disaffection becomes the
motive for action rather than apathy.

The success of candidates such as Wallace and McGovern suggests
a final approach to reconciling the two themes. Many people have
become disaffected from politics through opposition to federal policies on Vietnam, the economy, race, and social welfare issues. Candidates who have made these issues the focus of their campaigns have
attracted these cynical voters to their camps. Arthur Miller's analysis
of this issue basis of cynicism is illuminating.[37] He finds a significant
growth of disaffection among people who are well to the left and to
the right of the government on these issues. He labels the two groups
"cynics of the right" and "cynics of the left." In his neat phrase, cynics

[36] Converse, "Change in the American Electorate," pp. 334–337, and William A.
Gamson, *Power and Discontent* (Homewood, Ill.: Dorsey, 1968), pp. 39–52.
[37] Arthur H. Miller, "Political Issues and Trust in Government: 1964–1970,"
American Political Science Review, 68 (March, 1974).

of the left prefer more social change; cynics of the right, more social control. (By social control, Miller means that "cynics of the right" prefer the system as it is and support policies and police action against those who would disrupt it.) Thus, there is no necessary contradiction between a trend toward more concern for political issues and a growth of cynicism. Quite the contrary, the opposition of the left and the right to current government policies has been a cause of increased disaffection.

What then is the prospect for renewed trust in the political system? Suggesting a renewal of trust is the fact that political cynicism is not endemic to American politics. As late as the mid-'60s people were fairly confident of their own political influence and the integrity of public officials. For the short run many people may tap a reservoir of faith in the political system that will allow them to believe that though they distrust officials in office, the challengers to those incumbents may be more worthy of trust. The maverick candidates of recent elections— Goldwater, Wallace, McCarthy, and McGovern—have all been partially successful in appealing to the latent faith of the disaffected.

More likely, however, political disaffection will continue through the present decade. As Arthur Miller has shown, cynicism is centered among people who have opposed many of the major themes of government policy—on the Vietnam War to be sure, but also on race and social welfare. The problem is not simply that people believe that, on the war and Watergate, political leaders have mocked reasonable standards of official conduct. When disaffection is also tied to disagreements on policy, it is not clear that a government, however attentive to high standards of democratic procedures, can quickly regain the trust of dissidents. What policies will simultaneously satisfy the right and the left, when opinions are as intensely held as they presently are? For example, during the '72 primaries it was often remarked that McGovern was establishing a "coalition of the alienated." The disaffected on the right were said to be either insensitive to or willing to overlook their policy disagreements with McGovern because of their faith in his personal integrity. Reflecting on the '72 election, this all seems rather foolish. Honest candidates will not rapidly mute the disaffection of dissidents when policy disagreements between the right and the left remain intense. For perhaps a decade public officials can anticipate that many will react to government actions with reservations about the good faith and integrity of their proponents. This, in turn, suggests that policies that depend upon the cooperation of people who oppose their enactments will likely fail. This is not a sanguine prospect for the coming years in American politics.

Index

Adams, John Quincy, 72
Advisers, presidential, 9, 26–28, 49
Agnew, Spiro T., 1, 5, 44, 104, 125
Agricultural leadership, model of, 30–31
Armed Services Committees, 12
Arrow, Kenneth, 37
Assassination, 123–124, 142–143
Authority
  democratic style of, 21–25
  presidential style of, 9

Baker, Howard, 104
Baker, Russell, 137
Barber, James David, 1–6, 147
Barkley, Alben, 44, 45
Bay of Pigs invasion, 7, 23
Bayh, Birch, 47
Beirne, Joseph A., 109
Bennis, Warren G., 30
Boorstin, Daniel, 160
Borah, William, 58
Boyd, Richard W., 6, 122, 175–201
Bricker, John, 40, 56, 97–98
Bryan, William Jennings, 97, 109
Buchanan, James, 75
Bundy, McGeorge, 23

Cabinet officers, 48–50, 66
Calhoun, John C., 72
California primaries, 84, 91
Cambodia, 10, 11
Campaigns, presidential, 96–119
  advertising costs, 165–167
  candidate strategies, 167–169
  citizen participation, 195–198
  deliberate manipulation in, 158–160

Campaigns, presidential (*cont.*)
  Democratic
    1964, 100–103
    1968, 107–109, 117
    1972, 109–113, 117
  financing, 5, 43, 64, 88–89, 92, 165–167, 196
  incumbency, advantage of, 169–171
  media, special targets of, 164–165
  Republican
    1964, 98–100
    1968, 103–105, 109, 117
    1972, 113–116, 117
  symbolic media products, 160–164
  symbolic politics, 155–157
Campbell, Angus, 6, 187–188
Canada, 15
Cantril, Hadley, 181
Caucus system, 60–61, 72
Central Intelligence Agency, 23
Chapin, Dwight, 170
Character, presidential, 8–9, 17–21, 31–33
Checks and balances, 16
Children, and images of Presidency, 129–134
Civil rights movement, 31
Clay, Henry, 72, 75
Cleveland, Grover, 75, 186
Clifford, Clark, 25
Closed primary, 76–77
Coalitions, 4, 13, 41, 96–119
Colodzin, Robert, 2
Colson, Charles, 170
Commission on Party Structure and Delegate Selection, *see* McGovern-Fraser commission
Committee on Delegates and Organization, 76, 86

About The American Assembly

The American Assembly was established by Dwight D. Eisenhower at Columbia University in 1950. It holds nonpartisan meetings and publishes authoritative books to illuminate issues of United States policy.

An affiliate of Columbia, with offices in the Graduate School of Business, the Assembly is a national educational institution incorporated in the State of New York.

The Assembly seeks to provide information, stimulate discussion, and evoke independent conclusions in matters of vital public interest.

AMERICAN ASSEMBLY SESSIONS

At least two national programs are initiated each year. Authorities are retained to write background papers presenting essential data and defining the main issues in each subject.

About sixty men and women representing a broad range of experience, competence, and American leadership meet for several days to discuss the Assembly topic and consider alternatives for national policy.

All Assemblies follow the same procedure. The background papers are sent to participants in advance of the Assembly. The Assembly meets in small groups for four or five lengthy periods. All groups use the same agenda. At the close of these informal sessions, participants adopt in plenary session a final report of findings and recommendations.

Regional, state, and local Assemblies are held following the national session at Arden House. Assemblies have also been in England, Switzerland, Malaysia, Canada, the Caribbean, South America, Central America, the Philippines, and Japan. Over one hundred institutions have co-sponsored one or more Assemblies.

ARDEN HOUSE

Home of The American Assembly and scene of the national sessions is Arden House, which was given to Columbia University in 1950 by W. Averell Harriman. E. Roland Harriman joined his brother in contributing toward adaptation of the property for conference purposes. The buildings and surrounding land, known as the Harriman Campus of Columbia University, are fifty miles north of New York City.

Arden House is a distinguished conference center. It is self-supporting and operates throughout the year for use by organizations with educational objectives.

The background papers for each Assembly program are published in cloth and paperbound editions for use by individuals, libraries, businesses, public agencies, nongovernmental organizations, educational institutions, discussion and service groups. In this way the deliberations of Assembly sessions are continued and extended.

The subjects of Assembly programs to date are:

1951——United States–Western Europe Relationships
1952——Inflation
1953——Economic Security for Americans
1954——The United States' Stake in the United Nations
——The Federal Government Service
1955——United States Agriculture
——The Forty-Eight States
1956——The Representation of the United States Abroad
——The United States and the Far East
1957——International Stability and Progress
——Atoms for Power
1958——The United States and Africa
——United States Monetary Policy
1959——Wages, Prices, Profits, and Productivity
——The United States and Latin America
1960——The Federal Government and Higher Education
——The Secretary of State
——Goals for Americans
1961——Arms Control: Issues for the Public
——Outer Space: Prospects for Man and Society
1962——Automation and Technological Change
——Cultural Affairs and Foreign Relations
1963——The Population Dilemma
——The United States and the Middle East
1964——The United States and Canada
——The Congress and America's Future
1965——The Courts, the Public, and the Law Explosion
——The United States and Japan
1966——State Legislatures in American Politics
——A World of Nuclear Powers?
——The United States and the Philippines
——Challenges to Collective Bargaining
1967——The United States and Eastern Europe
——Ombudsmen for American Government?
1968——Uses of the Seas